The Mystery of the Madonna of Medjugorje

Spark from Heaven

Mary Craig

AVE MARIA PRESS Notre Dame, Indiana 46556

Thou waitest for the spark from heaven! and we,
Light half-believers of our casual creeds,
Who never deeply felt, nor clearly willed,
Whose insight never has borne fruit in deeds,
Whose vague resolves never have been fulfilled;
For whom each year we see
Breeds new beginnings, disappointments new;
Who hesitate and falter life away,
And lose to-morrow the ground won to-day –
Ah! do not we, wanderer! await it too?
Matthew Arnold, *The Scholar Gipsy*

First published in the United Kingdom by Hodder and Stoughton, Limited, Sevenoaks, Kent, England.

Published in the United States of America by Ave Maria Press.

Copyright © 1988 by Mary Craig.

International Standard Book Number: 0-87793-386-3

Library of Congress Catalog Card Number: 88-71358

Cover design by Katherine Coleman.

Manufactured in the United States of America.

FOR ANGELA TILBY, ROGER STOTT AND TONI OJVAN-JOLIĆ

Acknowledgments

To:

Stella Alexander, Chris Cviic, Guido Sagamić and Kreśmir Sivor for information and advice on the Croatian background to the Medjugorje events.

John Bird of Westernhanger Productions and Richard Foley, SJ, who introduced me to much of the written material on the subject.

Peter and Margaret Hebblethwaite with whom I discussed the theological implications of Medjugorje; and Dr Jill Robson who generously shared her theories on the psychology of apparitions.

Jozo Kraljević of Mostar, Yugoslavia, for information regarding the early history of the Franciscans in Bosnia and Hercegovina.

Toni Ojvan-Jolić for acting as interpreter, companion and patient translator of numerous documents.

Maja Samolov for translating the article by Josip Curić.

John Harriott, Angela Tilby, Roger Stott and my husband, Frank, for reading the entire ms; Stella Alexander, Chris Cviic and Vlado Pavlinić for checking Chapter 2.

My editor, Maria Rejt, for her interest and encouragement at every stage.

Contents

Author's Note

In Serbo-Croatian:
> c = ts, as in cats
> č = ch, as in church
> ć = ch, as in cheap
> dž = j, as in June
> j = y, as in yoke
> dj = j, as in jeep
> š = sh, as in ship
> si = shee, as in sheep
> ž = zh, as in pleasure
> a = āh, as in father
> e = eh, as in get
> i = ēē, as in feet
> o = ŏ, as in hot
> u = ōō, as in boom

MEDJUGORJE: med-yu-gor-ye
IVAN, IVANKA: ee-van, ee-van-ka
JAKOV: ya-kof
JELENA: ye-le-na
JOZO: yo-zo
MARIJA: ma-ree-ya
MIRJANA: mee-rya-na
VICKA: vee-tska
VLASIĆ: vla-sheech
ŽANIĆ: zha-neech

Ustaša becomes Ustaše in the plural, although the phrase 'Ustaše terror' has passed into common usage (see Chapter 2).

Author's Introduction

It was, I think, some time in 1982 that I first heard of Medjugorje. I had chanced on an article which told of the extraordinary happenings in a remote mountain village of Yugoslavia. A group of six children, aged from eleven to sixteen, were claiming that for almost a year the Virgin Mary had been appearing to them every day, calling for peace in the world. Crowds of people were, inevitably, flocking to the place with the strange, unpronounceable name. Well, similar claims had been made for other places, Lourdes and Fatima, for example. What made Medjugorje so remarkable was not only that the apparitions were more frequent and longer-lasting than anywhere else, but that all this was happening at the heart of a Communist country, to children brought up on the principles of Marxism–Leninism. The authorities, it seemed, were clamping down heavily on the phenomenon; while the Roman Catholic Church was embarrassed and nonplussed. I made a mental note to watch out for further developments. Then I forgot all about it.

To be honest, it was the political implications that had intrigued me. Although a Roman Catholic from birth, I had never been attracted to stories of apparitions. I knew, of course, that many people found great strength and encouragement in visiting shrines such as Lourdes. But, though I had once visited Lourdes with my handicapped son, I was not of their number. During the seventies, when I worked as a regular reporter and feature-writer on BBC Radio 4's weekly ecumenical religious programme, *Sunday*, I was willing to tackle almost any subject that came along – except for apparitions and the like. I was wary of supernatural manifestations.

So when the telephone rang in my study one morning in June 1986 and a voice asked: "Mary, how does the idea of Medjugorje grab you?" I answered instinctively: "It doesn't." From time to time, I had heard that the apparitions were still going on, the number of pilgrims dramatically multiplying. If people wanted that kind of thing, they were welcome to it. "Pity," said the voice, which was that of Angela Tilby, a former radio colleague who was now a producer with the BBC *Everyman* unit. "I'm going there to make a film, and rather hoped you might come too." Angela, it transpired, had just been out to Medjugorje with the film's researcher, Roger Stott. "*Something* is happening there," she said, "and

7

the exciting thing is that it's happening right now, and we have the opportunity to film it."

Angela's idea was that I might write the film-script. Almost as an after-thought she added: "There might be a book in it too." But did I really want to write a film-script, let alone a book, on such a subject? My instinct was to say no, and turn my back on the whole project. On the other hand, Angela seemed to have been impressed, and she was nobody's fool. What if something really *was* happening in Medjugorje! I should at least be prepared to go there – and draw my own conclusions.

When I joined the film crew in Medjugorje on 1st September, I knew somehow that I was embarking on a kind of personal quest, and would have to write that book in order to pursue it. In fact, Hodder and Stoughton had already commissioned me to write it. Having decided to go there, would I find in Medjugorje what so many pilgrims insisted they had found – interior spiritual peace and a renewed faith? I hoped I might, although, as an honorary member of the BBC team, with a varied programme and privileged access to sites and personalities denied to the majority, I could hardly describe myself as a typical pilgrim. Yet, however dimly, I began to sense that what was happening in Medjugorje was a growing force that could affect the whole world. I knew I could no longer afford simply to dismiss it.

With that visit, my search was only just beginning. For one thing, it was far more complicated than I had suspected. There was intrigue, controversy and excitement in abundance. And I realised, almost immediately, that if the search was to be truly honest and objective, it would not be enough simply to focus on what had happened since 1981. The people of this village in the republic of Bosnia-Hercegovina were steeped in their own violent and blood-stained history, and today's events could only be fully understood in the context of that violent past. The Madonna of Medjugorje (known locally as *Gospa*, the Lady), was pleading for peace, yet peace was a commodity virtually unknown in that particular part of the world, the Balkan peninsula. The Second World War had followed an especially bloody course in that region.

A passage from Rebecca West's pre-war book on Yugoslavia, *Black Lamb, Grey Falcon*, struck me as both graphic and significant. Writing of an unbroken continuity of pain, appalling (and incomprehensible) to anyone nurtured in the security of an English or American past, she continued:

> Were I to go down to the market-place, armed with the powers of witchcraft, and take a peasant by the shoulders, and whisper to him, "In your lifetime, have you known peace?" wait for his answer, shake his shoulders and transform him into his father, and ask him the same

question, and transform him in his turn to his father, I would never hear the word "Yes", if I carried my questioning of the dead back for a thousand years.

I felt it was essential to try to understand something of this background, and have therefore included a brief outline of Bosnia-Hercegovina's tumultuous past, the massacres and hatreds that have beset its volatile mix of peoples, the historic rivalry between Serb and Croat which owes much, if not all, of its force to the religious differences between them. It is from this tragic land that the appeal for the world to save itself from destruction has recently gone out, and if Medjugorje can heed its own message, there may well be hope for us all.

The Madonna has told them, the young visionaries claim, that these are the "last apparitions on earth", the last chance the world will be given to mend its ways. When I read those words, I remembered with a shiver some lines of T. S. Eliot in *The Four Quartets*. Unless, the poet had written, human life is lived in the light of something greater than itself, it is a voyage

> In a drifting boat with a slow leakage,
> The silent listening to the undeniable
> Clamour of the bell of the last annunciation.

Are we, then, living in the last times, on the edge of extinction? Few could deny the possibility of it. So does Medjugorje represent the "bell of the last annunciation", a last-ditch attempt to save us from ourselves? To decide about that, we would first have to decide if the claimed apparitions are authentic. Are they the twentieth century's most momentous happening, of earth-shattering importance – or are they its most ingenious and cruel hoax? Even if the answer is elusive, we can at least examine the available evidence both for and against. This book represents, I hope, a search that has remained open-ended and objective. My quest may not have led me into certainties. But then I am not at all convinced that faith requires certainty. Doubts are merely the shadow side of faith.

Those who are unreservedly committed to Medjugorje and who derive great solace from their commitment, may find this approach disappointing. For such as these, countless books on Medjugorje have already been written. I make no apology. For I suspect that there are many more who, like myself, "hesitate and falter life away", yet half-consciously long for some "spark from Heaven" to light up the darkness. There is always, however, the fear that we may not recognise that spark if and when it appears. And this, perhaps, is our greatest dilemma.

MARY CRAIG
December 1987

9

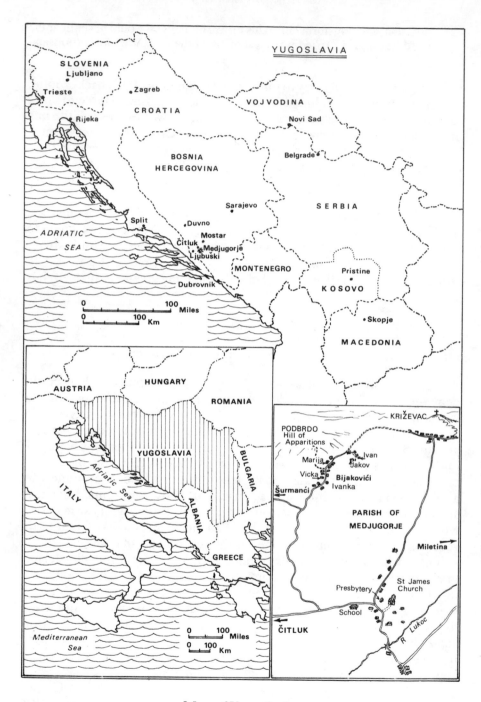

Map of Yugoslavia

1

The First Three Days

If the doors of perception were cleansed,
everything will appear to man as it is, infinite.
William Blake

Leave the spectacular beauty of the Adriatic Riviera which forms part of
the Republic of Croatia in south-western Yugoslavia, and plunge inland
along the west bank of the green Neretva river. The contrast is dramatic
and extreme. Translucent sea gives way to an arid wilderness of limestone
Alps, dense with scrub and haunted by the ghosts of ferocious wartime
Partisans. Little white stone houses dot the landscape at intervals and
huge boulders line the road. Centuries ago the sea used to cover the flat
valley floor that separates the parallel ranges, and even today it is still
flooded in autumn and winter from innumerable hidden underground
waters.

But only a little further inland, on the right side of the river, is a
different world – of lush foliage, flowering hedgerows and trailing vines.
For having passed the little village of Vasarović we are on the wide Brotnjo
plateau of Western Hercegovina and the inhospitable mountains have
been left behind. Economically speaking the poorest and most unde-
veloped region of all Yugoslavia, Western Hercegovina has little industry
but a wealth of trees; oak, ash, hornbeam, maple, spruce, pine, cypress
and laburnum being the most common. The area's own climate may
alternate between torrid and freezing, but the healing waters of the
Neretva bring with them the blessings of the mild Mediterranean climate
of the Adriatic so that peaches, cherries, plums, almonds, water-melons
and figs grow here in abundance. Best of all, high-quality tobacco –
Hercegovina Gold – can be grown on the rich red soil, and the vines which
produce the much sought-after Hercegovinan wines, the white Žilavka
and red Blatina which have been grown here ever since Roman times
and were given a seal of approval from the Austrian royal house in
1886.

Yet, away from this splendid Mediterranean profusion, most of the
Brotnjo earth is stony and good arable land for crop-growing is hard to

come by. Since the Middle Ages, men of these parts have had to abandon their homes and go elsewhere to wrest a living from the land. Since the 1960s they have gone as migrant workers to West Germany, Belgium, Sweden and Switzerland, leaving their wives and children to tend the tobacco and vines, the cows and the sheep. It is they who now pit their wits against alternating floods and drought and the unyielding rocky soil. When the men return, they bring the late twentieth century with them, turning their backs on farming, setting up as electricians, mechanics or tradesmen in the nearby towns of Mostar or Čitluk, and "not doing badly at all". Some of them build modern houses with up-to-date kitchens and tiled bathrooms; they have cars, colour TV, washing machines and video recorders. The state system ensures that their children have at least eight years (primary) education, followed by an optional four years at a technical, medical or general cultural school. The peasant children of the Brotnjo region can no longer be classified as ignorant, superstitious and illiterate.

At the south-eastern end of the plain, far from any modern roads or railways, five small hamlets nestle around an ugly twin-towered church built of breeze-blocks and concrete slabs. Sheep, hens, goats, donkeys and small mountain-cows wander around streets which are not much more than cart-tracks, and never more than three metres wide. In these villages – Medjugorje (the biggest of the five and the only one to have a post office), Bijakovići, Miletina, Vionica and Šurmanći – about 400 peasant families do battle with the intractable land. The government allows them to possess ten hectares of ground, but few of them own the maximum amount.

The church of St James towers above the tall tobacco plants and spreading vines in the village of Medjugorje, too large, one would have thought, for the needs of five villages such as these. But large churches are not unusual in Western Hercegovina, the most fervently Catholic region of Yugoslavia. The republic of Bosnia-Hercegovina is renowned for its explosive mix of races and religions, but the inhabitants of Western Hercegovina are almost all Croats, which is to say that they are virtually all Roman Catholic. The 1.2 per cent of ethnic Muslims and 0.5 per cent of Serbs who also inhabit the area are not necessarily worshippers, but it can virtually be guaranteed of the Croats. Throughout the ages they have guarded their religion against foes without and within, and violence has been no stranger to them.

Opposite the church is the eastern flank of a small mountain, 1,200 metres high, home to the long, poisonous snakes known as *poskoci* ("jumpers"); and, on its Čapljina and Metković sides, to wild boar and wolves. Once it was called Šipovac – Rose-hip Hill – but since 1933 it has been known as Križevac, Hill of the Cross. The huge concrete cross, fourteen metres high, was erected in that year to commemorate the nineteen hundredth anniversary of Christ's crucifixion, but the peasants tell a more colourful story of its origins. They say that for years they had been plagued by fierce hailstorms which destroyed the tobacco and vines, bringing disease and even death. Early in 1933, designated by Rome as a Holy Year, their priest, Brno Smoljan, was summoned to Rome by Pope Pius XI. It appeared that Pius had been instructed in a dream to raise a cross "on the highest Golgotha in Hercegovina", a region he knew not at all. Fr Smoljan returned home with a commission to turn the dream into reality, to build a huge cross which could be seen for miles around. The parishioners dug up and broke stones with a will, carting them on their backs over the karstic rocks of Šipovac and building them into a cross when they reached the summit. And if their secret hope was to ward off the destructive storms, their faith was not misplaced. The killer-storms stopped; and the vineyards flourished again. The "white magic" continues to hold good to this day. "When a storm begins to gather and hail threatens, we ring the church bells," says a local farmer. "Then you can see the clouds change direction and unload on the hills around us, sparing the villages."

Medjugorje – a word of Slavic origin meaning "among the hills" – lies right at the foot of rocky Križevac. Facing it and across the fields is the hill of Crnica which has another smaller hill, Podbrdo, growing out of it like a pregnant hump. At its base is Bijakovići, a village almost indistinguishable from Medjugorje with its white stone houses and its solitary cart-track street. The two villages, however, have for centuries glowered at each other across the valley floor; until recently there was little love lost between them. The Croatians are a Balkan people, as fierce and unbiddable as their land. Personal feuds and vendettas lie deep in their bloodstream.

The drama which was to shake both villages to the roots began on Wednesday, 24th June 1981, the Feast of St John the Baptist. And it had a fine, crashing, orchestral overture, well-suited to this region of violent contrasts and untamed emotions. The night before had been sticky-hot and oppressive, heavy with menace. At one in the morning, a storm of Homeric force split the sky. It woke Iva Vasilj, wife of a peasant farmer in Medjugorje, and she rushed outside to see what was happening, then back inside again to shake her husband, Pero, awake. "It's like the Day of Judgement out there," she shouted.

> Everything seemed to be on fire [she recalled later] and the thunder was crashing round the sky. I grabbed a crucifix and a bottle of holy water and went round sprinkling half the village. Then I saw a house on fire. "Look," I screamed at my husband, "it's poor Pesko's house, and him with all those

13

children!" By this time, my husband had come out and he too was trembling. "No," he said, "that's not Pesko's house, it's where the young people have their discos." The post office was on fire, and suddenly smoke began belching out of the pine trees below our house. The firemen came but they had a hard time coping with all the fires – and they only managed to save half the post office. When the storm died down, I went back to bed, but I couldn't sleep, I was too frightened.

It would not, however, be in Medjugorje but in Bijakovići that the drama would unfold, later that same day, in the atmosphere of calm tranquillity that followed the storm. Two young girls were at its centre. Ivanka Ivanković, a dark, attractive girl of fifteen, lived in the provincial capital, Mostar, but spent her summer holidays in Bijakovići helping her grandparents in the vineyards and tobacco fields they still owned. She and blonde Mirjana Dragicević, a sixteen-year-old from Sarajevo, who also spent her holidays with her grandmother in Bijakovići, were always together. Usually inseparable from them was Vicka Ivanković (no relation to Ivanka), another spirited but much less sophisticated sixteen-year-old who lived across the road – the unpaved track – from Mirjana's grandparents' house.

On that feast-day afternoon, Ivanka and Mirjana decided to collect Vicka and go for a walk. But Vicka, having failed her first-year textile-school exam in mathematics, had spent the morning in Mostar at a special summer-school class. Having got home at about twelve, after a miserable journey on a hot and crowded bus, she had now gone for a rest. Leaving her a message the other two went off without her – up the hill of Crnica, by way of the smaller Podbrdo which rises just behind Vicka's house. Although, when questioned later, the girls at first denied having gone up the hill for a quiet smoke, they later admitted to it.

At about five o'clock they were on their way down again. As they passed Podbrdo, something made Ivanka look up. In the distance she could see a luminous shape, the shadowy figure of a young woman, apparently hovering some way off the ground. "Mirjana, look there, it's the Madonna," she said in excitement. ("To this day, I don't know how I knew, but somehow I just did," she says.) Mirjana, though she could see that Ivanka had gone pale with fright, refused to look where her friend was pointing. "Don't be idiotic," she retorted, "why on earth would the Madonna appear to us?" But the sight of Ivanka's face had scared her, and both girls ran back to the village as quickly as they knew how. As they reached the houses at the bottom of the hill, another friend, Milka Pavlović, was setting out to round up her small flock of sheep who'd been left grazing at Podbrdo. They could hardly refuse when she asked for their help; so, with some reluctance, they retraced their steps.

Milka let the sheep out of the pen; and they all three began to head for home. The time was about six-fifteen. When they reached the spot where Ivanka had looked up and seen the mysterious figure, the girl again cried, "Look, there she is." Mirjana and Milka, following her pointing finger to a distance of 200 metres or so, saw a young woman in grey, holding something in her hand which she seemed to be protecting.

"She was a long way away," says Ivanka. "We couldn't see her close to, just the outline of her body."

"We couldn't see her face," confirms Mirjana, "and anyway, we didn't know what the Madonna would really look like! But something inside us insisted that it was the Madonna.* We knew it was her, but we felt confused, and just stood there looking at her."

Ivanka agrees: "We didn't know what to do, where to put ourselves. We felt a mixture of joy and fear. So much joy, yet so much fear, it's impossible to describe it."

Vicka, meanwhile, had woken up and, finding the message from her friends, had set off to look for them:

> So there I was, coming up the path, and I could see Ivanka and Mirjana up there, standing on the path and calling me to come quickly. I came up closer and then – well, they were gazing at something higher up on the hill. I thought perhaps it was a snake or something like that. But when I caught up with them and they said "Look, it's the Madonna," I was so frightened that I just kicked off my slippers and ran like crazy down the hill. I just couldn't believe what they were saying.

Reaching the houses along the road, she burst into tears. Then along came twenty-year-old Ivan Ivanković† and sixteen-year-old Ivan Dragicević, carrying apples in a plastic bag. Nervously Vicka asked them to go up the hill with her. "Something was drawing me back there," she says. "It was pulling and pushing me to where the others were. But I was very scared."

"What on earth is there to be scared of?" asked the younger Ivan, but when they reached the spot where the others stood, within seconds he had climbed over a fence and taken to his heels, abandoning the apples in his haste.

"Can you see anything?" Vicka asked the other Ivan, still not daring to look herself.

"I can see something completely white, turning," he replied.

Vicka was still rooted to the spot in terror, not daring to raise her eyes.

---

* The Croatian word is *Gospa*, meaning "the Lady".
† Once again, no relation; Ivanković is a common patronymic, like Johnson or Jackson.

But then, all of a sudden, I looked up and saw her standing there, just as clearly as I can see you now. She wore a grey dress with a white veil, a crown of stars, blue eyes, dark hair and rosy cheeks. And she was floating about this high in the air on a grey cloud, not touching the ground. She had something in her left hand that she kept covering and uncovering – but you couldn't see what it was. She called us to go nearer, but none of us dared to.[1]

Shaken, the children returned home. "I was tremendously happy, but frightened too," said Vicka. "When I got home, I just sat on the couch and started to cry again." They told their families what they had seen, and were not really surprised when they weren't believed. "They just laughed at us," remembers Ivanka. "They said we must have seen the glow from a shepherd's torch or a will-o'-the-wisp." Vicka's sister said it was probably a flying saucer, and her parents told her to keep quiet about all this if she didn't want people to think her mad. "Why didn't you grab hold of the lady?" Milka's Uncle Simun teased. "Did she send her regards to the rest of the family?" Milka's older sister, Marija, laughed along with the rest.

"It wasn't really surprising," admits Vicka. "How could they be expected to believe us? In their place, I wouldn't have believed us either." Only Mirjana's grandparents accepted the story, but her uncle was tense with worry. How could she talk such nonsense, he berated her; if she didn't watch out, they'd all be in a lot of trouble.

Word spread and soon the whole village was agog. Across the fields, in Medjugorje, Iva Vasilj heard the news without surprise. "When one of the boys from the village came and said, 'The Madonna has been seen in Bijakovići', I said, 'Ah, so that's why there was all that thunder and lightning last night. The mother of God is visiting the earth.'"

Marinko Ivanković lived next door to Milka and Marija on one side and Vicka on the other. He was a car mechanic, working at a garage in Mostar. On that Thursday morning he gave a lift to Vicka and Marija, knowing nothing of the previous day's excitement. (The girls had, as usual, been up at dawn to pick the tobacco and feed the animals before going to school.) When Marija told him what had been happening, he all but drove the car into a ditch. "I was so shaken I came out in goose pimples all over," he said. "Vicka went on to tell me the whole story. When she said that Ivan Ivanković had seen the vision too, I said I'd ask him about it when I got home at midday. Ivan's a sensible boy, and as I said to Vicka: I'd trust his word more than that of a hundred girls."

Marinko was even more shaken when Ivan corroborated Vicka's story. He decided to keep an eye on the children if they went back to the hill. What actually induced them to go back next day, Ivanka and Mirjana have never been able to explain, except that some indefinable force propelled them there. They had worked as usual in the tobacco fields till late afternoon, collecting the leaves. Vicka says that it was Ivanka who suggested that in the early evening, when work was over, they should go towards the hill. If they saw the Madonna again, well and good, if not, well, there was nothing lost, and at least they wouldn't have to be laughed at any more. Ivan Dragicević agreed to conquer his fears and go along, though the older Ivan Ivanković had decided that enough was enough. "He's a bit older than us," Vicka excused him. "Why would he want to hang around with kids like us?" Mrs Pavlović said that Milka was needed for the sheep, but there was nothing to stop her older sister, Marija, going along if she wanted to. Marija, a calm, rather shy girl of sixteen, who was training to be a hairdresser in Mostar, was keen to go. "If you see the Madonna today, call me," she begged Vicka. "I don't mind if I don't see her, but I'd love just to be there."

When Iva Vasilj heard that the youngsters were going up the hill again at dusk, there was no holding her. "I didn't even stop to lock up," she says. "If any thieves had come along, they could have cleared us out." With Mirjana's uncle and a couple of curious children, she followed at a short distance from the main group. It was six o'clock. Ivanka led the way, with Mirjana walking behind. Once again, it was Ivanka who stopped and said, "Look, the Madonna." Mirjana and Vicka both looked up, and both cried out in amazement. "It was still light," recalls Vicka. "This time I could see her face, eyes, hair and gown."

Remembering her promise to Marija, Vicka rushed down the hill to call her, and found her with ten-year-old Jakov Čolo. Both of them dropped what they were doing and ran after Vicka.

At first Marija could discern only a vague outline, which gradually came into focus, "like a mist clearing". "Then I saw her: in a long grey dress and white veil. I could see the outline of her face quite clearly, though she was a long way away at the top of the hill."

The apparition beckoned them and they ran towards her, "as though we had wings, in spite of the sharp stones and brambles". "It takes at least twelve minutes to get up there," said Mirjana's uncle, "yet they did it in two. It scared me to death."

When you look up there from the bottom of the hill, it doesn't look far, [says Vicka] but in reality it's quite a way. We ran up that hill. It didn't seem like walking on the ground, and we didn't bother to look for the path. We just ran towards the Madonna, as if something was pulling us through the air. I was terrified. I was also barefoot, but the thorns didn't scratch me. When we were a few feet away from her, we felt as though we were thrown to our knees. Jakov was kneeling right in the middle of a thorn bush and I was sure he'd be hurt. But he came out of it without a scratch. We began praying, because we didn't know what else to do. We were crying and praying all at the same time.

By the time the handful of villagers had also reached the top, the children were kneeling on the rocks in prayer. "We prayed Our Fathers, Hail Marys and the Glory Be. We couldn't think of anything else to do," said Vicka. It was Ivanka who plucked up courage to address the vision first, asking, out of the depths of grief, a question about her mother, Jagoda, who had died a few weeks earlier. The vision assured Ivanka that her mother was well and happy. Since her mother had actually died alone in hospital, the girl was anxious to know if she had wanted to say anything special to her children before she died. "Just that you should obey your grandmother," smiled the vision, "and take special care of her now that she's old and unable to work."

Mirjana, the cleverest of the group, was already worrying about what the neighbours were going to think. "Dear Madonna, they won't believe us, you know. They'll say we're mad." In reply, she said, the Madonna just smiled.

They were on the hill for about fifteen minutes, before the apparition left them, with the words, "Go in the peace of God". They gazed after her for a while, then slowly walked down the hill. None of them spoke, but Ivanka was overwrought and weeping hysterically.

Marinko, who had intended to go with them that evening, had got the time wrong and arrived home just as the group of scared teenagers came down the hill: "Ivanka was sobbing, terribly upset. I ran to her and asked what the matter was, and she told me all that had passed between her and the apparition. I tried to tell her that if the vision had said her mother was well and happy, then she should be laughing not crying. But she was inconsolable."

It was too much for Marinko to handle on his own, so he went for the priest. "If there is some evil power at work here, they should not be playing around with it," he thought. But as bad luck would have it, the parish priest, Fra Jozo Zovko, was away, and his assistant chaplain, Fra Zrinko Čuvalo, a robustly down-to-earth, choleric man who did not suffer fools gladly, gave Marinko short shrift. "He just wouldn't listen," sighs the latter:

> so I went back home and talked to the children myself. Ivanka had calmed down by that time and was able to talk quite rationally. And that was when I began to believe the whole fantastic story, because I knew Ivanka well, and she was a level-headed, studious girl. I knew Milka and Marija too; every night the girls used to come and help my wife, Dragica, with the washing-up, and then stay to watch our colour TV. They were good girls.

So ended the day which would eventually be considered the anniversary of the apparitions – 25th June. For it was the six young people who went to the hill that day – Ivanka Ivanković, Mirjana Dragicević, Vicka Ivanković, Marija Pavlović, Ivan Dragicević and Jakov Čolo – who would constitute the permanent group of visionaries. Neither Milka nor the older Ivan ever saw the Lady again.

On the following day, Friday, the heat was intense. Marinko was taking no chances. Carrying some salt and a bottle of holy water with which to ward off evil spirits, he arranged to meet the children at the bottom of the hill. At a quarter past six, the village of Bijakovići and the surrounding area for miles around were lit up by three flashes of brilliant light. Seeing the light – and then the Lady – the children ran up the hill, followed by a large crowd of excited people. It had, of course, not taken long for news of these strange happenings to spread. Stragglers had already begun arriving on the second day. But now on this third day, several thousand people, the curious as well as the pious, had come in from the surrounding villages and from Čitluk, five miles away.

Such was the children's speed that they got separated from each other. Nevertheless, about 300 metres higher than the day before, in front of a rock where there was an old wooden cross, they all six suddenly stopped, turned to the north-east and dropped to their knees at the same moment. Vicka, threw the salt and sprinkled the apparition with the holy water as Marinko had told her, saying firmly, "If you really are the Madonna, please stay with us; but if you are not, go away and leave us alone." The vision smiled – and stayed where she was.

"Who are you?" the children pressed her.

"I am the Blessed Virgin Mary."

"And why have you come here?"

"I have chosen this place specially, because there are many faithful believers here."

She told them to stand and join her in prayer. Prompted by Mirjana's grandmother, who was standing nearby, they began to recite a traditional prayer sequence of seven Our Fathers, seven Hail Marys and seven Glorias. At the Madonna's request, they added the Creed.

The whole crowd joined in. In a *Sunday Times* article,[2] journalist Gitta Sereny would later write about that evening:

> Tapes made on the day vividly record the tumult as the children described to the crowd what the Madonna looked like and valiantly tried to transmit questions to her and report her replies. Many wanted news of departed relatives; others begged for help for their loved ones, often pushing severely handicapped infants into the children's arms.

The Madonna told the children she would come to them again next day, at the spot where they had seen her on the first day, lower down the hill. Then she left them, with her now familiar valediction, "Go in the peace of God".

It was already seven o'clock in the evening, but the heat was still unbearable. Mirjana and Ivanka felt faint and Marinko cleared a way for them out of the crowd. The others made their way down over the rough boulders and stones, the crowd following behind. Marija, walking along with a small group of women, felt a sudden overpowering compulsion to leave them and go down by a path to the left. Obeying the impulse, she had a vision of a cross, shining with a whole spectrum of colours but empty. In front of the cross, weeping, stood the Madonna. "Peace, peace, you must seek peace," she cried. "There must be peace on earth, you must be reconciled with God and with each other. Peace, peace, peace."

"It was an overwhelming experience," says Marija. "I saw the Madonna weeping, and the sight drove me to commit myself totally to her request. She had come to inspire all of us to search for peace – peace in our own hearts, peace within our families, peace in the world."

Thus was the essence of the Medjugorje message revealed. The Madonna's desperate plea for peace would go echoing round a world which, in that summer of 1981, seemed to hover on the brink of self-destruction. Relations between the superpowers were at their lowest ebb; and there were real fears of a Soviet invasion of Poland – they had invaded Afghanistan the previous year – that might engulf the world in nuclear war. In those dark days, few people would have rated the chances for peace as being very high. Though the very idea chilled the blood, the time for building fall-out shelters seemed to be at hand.

2

In Your Lifetime, Have You Known Peace?

> I had come to Yugoslavia because I knew that the past had made the present, and I want to see how the process works. It is plain that it means an immense amount of human pain, arranged in an unbroken continuity appalling to any person cradled in the security of the English or American past. Were I to go down to the market-place, armed with the powers of witchcraft, and take a peasant by the shoulders, and whisper to him, "In your lifetime, have you known peace?" wait for his answer, shake his shoulders and transform him into his father, and ask him the same question, and transform him in turn into his father, I would never hear the word "Yes", if I carried my questioning of the dead back for a thousand years. I would always hear, "No, there was fear, there were our enemies without, our rulers within, there was prison, there was torture, there was violent death."
>
> Rebecca West, *Black Lamb, Grey Falcon*

With that cry for peace to a people who have almost never known the meaning of the word, we need to pause and take stock for a moment. From now on, because the story is lifted right out of the private and innocent domain to become enmeshed in the politics and conflicts of both Church and State, we must journey back into history in search of understanding. No events, not even religious revelations, take place in a vacuum. Placing them in some kind of context is necessary.

Behind the realities of present-day Yugoslavia, we see a people with an epic history, replete with suffering and violence. We see a land occupied and torn apart by successive waves of invaders and tyrants, individuals and empires. There are those who say of this land that it is only truly itself when in the grip of catastrophe. Down the centuries the area that only in this century has become known as Yugoslavia – land of the Southern Slavs – has been not only a meeting-point between many civilisations, cultures and faiths, but also the scene of their violent collision. It marked the historic divide between East and West; and still does.

Yugoslavia never succeeded in becoming a melting-pot; rather was it a cauldron in which a host of nationalities seethed and bubbled but never managed to coalesce. To outsiders the main language spoken is known as Serbo-Croatian (except in Slovenia and Macedonia which have their own languages). But any Serb will tell you he is speaking Serbian, any Croat that the language is Croatian. Such issues carry an emotional charge that is scarcely affected by government demands for uniformity.

Medjugorje and its sister villages of the Brotnjo plateau, are, as we have already seen, in Hercegovina, part of Bosnia-Hercegovina, one of the six republics of post-war Communist Yugoslavia. Originally the Brotnjo area was settled by Illyrians, Celts and Greeks, but by the first century AD it had become part of the Roman Empire. The Empire's days were numbered, however, and its territories were soon to be overrun during the great migration of peoples which began in the third century. Migrant Slavonic tribes scattered all over Europe: one branch went east to settle Russia; another westward to found Poland and Czechoslovakia; while a third branch went south in the sixth and seventh centuries and made the Balkan territories of the Roman Empire their own. Within one hundred years these Southern Slav tribes had expelled or assimilated the native Illyrians and were permanently settled throughout the entire peninsula, Slovenes to the north, Croats to the centre and west, and Serbs to the east of the frontier established in AD 395 between the Greek-speaking Eastern (Byzantine) and the Latin-speaking Western Roman Empires, based respectively on Constantinople and Rome. Their arrival widened the already yawning gulf between East and West.

Nor did their own unity last long. The Serbs and the Croats belonged to the same ethnic group and spoke different dialects of the same language; both tribes came from the swamps and forests beyond the Vistula river and the Carpathian Alps to the east. But history would decree that the relationship between these two brother-tribes would be a fratricidal one: a recognised symbol of human divisiveness, a chronic threat not only to their own peace but to that of Europe. And it is in their location east and west of the old imperial dividing line, and still more in their conversion to strongly diverging branches of Christianity, that we find the key to their tragic enmity.

The Serbs were converted to Christianity in the ninth century, and succeeded in translating the Scriptures from the official Greek into a Slavonic tongue. But in the middle of the seventh century the Slovenes and Croats had come under the influence of the newer Latin Christianity which had gradually been establishing itself in Europe and Africa. For a time, both the Latin and the Slav rites were used in the Croatian kingdom; but the Roman bishops objected to saying Mass "in barbaric tongues"; and in the twelfth century, when the kingdom passed into the control of the Roman Catholic Magyars, the Slav rite and the Slav language were banned from the Roman liturgy.

Reacting strongly against both variants of organised Christianity were the strange mystical group known as the Bogomils. Bogomilism had originated in Bulgaria in the tenth century and was probably imported from Constantinople by Bosnian and Dalmatian merchants. It was an offshoot of the Manichaean heresy which in the twelfth and thirteenth centuries was spreading over large areas of Europe under different names, such as Catharism, Albigensianism and Patarenism, offering a radical solution to the problem of Evil in the world. Deeply pessimistic and anarchic, the Bogomils believed that the world, with all its injustices and servitudes, was not created by a good God, but by Satan, a totally separate force of Evil, hostile to the godhead. The material world of Satan and the spiritual world of God were two distinct, warring entities. Only a small elect of those who sought only the spiritual life – "the perfect" – could hope to be saved. To defeat Satan's purposes, this élite must adopt a lifestyle of rigid asceticism, eschewing marriage (a form of adultery); all sexual intercourse; the eating of meat and the drinking of wine. The Bogomils called themselves the Bosnian Church, or simply Christians, though they rejected the basic doctrines of Christianity such as the Incarnation and the Trinity. They would have nothing to do with infant baptism, the sacraments, the Communion of Saints, all use of images, church buildings, and an ordained priesthood. They admitted no authority; and no obligation, whether moral or material.

With their rejection of marriage, the basis of all Western social custom and law, the Bogomils posed a threat to the fundamental structure of society as well as to the Christian faith. It is not surprising, therefore, that both the Orthodox and Roman Churches regarded them as a dangerous "fifth column", a subversive heretical minority to be destroyed.

The Bogomils had first settled in Serbia. But the Eastern Orthodox Church had persecuted and, by the end of the twelfth century, expelled them. Escaping into Bosnia, they had found their true home, a fertile soil for their harsh, fanatical doctrines. The king of Bosnia had actually renounced the Roman Church and became a Bogomil, until pressure from the Papacy and a Crusade led by the king of Hungary forced him to recant. (This Crusade was a spin-off from the famous Albigensian Crusade preached against the Bogomils' spiritual kin in France, the Cathars.) Christian soldiers obeyed the summons to march against the heretical Bogomils; and Bosnia was laid waste by fire and sword. But recovery was swift. By the end of the thirteenth century, Bogomilism was established as the state religion of Bosnia, to the exclusion of the Roman Catholic Church.

In the fourteenth century, during the reign of the Bogomil king, Stephen II, Bosnia acquired the principality of Hum, the future Hercegovina, which had led a more or less independent existence since the tenth century. (Herceg means "duke", and Hercegovina simply means "the dukedom".) The Hercegovinan nobles were influential at the Bosnian court, so they too must have been Bogomils. When the head of the Franciscan Order passed through Bosnia in 1339, in order to establish his itinerant friars there and restore "the true faith", he found it without priests of any kind and "infested with heretics". But, much to the fury of the powerful Bogomil barons and landowners, he succeeded in converting the king to Roman Christianity. From then on, the Franciscan friars had a secure foothold in Bosnia-Hercegovina; and by 1343 they already had thirty-six monasteries in the region.

The Ottoman Turks, however, were spreading relentlessly into Europe, their progress made easier by the internecine feuding among the various states. In the Balkan peninsula they conquered Macedonia and trounced the Serbians at Kosovo in 1389, before turning their attention to Bosnia, which they invaded for the first time in 1398. Divided amongst themselves and weakened by religious strife, the Bosnians offered little resistance. Throughout the first half of the fifteenth century, with the Turks at their very gates, they continued to destroy themselves from within.

In 1450, the king, a Bogomil, made a fateful decision. Believing his country's only salvation to lie with the West, he became a Catholic. Encouraged by the Pope, to whom the Bogomils within were no better than the Turks without, he began to persecute his former co-religionists. Thousands of extraordinary tombstones (known as *stecaks*), which one comes across today near Medjugorje and elsewhere in Bosnia-Hercegovina, bear eloquent and defiant witness to their sufferings. Carved with running stags, hinds, birds and rustic knights, and vividly reminiscent of the celebrated cave-paintings at Lascaux, they shock by the stark simplicity of their message. Epitaphs such as: "Here lies Ozrislav Kopijević. I have been pierced, I have been slashed, I have been skinned", say it all. Another one reads: "Here I stopped, praying to God and thinking no evil, but lo, thunder struck me."

Many of the Bogomils fled abroad. Others, made desperate by this latest bout of persecution, turned to the Turks for military protection, accepting them as liberators. When it became clear to the Bogomil nobles that, under Turkish rule, they would be allowed to keep their lands, rank and exemption from taxes, if they converted to Islam, they scarcely hesitated. Preferring the prospect of Islamic conquest to that of militant Catholicism – "better the Turk's turban than the papal tiara" – they were more than ready to embrace a faith whose harsh unforgiving doctrines had so much in common with their own.

Much of today's Yugoslavia was overrun. Serbia was overthrown in 1459. And in 1463, when the new king of Bosnia refused to pay tribute to Sultan Mohammed II, Mohammed invaded Bosnia in person, capturing and executing the king, reducing the country to the status of a Turkish province. Hercegovina resisted for a little while longer but by 1483 it too had fallen to the Turks.

As the last Catholics fled from the northern areas of Bosnia into what remained of the former kingdom of Croatia, hundreds of thousands of Orthodox peasants, fleeing the conscription of their children, came to replace them. The future republic of Bosnia-Hercegovina was already forming that chaotic and inflammable mix of religions that for centuries to come would tear it apart and make it uncertain of its real identity.

Under Turkish rule, Bosnia and Hercegovina formed a tight little world of their own, cut off not only from the rest of Europe but even from Constantinople. In contrast with Serbia, where the Muslim Turks were alien occupying invaders, the Bogomil landowners of Bosnia converted as a class to Islam, and henceforth the Christians referred to them as Turks. Few true Turks were needed to settle the territory. Though a Turkish governor in Sarajevo was in nominal control, he interfered little in local affairs so long as taxes were paid on time. Real power lay in the hands of the forty-eight hereditary nobles who exercised feudal rights over their mainly Christian peasants. (Those nobles who had not converted to Islam were demoted to second-class citizens.) Adopting Turkish manners and dress, the new Muslims of Bosnia and Hercegovina were more zealous for Islam than any true Turk from Constantinople would have been. Yet their faces were Slav and they spoke the language of the Slavs.

The mainly Christian masses were left in peace so long as they paid their (exorbitant) taxes and gave their new masters one third of all their land produced. One of the worst terrors that faced them was the kidnapping of small boys from Christian families for the Sultan's standing army of Janissaries. These young boys were taken from their homes, trained in military discipline and in total loyalty to the Sultan's wishes, brain-washed into forgetting parents, religion and country, until such time as they were required to return home and establish a harsh alien rule.

What remained of the old national consciousness was fiercely guarded by these peasants. It was they who kept the old traditions alive, and who passed on the old songs and legends. Priests and people alike fled to the Dalmatian coast and only small pockets of Roman Christianity survived – mainly in the barren, mountainous regions of Hercegovina to the south-west. That it did not die out completely was due to the Franciscans, a band of devoted and zealous men who continued to labour in the arid limestone karst of Hercegovina – in the district of Brotnjo, for example, which had fallen to the Turks in 1468. Hunted, persecuted and martyred, their monasteries set on fire, they obeyed the commands of their founder, Francis of Assisi, to stay close to the poor and share their hardships – as bishops, priests, teachers, doctors, pharmacists. Of peasant stock themselves, they were well able to represent peasant interests. The contribution of the Franciscans to the history of the people of Hercegovina cannot be overestimated. They were deeply-rooted in the national psyche.

The harsh Muslim rule was to last for more than 400 years. Guerrilla warfare would never really cease, but it was not until the nineteenth century that Turkish power began to crumble. Serbia rose in 1804 and gave the signal for insurrection all over Europe. In 1815, though still a Turkish vassal-state, Serbia established itself as a principality which grew steadily larger and more independent. But in Bosnia and Hercegovina, though unrest was widespread and desperate, all attempts at revolt were bloodily put down.

As the power of the Ottoman Turks declined, three other powerful Empires, Austro-Hungary, Germany and Russia, jostled for influence in Central Europe. It did not suit the Austro-Hungarian Dual Monarchy that Bosnia-Hercegovina should be free to unite with Serbia, possibly under Russian protection, in some sort of pan-Slav alliance which would threaten the expansionist aims of Germany and Austria in the East. Potential Slav unity had to be nipped in the bud at all costs. In 1875, the whole of Bosnia-Hercegovina at last rose in revolt, and the Great Powers grew nervous. Three years later, against the wishes of Serbia and of the two nations involved, the Congress of Berlin allowed Austro-Hungary to occupy Bosnia and Hercegovina.

The new regime brought economic progress in its wake (and Hercegovinan tobacco was suddenly in great demand), and the new masters were less repressive than the old. But every attempt was made to encourage dissension between Serbs and Croats, and widen the divide between Orthodox, Muslim and Catholic. No contact with Serbia was allowed to the Serbs. Serbian resentment spilled over into fresh insurrection and in 1908 Austro-Hungary abandoned the fiction that it was merely administering the territories of Bosnia-Hercegovina, and without warning formally annexed them. This further humiliation, which slammed the door on Southern Slav unity and made permanent an arrangement that had been regarded by all parties as temporary, infuriated Serbia and gave it a grievance against Austro-Hungary that would before long shatter the peace of the world.

Serbia had grown into a self-confident state. Its defeat of the Turks in the Balkan Wars of 1912–13 excited and aroused all the South Slavs and drove them into a rare and passionate unity. Tensions grew. On 28th June 1914 the heir to the imperial throne of Austro-Hungary, the Archduke Franz Ferdinand, visiting Bosnia to attend troop manoeuvres on the border with Serbia, was assassinated by a Serb as he drove through Sarajevo. Austro-Hungary declared war on Serbia; the other nations lined up; and within two months Europe had been swept into the conflagration of the First World War.

When that war ended, the Slav dream seemed about to come true: all the old empires, including that of Austro-Hungary, had collapsed, and the kingdom of Serbs, Croats and Slovenes, came into being. The Croats, of whom many were to be found in Bosnia-Hercegovina, and most of whom were peasants, were confident that at last they were emerging from 450 years of slavery into a paradise of Southern Slav equality. But the new kingdom had a Serbian king at its head, and the Serbs were in a powerful majority, determined to prove their superiority over the Croats and Slovenes. Disillusionment set in almost immediately for the Croats, as the Serbs strove to consolidate their advantage. It was they who got the best jobs, whether in government, the armed forces, the police or commerce. The Croats, who in fact despised the Serbs for their alien Byzantine culture, had to face the fact that the Serbs regarded the new kingdom as an extension of Serbia; and their sense of burning injustice drove them to demand a separate Croat state of their own. In 1928, Vladko Maček spoke at the funeral of the Croat peasant leader, Stjepan Radić, murdered in the Belgrade Parliament, whom he was to succeed. He spoke bitterly of "millions of abused and oppressed peasants"; of "a nation which desires to be recognised as such"; of the right to have their own free state of Croatia, "where oppressed individuals and, even more, oppressed national groups, would be non-existent".[1]

In the light of what happened thirteen years later, his words hold a terrible irony.

The Serbian King Alexander ran out of patience and decided to impose unity by force. In 1929, he suspended the Constitution and declared a dictatorship, hopefully re-naming the country Yugoslavia, land of the Southern Slavs. Vladko Maček voiced the hopes of all Croats that by the wisdom of the king, they would become "free in their free Croatia".[2]

Alexander, unfortunately, was more at home with coercion than persuasion. He did not seem able to understand that unity could not be imposed, that it had to be given time and space within which to put down roots and grow. All opposition to his policies was suppressed; and bands of brutal Serbian Četniks,* an auxiliary arm of the state police, roamed the country, terrorising the Croat villages, and increasing the desperation of the Croats. "The Četniks in Čapljina threw babies and children up in the air and caught them on their swords," shuddered a peasant woman

---

* Četnik is a generic Serb name for freedom-fighter and in this sense it was later adopted by Colonel Draža Mihailović's Serbian royalist guerrillas during the German Occupation. Unfortunately its use by the excessively brutal thirties police blackened its name for all time.

in Medjugorje. "There was a house near Ljubuški and another near Čapljina which the Četniks specially built for hanging Croats in. They would have liked to hang every single Croat if they could, but the Blessed Mother didn't let them." A memorandum submitted to the League of Nations by exiled Croats in 1931 listed innumerable people held without trial, the use of torture, police brutality and other forms of oppression.[3] In setting out to break the passive resistance of the Croats, Alexander had succeeded only in embittering them still further.

The people of Medjugorje remember these as desperate years, when it was almost impossible for a Croat to find work, when poverty was intense. As the price of tobacco dropped on the world market, the Hercegovinan growers were unable to pay their taxes. Many of them were forced to emigrate – to America, Canada or Australia.

Yet few resorted to violence. Those extremists who belonged to the outlawed nationalist Ustaša group had already fled to Italy with their leader, Ante Pavelić. They were welcomed by Mussolini and placed under his special protection. The running sore of Croat nationalism was seen by the Fascist dictator as a useful weapon for the Axis Powers to use against Yugoslavia. Pavelić and his Ustaše were given funds and established in terrorist-training camps where they learned to handle bombs and small arms and were encouraged to make hit-and-run guerrilla raids on their homeland.

In October 1934, Pavelić agents assassinated Alexander. He bequeathed a legacy of political bitterness and considerable economic distress, but, to Mussolini's chagrin, Yugoslavia did not fall apart. Nor, in spite of the murder, were the nationalist Ustaše yet being taken seriously as a political force. It was not until 1938, when the Nazis had already seized power in Austria, that rumours of a possible link between the Ustaše and the Nazis began to gain ground.

In April 1941, rumour became fact, after Yugoslavia was bombed into unconditional surrender and carved up among the Axis Powers: Germany, Italy, Bulgaria and Hungary. The largest fragment of what remained was given the title of Independent State of Croatia, and included Croatia-Slavonia, parts of Dalmatia and all of Bosnia-Hercegovina. It was a puppet state, controlled by German and Italian arms, but with immediate power vested in Pavelić and his Ustaše. The new state's name was a misnomer, since it was neither independent nor sovereign, and many of the people who belonged to it were not Croat. Included in the population were many Muslims and at least two million Serbs, now, unluckily for them, at the mercy of their sworn enemies.

Though many Croats were sickened by the triumph of the extremist Ustaše, most people in Bosnia-Hercegovina rejoiced at this apparent reversal in their fortunes. Just two days after the proclamation of the new state, word had reached the capital, Zagreb, that Četnik paramilitaries had completely destroyed two Croat villages and massacred their inhabitants. Such horrors would not lightly be forgotten. "We weren't sorry when Hitler bombed Belgrade," a woman in Medjugorje told me forty-five years later, recalling the event as though it had happened yesterday. Refugees from Serbian terror in Hercegovina poured into Zagreb to enrol in the Ustaša militias, in the hope of revenge.

Dr Alojzije Stepinac, the Catholic Archbishop of Zagreb, formally welcomed the new state which was to mark the end of the hated Serbian domination. The small extreme nationalist wing of the Peasant Party threw in their lot unreservedly with the Ustaše, but the much larger group of moderate Peasant leaders stayed neutral.

It is an enduring tragedy for the Croats that they so cruelly misjudged the moment. For what lay in store for them was not the hoped-for journey into freedom but a nightmare descent into pure barbarism. In their enthusiasm for the New Order, they were blind to the fanatical racial hatred which drove Ante Pavelić and his Ustaše. Pavelić wanted to "purify" Croatia from its alien Serbs – whom he hated – and, as a sop to Hitler, from its Jews, although his own wife was Jewish. Like Hitler, he would stop at nothing, not even mass extermination, to achieve his aim. The terror promptly unleashed by the Ustaše was aimed both against Jews and Serbs; and against the thousands of Croats who found the courage to resist the tide of evil.

Croatia was to be a two-religion state – Catholic and Muslim – again. On that Pavelić was determined. There began a barbarous persecution of the Orthodox Churches. Mile Budak, the Minister of Education, announced that one third of the Serbs were to be deported, one third (mainly the intelligentsia) killed, and one third (the peasants and the uneducated) converted to Catholicism. When the deportations began, whole families were picked up at night, given half an hour in which to get ready, then taken to a transit camp and stripped of all they possessed. Within a very few weeks, as transport arrangements collapsed, these camps had become dangerously overcrowded and a huge health-hazard. The Germans eventually put a stop to this traffic, but not before 120,000 Serbs had been deported.

Bands of Ustaša thugs were sent all over Bosnia-Hercegovina with orders to burn down Orthodox villages and cut the throats of their occupants. In several cases, all the males were driven into the church – which was then burned down, while the Ustaše stood outside, guns at the ready, waiting to shoot any would-be escapers. Corpses were strung up on trees and lamp-posts as an object-lesson to the whole population. Everywhere "the slaughter was carried out with sadistic cruelty; the victims were hacked to death, buried alive after being forced to dig their own graves, hideously tortured and mutilated before being despatched."[4] So excessive was Ustaša cruelty towards Serb women and children that even the Germans disapproved, not least perhaps because the Ustaše terror was driving the Croatian Serbs (and huge numbers of conscience-stricken Croats) into the mountains and forests, where Josip Broz Tito (himself a Croat) and his Partisans were putting up a valiant resistance. The latter had sprung into action only after June 1941 when Germany invaded the Soviet Union, and the "Imperialist War" suddenly became the "Great Patriotic War of Liberation".

As head of the Roman Catholic Church, Archbishop Stepinac was trapped in a cruel dilemma. He was now receiving first-hand accounts of appalling atrocities in which, it was clear, a number of his priests were implicated. (After the war, the evidence for this came not only from Communist but from Vatican, Italian and British sources.) Indeed, some of the Catholic clergy had given the new Croatian state their whole-hearted approval and had actively supported the compulsory conversion of Orthodox Serbs to Catholicism. Evidence of Franciscan involvement in Ustaša crimes against the Serbs was unfortunately beyond doubt. Some friars even served in the Ustaša government. Many of these men had joined the Ustaše before the war. In an official report to his brigadier in 1945, the Catholic writer Evelyn Waugh, who served in the British forces attached to the Partisans in 1944, had this comment to make:

> For some time the Croat Franciscans had caused misgivings in Rome for their independence and narrow patriotism. They were mainly recruited from the least cultured part of the population and there is abundant evidence that several wholly unworthy men were attracted to the Franciscan Order by the security and comparative ease which it offered. Many of those youths were sent to Italy for training. Their novitiate was in the neighbourhood of Pavelić's HQ at Siena where Ustaša agents made contact with them and imbued them with Pavelić's ideas.[5]

In 1945, the provincial of the Franciscans in Croatia said that nearly all the priests known for their Ustaša activity were in the army and therefore outside the jurisdiction of their regular Superiors.[6]

Too late, Stepinac realised what was happening. Estimates of the numbers of Serbs killed ranged from 60,000 to 750,000, with some-where between 200,000 and 300,000 forcibly (or willingly, to escape the slaughter) converted. It must have been a grievous blow to Stepinac that the longed-for Croatian state had turned out to be a machine operated by monsters. Croats generally were appalled, but for the most part dared not say so publicly, for the long arm of the Ustaše reached out to strike its internal as well as its external opponents, and even mild expressions of opposition were punishable by death or internment in a concentration camp from which few returned. In the notorious camp of Jasenovac were not only Serbs, Jews and gipsies but Croats who had dared defy the regime. Any Croat refusing military service in the Ustaša Army would have been summarily shot. Dissident voices were therefore few, but one Croat Catholic voiced the thoughts of many in a letter to Stepinac in July 1942:

> The inhuman and anti-Christian attitude of the many Croat Catholic priests has dismayed not only some of their brothers but the majority of Croat intellectuals to whom I belong. I have been struck by the absence of all public manifestation of a Christian and human sympathy from the Croat hierarchy to the victims of an indescribable regime of massacre and illegality against Orthodox fellow-countrymen. I have asked myself with anguish why Croatian Catholic circles have not disavowed publicly in the name of the Catholic Church the forced conversion of the Orthodox and the confiscation of their goods.[7]

In September 1941, the Franciscan Bishop Mišić of Mostar in Hercegovina (the diocese which includes Medjugorje) had instructed all his priests to tell their congregations that those who murdered or despoiled others would be refused absolution in the confessional. He later wrote to Archbishop Stepinac describing "a reign of terror":

> Men are captured like animals, they are slaughtered, murdered, living men are thrown off cliffs . . . From Mostar and from Čapljina a train took six carloads of mothers, young girls and children . . . to Šurmanći . . . they were led up the mountains and . . . thrown alive off the precipices . . . In . . . Mostar itself they have been found by the hundreds, taken in wagons outside the town and then shot down like animals.[8]

The harshness of the impoverished Hercegovinan territory bred extremism. Brutality and fanaticism went hand in hand with extraordinary courage and endurance. Šurmanci is a village within the parish of Medjugorje, where almost exactly forty years later a weeping Madonna would be seen on a hillside, calling for peace. A short distance away, and within sight of those dreadful cliffs, is the Orthodox monastery of Žitomislić, which was burned down during the war and later rebuilt. On the wall leading into its chapel is a plaque to commemorate the day, 21st June 1941, when the entire community of monks was taken outside by the Ustaše and buried alive.

Stepinac could not believe that Pavelić actually knew about such atrocities, and pleaded with him to restrain the violence of his followers. It was not true, as the Communists would later charge, that he underwrote

Ustaša crimes. For from 1942 onwards, he began to protest vehemently in his sermons against racial discrimination. In May 1942 he said, "Our true relations with our neighbour demand that we see in him a man . . . a child of God . . . our brother, whom we must love . . . It would be an absurdity to speak of a New Order in the world if the human personality is not valued within it."

From this time onwards, Stepinac more and more openly denounced the regime as evil, and warned the government that even the conscript soldiers in the Croatian Army were deserting to the Partisans in large numbers. (Many more claim that they would have done so, had they not been equally afraid of being treated as "class enemies" by the Communists.) Stepinac intervened wherever he could, to save both Jews and Serbs, and it is said that he provided Swiss passports with which they might escape the country. In 1942, he engineered the rescue of 7,000 Serb children from the internment camps, and put them into the care of private families. As time went by, and Ustaša cruelty did not abate, his tone grew sharper, and the official press began to attack "that high ecclesiastical dignitary who has recently, in his sermons, passed beyond the limits of his vocation and begun to meddle in affairs in which he is not competent".[9]

When Italy withdrew from the war in 1943, the Germans took control of that part of the Croatian state hitherto held by the Italians. The Western Allies ordered the Italians throughout Yugoslavia to hand over their arms and equipment to the Partisans. Tito's hand was thus immeasurably strengthened by the spoils from ten Italian divisions. Resistance in Yugoslavia had taken the form of civil war because its two main movements were engaged in active hostilities against each other even more enthusiastically than against the common enemy. The Partisans had grown in political and military importance, and from January 1944, regardless of the implications for the future of Yugoslavia, the Allies gave them full support: "We have proclaimed ourselves the strong supporters of Marshal Tito because of his heroic and massive struggle against the German armies."[10] What this meant was that in Allied eyes Tito was killing more Germans than Mihailović's Serbian Četniks. In fact, both groups were more interested in destroying each other than in fighting the Germans.

As the Partisans, Četniks and Ustaše engaged in their bloody three-cornered struggle for the future control of the country, the villages of Bosnia-Hercegovina were once again in the thick of battle. Today, the people are unwilling to talk about the war years, but just occasionally they drop their guard. Asked point-blank about atrocities, one woman angrily replied, "Well, the pre-war Četniks had thrown Croat people into pits and buried them, so we did the same to them."

The villages were under merciless pressure, constantly terrorised as first one side and then another gained the upper hand. Wherever the Partisans – whose slogan was "Brotherhood and Unity" – came into a village, they burned down the village hall, destroyed all public records and executed the leaders of the community.[11] Frequently they killed not only individual "enemies of the people" but whole communities which offered them resistance. Thus did they dispose of any who might later have opposed them. For the Partisans had now dropped their wartime façade of tolerance and emerged in their true Communist colours. The post-war ideological battle had already been joined, and the cost of "liberation" was high.

By 1945, almost all the countryside was under Partisan control and the Ustaše were at their last gasp. In Hercegovina, some of them fled to the hill-top Franciscan monastery of Široki Brijeg. When the Partisans surrounded and took the monastery, they killed everybody in it, Ustaše and priests alike. On 24th March five Croatian bishops wrote a pastoral letter rejecting guilt for wartime atrocities and accusing the Partisans: "Today we must decisively bear witness before God and the world against the systematic murder and torture of innocent Catholic priests and people, most of whom have led blameless lives, illegally condemned for imaginary crimes by those who hate the Catholic Church."

The letter concluded with a promise that Croats would continue to struggle for a national identity: "History is the witness that the Croatian people through all its thirteen hundred years has never ceased to proclaim . . . that it will never renounce the right to that freedom and independence which every nation desires."[12]

Worse was to follow. When the Ustaša government was forced out on 6th May 1945, about 200,000 Croat soldiers, civilian refugees from the Communist terror, and some Četniks retreated to the Austrian border, where the soldiers tried to surrender to the British military authorities at Bleiburg. But the British, who now officially recognised only the Partisans, sent them back again. They were put on to trains and driven back to Yugoslavia and – to certain death. It is estimated that 16,000 Croats were butchered in one day – mass graves had already been prepared for them. Prisoners were tied in pairs and mown down as they walked.[13] Vladko Maček, the ex-leader of the Peasant Party, reports eye-witness accounts of corpses of men, women and children trussed up with wire and floating down the river Drava, into which they had been presumably thrown alive.[14] Those who were not killed in this way were driven on foot through Yugoslavia to various concentration camps; those who dropped from exhaustion on the way were shot. Though some of the victims were undoubtedly guilty Ustaša criminals, the majority were simple peasants, innocent of crime. The ex-Communist leader, Milovan

Djilas, would later testify to this. "They had no murder on their hands," he wrote. "Their only crime was fear of Communism and the reputation of Communists. Their sole motive was panic."[15]

But, as Joseph Stalin said, history is as history is written. And as history is always written by the victors, the losers will always be vilified. Particularly when the victors scorn objective truth as "bourgeois" and define truth as that which suits their revolutionary purposes. Such own-goal horrors were, and still are, swept under the carpet by the new masters of the country. The subject has so far been taboo in modern Yugoslavia, where to talk of Partisan war-crimes, or to challenge the official Partisan record of the war, is a criminal offence. Today in a museum in Mostar, Medjugorje's provincial capital, one may see photographs of Partisans who were shot or hanged by the Ustaše, Germans or Četniks; but none of those who were murdered by the Partisans. Yet the truth remains, even though it may only be stated obliquely. In *The Knife*, a post-war novel, an old Yugoslav Muslim puts those bitter days in perspective: "All of them: Ustashas, Chetniks, Serbs, Croats and Moslems killed each other and when the knife is used, there is no difference between a cross, a crescent, a tricolour cockade, a letter U or a red star; the pain is the same."[16]

The war over, all internal resistance to Communist rule came to an end and full-blooded Communism could be imposed. The people were relieved that the Germans had gone, but increasingly frightened of the Communist secret police with its network of informers in every village, street or workplace. Yugoslavia was proclaimed a Federal People's Republic, with six constituent republics, of which Bosnia-Hercegovina was one, and with Josip Broz Tito as head of state. As, in a mixed state like Bosnia-Hercegovina, with its population forty per cent Serb, forty per cent Muslim and twenty per cent Croat, the Serbs and Croats identified themselves as Serb or Croat, and the Muslims refused to be described as either, the government decided to introduce a new ethnic category of Muslim. A Muslim in Yugoslavia is not necessarily a disciple of Allah!

The state-controlled media went on to the attack, branding all opponents of the new regime as Fascists and traitors; to be systematically eliminated as "enemies of the people". The arrests and liquidations echoed those of the hated Ustaše. All signs of ethnic "separatism" were rigorously suppressed. Religion was not abolished but was firmly detached from the State, in a determined bid to smash the power of the Church, whether Catholic or Orthodox. Religious worship was permitted, but religious education in secondary schools was gradually phased out and replaced by education in the principles of Marxism-Leninism; the religious press was banned, and a land reform reduced the Roman Catholic Church to penury. Most importantly, the "misuse of religion for political ends" – whatever that might be taken to mean – was rigorously proscribed. There were to be no privileges for the Churches in the new society.

Priests, whether innocent or guilty, were a special target. Many were executed or imprisoned on charges of having collaborated with the Ustaše. The most notorious of the ensuing trials (though by no means the worst) was that of Archbishop Stepinac himself. Tito had tried to persuade the archbishop to loosen the Catholic Church's ties with the Vatican and lead a more national Church under the control of the State. On his refusal, he was arrested and charged with having supported the Pavelić regime and with trying to undermine the present one. In 1946 he was sentenced to sixteen years' hard labour.* It was the start of a bitter and ruthless ideological war. Relations with the Vatican were severed; infamous show trials were arranged on fabricated evidence; bishops visiting their dioceses for Confirmation were obstructed and frequently beaten up. Pressure, both crude and subtle, was brought to bear on believers, to discourage them from practising their faith or bringing up their children as believers. Yet, through it all, the bulk of the population remained Christian.

When Tito asserted his independence from Moscow, Stalin expelled him from the Cominform in 1948. Stalin had long mistrusted ambitious foreign Communists who were capable of running their own show. Tito, though he had not expected the expulsion, put a brave face on it and set out to prove himself as good a Marxist-Leninist as Stalin.

Though matters slowly improved after Stalin's death in 1953, no very obvious change was noted until after the death of Cardinal Stepinac in 1960† and the general improvement in relations between the Communist Powers and the Vatican that followed the Second Vatican Council. The Council also opened the door to the renewal of dialogue with the Orthodox Churches.

But the desire for reconciliation was not universal. When in a sermon for Christmas 1963 the Bishop of Banja Luka humbly admitted that crimes had indeed been committed against the Serbian Orthodox Christians by those who called themselves Catholic, there was outrage among the Croats. "We acknowledge with anguish," the bishop said, "the terrible crimes of these misguided men, and we beg our Orthodox brothers to forgive us, as Christ on the Cross forgave all men. We in our turn forgive all those who have wronged or hated us. Today, gathered round Christ's cradle, let all debts be cancelled, and may love reign."[17]

Some priests in the bishop's diocese refused to read out the letter from

---

* Archbishop Stepinac served five years of this sentence, and was then released into a supervised house arrest.

† He had been made a Cardinal *in absentia* in 1953.

their pulpits. The treaty later signed with the Vatican in 1966 was hated for the clause in which Rome promised that its clergy would not indulge in politics and "condemned every act of political terrorism or similar criminal forms of violence, whoever its perpetrators be".[18] This much resented clause reflected government fears about the activities of certain priests working in Croat émigré circles throughout the world. Among the émigrés were a handful of Ustaša sympathisers who were mounting terrorist attacks on Yugoslav officials abroad. Fear of resurgent Croat nationalism seemed to haunt the regime.

Since 1963, the government had accelerated its attempts to liberalise the regime, moving away from sterile over-centralised Soviet-style economics towards a limited self-management and greater national autonomy. A new industrialisation programme meant the decline of agriculture – and of village life. As travel restrictions were lifted, about a million Yugoslav workers migrated to the West European factories to do most of the hard dirty jobs that nobody else wanted. But as the liberalising process gathered momentum, the Croats began to complain of political, cultural and economic discrimination.[19] Demonstrations and rallies followed. Tito let it be known, just three years after Russian tanks had rolled into Prague, after the brief Prague spring, that Brezhnev was threatening equally unwelcome fraternal assistance to settle matters in Yugoslavia.

In November 1971, students at Zagreb University went on strike and took to the streets. Police and troops moved into Zagreb and arrested the ringleaders. Over the next few months there were over 400 arrests, resulting in long prison sentences. Tito was so alarmed by this threat to national unity that he began to impose tighter controls, and to take measures to stamp out any incipient nationalism. The leaders of the Croatian League of Communists were sacked, and hardliners installed in their place.[20] Several issues of the Zagreb diocesan newspaper were banned for including "nationalist propaganda"; both the editor and a woman staff journalist were sentenced to one year of imprisonment each.* The secular press launched a fierce attack on Cardinal Kuharić of Zagreb.

Yet was this really a nationalist revolt nipped in the bud? Dusko Doder, a visiting American journalist of Serbian origin, doubted it. On all sides, he heard it said that the ethnic issue was being used by the ruling group to divide the country and to postpone indefinitely the granting of individual liberties:

> I heard both Serb and Croat intellectuals argue that the 1971 crisis was a popular movement against the authoritarian strands in Tito's regime, and

---

* The sentence was later quashed.

that the regime eventually fought back by casting the Croats into the role of separatists and spoilers, and telling others: "See what happens when you loosen up? The Croats want to destroy the State."[21]

By 1981, the large and restive Albanian majority in Kosovo, an autonomous state within the republic of Serbia, was regularly protesting on the streets. It was widely believed that it was the regime's repression of the normal outlets for political frustration – discussion and dialogue – that kept the ethnic minorities permanently on the boil.

Tito died, aged eighty-seven, in May 1980, and the state's future hung precariously in the balance. Apart from the ethnic discontent, the people were restive about the appallingly high rate of unemployment. Only the fact that roughly one in six of the entire work-force worked as migrant labourers abroad kept the situation from becoming intolerable. Inflation was the highest in Europe, and there was a chronic scarcity of consumer goods. In the socialist paradise, the rich were getting richer and the poor poorer. Fear that nationalist fervour might fuse with these social and economic grievances and ignite a general uprising kept the government awake at nights.

Then there was the Catholic Church. Since the election of a Slav Pope, the Polish Karol Wojtyła, in 1978, the Church had made great strides among the South Slavs – the Croats and Slovenes – particularly among the young. It seemed to be trying to model itself on the Church in Poland, and had to be reminded sharply from time to time that Yugoslavia was not Poland. In February 1981, Church-State relations reached a new freezing point when 7,000 Croats ostentatiously marked the twenty-first anniversary of Archbishop Stepinac's death round his tomb in Zagreb Cathedral. In view of what was happening in nearby Poland, where the Solidarity movement was making the Polish Communist Party sweat, the Yugoslav Communists felt nervous and insecure.

It was precisely at this point that reports began coming in that the Virgin Mary was appearing to a group of teenagers in Hercegovina, the very heartland of Croatian Catholicism. Is it surprising, therefore, that the government, insecure over the crumbling economy, and suffering from the loss of its legendary leader, should have reacted with such alarm?

3

A Diabolical Plot?

What have those lonely mountains worth revealing?
More glory and more grief than I can tell:
The earth that wakes one human heart to feeling
Can centre both the worlds of Heaven and Hell.
Emily Brontë

By Saturday, 27th June, Fra Zrinko Čuvalo was a worried man. He had sent Marinko Ivanković packing the previous evening. But Marinko's wife, Dragica, was made of sterner stuff and was a veritable tornado when roused. "Dragica came to see me early on the Saturday morning and really let fly," he recalls ruefully.

> She tore into me, shrieking that everyone was going to the hill, the police, the Mayor, doctors, friars, priests, bishop's secretary, and heaven knows who else. "You're the only stubborn one and you should be ashamed of yourself," she berated me. "Who do you think you are, behaving as though this had nothing to do with you? Are you human, are you a priest? You're no better than an atheist, you should be run out of the village." And so on. I shook her by the shoulders and said: "Dragica, calm down. One day you'll understand why it was important for us not to rush into this."

"Still, I *was* worried," he admits. "It wasn't that I actually believed the children's stories. What worried me was trying to decide what I was dealing with: was it a dangerous conspiracy, mere rumour, a piece of childish mischief – or irrational states of mind?"

Though in reality Fra Zrinko was kind-hearted and generous to a fault, few suspected it. He had a brusque and aggressive manner which made people, especially children, avoid him. "Children have always been frightened of me," he confesses disarmingly, "all children, not just these particular ones. My expression puts them off. They don't like my face. Well, that's too bad; I am what I am and I can't help my face." He now confronted the six like an avenging angel, accusing them of drug-taking and warning them to tell the truth while there was still time. Since he was more aware than they of the dire consequences that would befall them if this thing went any further, his anxiety found its outlet in anger: "One of these days, we'll find ourselves standing in the criminal dock together," he shouted. And, as ten-year-old Jakov obviously found that funny, Zrinko rounded on him: "And that means you too, little boy. It's no laughing matter."

Matters had reached this point when, to Fra Zrinko's undisguised relief, the parish priest, Fra Jozo Zovko, returned.

Forty-year-old Jozo Zovko, an attractive, burningly idealistic Franciscan, had been in charge of the Medjugorje parish only since the previous November, and as yet knew very few of his flock, even by sight. Jozo, an enthusiast for the charismatic movement, was disappointed by Medjugorje's lukewarm response to the changes he was trying to bring about in its prayer-life, and was inclined to dismiss the village's spiritual state as "stunted and anaemic".

Before his transfer to Medjugorje, Fra Jozo had arranged to preach several eight-day retreats, one of which had been fixed for June, in a convent near Zagreb, 400 kilometres away. On the eve of his departure, his mother broke her leg and was rushed off to hospital in Mostar. Paying her a hasty visit, Jozo promised to come back as soon as the retreat was over. For the next eight days he was shut away from all news of the outside world, praying – and asking the sisters to pray – that his uninspired parish might somehow discover a source of spiritual energy.

On the twenty-fourth, the day of the first apparition, he went into Zagreb for a Christian Renewal Group meeting. "Father Jozo," one of the group greeted him excitedly, "have you heard that Medjugorje was struck by lightning during the night? They say the post office has been burned down, and a lot of other damage has been done." Alarmed, Jozo rushed to telephone Zrinko, only to find that the lines were down.

From Zagreb next day he flew to Split, arriving at the nearby Franciscan monastery at about ten in the evening, to be told that Zrinko had been there, looking pale and withdrawn; but had left no message. Next morning found him at his mother's bedside in the Mostar hospital; and it was as he was leaving there that an ambulance from Čitluk drew up, with the excitable Dragica, swathed in bandages, inside. (At work earlier that morning, a metal slab had fallen on her, injuring her hand and breaking her leg.) "What's the matter with Father Zrinko?" she yelled at him, from the ambulance. For a moment, the startled priest thought his colleague must have met with an accident, but Dragica soon set him straight. "No, no, nothing of that sort," she said impatiently. "Nothing's happened to *him*. But you get on over to Medjugorje as fast as you can. Our Lady has been appearing to some children."

Jozo, who barely knew Dragica, decided she must be mad. None the less, he made his way with all speed to Medjugorje, arriving there just before noon. When his Franciscan housekeeper, Sister Marcellina, greeted him much as Dragica had done, he was profoundly shocked. "People are coming from everywhere," she told him. "They say Our Lady's been appearing to some children up on the hill." "Has Father Zrinko spoken to them?" he asked. "Yes, and he's recorded the conversations." Jozo found the cassette and listened to a play-back, noting abstractedly that Zrinko interrogating the children sounded like an official of the SUP (state security police). Impatiently he waited for his assistant to return from the village.

As soon as he saw Jozo, Zrinko blurted out his fears that the whole farrago was either drug-related or a Communist plot to discredit the Church: "One of the girls, Mirjana Dragicević, comes from a grammar school in Sarajevo and they're saying she brought drugs with her, maybe in cigarettes. She's started giving drugs to the children, and now they're claiming to see visions. The crowds are pouring in, and I'm at my wits' end. Whichever way you look at it, we've got a big problem on our hands. What made that girl decide to come from Sarajevo just now? Someone must have put her up to it."

"Do you know these children?" Jozo interrupted the flow.

"No, I've talked to them, but I can't say I know them."

"Well, you'd better bring them here."

When the children stood before him, Jozo couldn't recall having seen any of them before. He was unsure which thought disturbed him more: that they were dabbling in drugs or part of a Communist conspiracy. He decided to tackle the drugs possibility first, and called Mirjana in to his office, firing questions at her, staccato fashion: who was she, where did she come from, why was she in Bijakovići, did she go to church? After a few minutes he had concluded, to his own surprise, that Mirjana was a very normal teenage girl, interested in boys, not at all devout, but not devious either – and with no obvious symptoms of drug addiction. That left him with the conspiracy theory:

> I reasoned like this: she comes from a long way away. I don't know her at all. For that matter, I don't know any of the others either. Most of them go to school in Mostar or Čitluk. Anybody could have got at them and put them up to this nonsense. There has to be someone stage-managing them.

He was convinced that some enemy of the Church had hit on this method of bringing it into disrepute. So he began tape-recording all his conversations with the children:

> so that I could listen to them again at night and discover the inconsistencies in what they said. I spoke to them for hours on end, trying to get at the truth. But the more they told me, the more confused I became. They were

absolutely overwhelmed by what they'd seen: and they couldn't understand why I wouldn't believe them. But the more I listened to them, the more insoluble the problem seemed to get.

Helplessly he suggested they should pray more and read the Bible. He tried to find out what they knew about Lourdes and Fatima, places where the Virgin had appeared to peasant children before: but they appeared to know nothing at all. "I'd never heard of any other apparitions," said Mirjana. "I didn't know about Fatima or Lourdes. I suppose I'd never been interested in that kind of thing. In those days I only went to church when I had to." Marija, for her part, appeared astounded to learn that the Virgin had ever appeared on earth before. Depressed by their ignorance, Fra Jozo hastily distributed some prayer books and rosaries among them, together with a book entitled *The Apparitions of the Blessed Virgin*.

Early in the afternoon, cars began to stream in, filling every available square inch around the church. "My God, what *is* this?" the priest asked himself in despair:

> All those crowds, yet no one interfering with them. The police didn't seem to mind where they were going or what they were doing, they were only concerned with directing the traffic. There had to be something behind it. You couldn't see the road for people and cars; the hill was full, the fields all around were full. The crowds were swarming up the hill like bees. Thousands of gullible idiots, waiting for something spectacular to happen. Why couldn't the truths of the Gospel move them like that? What was wrong with them? I felt I was being threatened by a river in full flood, or by a huge landslide that was rushing at me to swallow me up. I felt very afraid and helpless.

Had he but known it, the authorities' collective state of mind was not very different from his own. The Communists, too, suspected a plot – on the part of the Croat clergy. And on the afternoon of Saturday 27th June the police made their first move, arriving in Bijakovići and removing the children to Čitluk for medical tests. "When I need a medical check-up, I'll arrange one for myself," Vicka, the most ebullient and outspoken of the six, had furiously protested. But all protest was vain. Zlata, Vicka's mother, rushed distraught to the presbytery.

"The SUP have taken the children away."

"What for?"

"To see a doctor."

"Don't worry," said Zrinko, "they've got to do that." He himself was arranging to have the children medically examined.

Vicka later described what happened that afternoon:

First of all, they took Ivan in . . . about four o'clock in the afternoon. Poor guy, he let the doctor ask him questions for more than an hour . . . Then *I* went in and said, "Have you finished?" Actually, they'd called for Mirjana, but I went in instead . . . [The doctor] said it wasn't my turn but I could sit down if I wanted. I told him: "I'm young and healthy, thank God, and I'll stay standing."[1]

The doctor they saw that afternoon was an ordinary GP, and therefore unqualified to pronounce on their sanity. As far as he could judge, however, the children were normal, well-balanced and healthy human beings. It was not the verdict the authorities had hoped to hear. For his part, Zrinko was disgusted to learn that so few tests had been done. No blood and urine tests for drugs, for example. "Look," he insisted, "we've heard that the girl from Sarajevo brought in drugs. And another thing, they say that one of the children is an epileptic and a hysteric. We'll have to call in the experts on that one." It seemed that the clergy were more eager to conduct a stringent investigation than the police.

It was six in the evening when the children were released, and they had to take a taxi back to Medjugorje. All of them except Ivan (whose anxious mother had prevailed on him to stay at home out of trouble) were on the hillside at six-thirty. As on the previous evening, everyone saw a brilliant light appear, flooding the village. Accounts of what happened on that evening and the next are a little contradictory, reflecting the general state of confusion at the time – and the fact that the authorities later confiscated the written accounts, filmed material and cassettes relating to those early days. When the crowd saw from the children's rapt faces that the vision had appeared again, they surged forward, almost crushing the visionaries in their excitement. Seemingly disoriented by the fuss, the vision kept appearing and disappearing. Disappointed, the children began to descend the hill, protected by the stalwart Marinko and some of his friends. "A few of us had got together to guard the children," he says. "Suddenly they broke away from us, shouting, 'There she is.' At that we made a circle round them so that the crowd wouldn't come too close again." Mirjana apparently told the vision that she was accused of being on drugs, and was told to pay no attention since people would always be ready to make unjust accusations.

This visitation seems to have been less satisfactory than its predecessors. Ivan, however, was consoled for his enforced absence, for while he was standing at the foot of the hill, looking longingly upwards, the vision appeared to him and told him to be at peace. Seeing how happy this made him, his mother felt unable to continue her objections to his joining the others on the hill. In fact, she had still not got over her surprise at discovering a rosary in his trousers pocket on the day after the first apparition; until this time, she had had no occasion to associate her son with spiritual fervour.

Sunday the twenty-eighth was a glorious day, but Fra Jozo was determined to dampen his flock's enthusiasm for hill-walking. At Mass, with a captive audience, he preached about revelation, recognising that God might choose to reveal Himself to the world at any time and in any place, but warning of the dangers of fraud and self-deception and advising care. True divine revelation would always be recognisable by its fruits: "A revelation that does not inspire me to be a better person and to pray more is not a revelation from God," he scolded. Had not Christ Himself, the most complete revelation of the Godhead, warned of false prophets who impress by the signs and wonders they perform, but who leave the essential human condition unchanged?

After Mass, he held his usual catechism class for older pupils attending state schools in Čitluk, Mostar and Čapljina, where, like everywhere else in Communist Yugoslavia, atheism was the prevailing ethos and religious instruction was not allowed. Then he took the class into the church to pray for the strength to resist Satan, if indeed it was Satan who was behind the strange happenings in Medjugorje. Someone pointed out Ana, Vicka's sister. "Ana," he protested clumsily, "I'm afraid your sister and the others are trying to make fools of us. How long are they going to keep up this hoax?" Ana burst into tears: "I know my sister," she stormed at him. "She doesn't tell lies."

It was already 5 p.m., and outside in the golden sunlight, the crowds were weaving their ant-like way up the hill. Jozo, quietly congratulating himself that his youngsters were all here in the church with him rather than on the hill, knelt and prayed aloud. Alas for his hopes: "When I finished the prayer, I turned round and – they had all gone, every one of them, to the hill."

Alone in the church, he felt desolate. "I wanted to cry out: God, what do you want of me? All these people are convinced you're up there on that hill. What am I supposed to do about it?"

Fra Zrinko, in civilian garb, was one of about 15,000 people on the Crnica hill that night. Fearful of the police, he stood at the bottom of the hill, urging all the Franciscans he met to follow his example and exchange their brown habits for something less provocative. "Some of the nuns didn't have anything to change into, so I told them to go and borrow something from our Medjugorje sisters, to help themselves to whatever they could find." He shared Jozo's fears: "It's as though you see something coming at you, but you're not sure what it is, what you should be doing about it, or how you can protect yourself. But you know that, whatever it is, it has the power to destroy you."

By noon, the pilgrims had begun arriving, hot, dusty and thirsty. "They baked in the sun," remembers Vicka, "without water or food or anything." The six children arrived a little after six, and once again the village was bathed in that special light that seemed to act as a beacon to them. A visiting Franciscan, Viktor Kosir, reported:

> Marija and Jakov were walking with me when suddenly Marija's face flushed scarlet. "Look! Look! Look!" she said. Jakov said nothing, but together they ran ahead at what seemed to be a superhuman speed. Marija was wearing a white blouse and red skirt, so I could see her distinctly as she ran, almost seeming to fly. It was impossible to keep up with her.[2]

Fra Zrinko heard a plain-clothes policeman in the crowd blaspheme loudly because he couldn't keep up with Marija. The Franciscan felt a deep loathing for this crowd: "They'd all hurried past the church to get to the hill, and there they all were with their clicking cameras, untouched by any spiritual experience." When a woman uttered an obscene oath because the Madonna hadn't appeared to *her*, Zrinko rounded on her. "And if *I* were the Madonna, I wouldn't appear to the likes of you," he said in exasperation.

"What do you want of these people here?" the children asked the apparition.

"That they should persevere in their faith," came the reply. "Let all those who do not see me believe just as though they *did* see." As for the priests, "Let them be strong in their faith and give you all the help they can."

"Dear Madonna," they persisted, "won't you leave some sign for us, so that people will believe we're not just playing tricks?"

"Go in the peace of God" came the only reply, but the light remained for an instant after she had gone.

The crowd followed the children in prayer and they sang Croatian hymns together; it was all a bit confused and aimless. Fra Zrinko's fears had most certainly not been laid to rest, and he sought out the children to question them further, hoping to trap them into contradicting themselves and each other:

> I was disappointed with what they told me. There was so much nonsense. The conversations they were apparently having with the vision were so flat and boring. It all seemed so pointless, there was no sense of the numinous, not the merest whiff of anything divine, as far as I was concerned.

It seemed, as the children pointed out, that everyone believed them except the priests and the police: "Everyone in the village knew we couldn't be lying," said Marija, "because they knew we'd never make a joke out of religion. We always put God in first place, in theory, at least."

In the parish of Medjugorje that night, theory was being translated into practice. As the crowd streamed down the hill in search of water, bread and wine, the villagers abandoned their suspicion of all strangers, and tentatively opened their doors and turned on their precious cold-water taps, to provide drinks for the thirsty. "The people gave so long as they had anything left to give," said Vicka. "But the water soon ran out. I know of a man – (it was, in fact, Marinko) – who gave not only water but wine and whisky too, until he had nothing left. He even went out and bought seven or eight cylinders of water to give out to the pilgrims."

Monday the twenty-ninth was the feast of St Peter and St Paul, an important day in the Church's calendar. Jozo went into his office and wrote out a declaration to be read aloud by himself and Zrinko after their respective Masses:

> We have been disturbed by . . . the statement of six children about the apparitions of Our Lady on the hill of Bijakovići. I have refrained from passing judgement on the matter, but I have been watching carefully and listening to the children and other eye-witnesses.
>
> After much prayer, I wish to state:
> a) I believe firmly in God and in God's self-revelation to his people.
> b) I hold God's Revelation and the Church's teaching to be good and true.
> c) I respect and honour Mary as Mother of God, of the Church and of us all.
> d) I respect the revelations, signs and miracles that God has wrought through her and at her intercession.
>
> As regards the present happenings in this parish, I declare that my conscience is clear:
> 1) First of all, I have prayed earnestly, especially while the people gathered on the hill.
> 2) I have talked to the children several times and recorded the conversations. Having listened again to the cassettes, I must insist that there is no public revelation here. If anything is being revealed, it is of a private nature, for the children's benefit alone. Whether this will change I do not know. So far, Our Lady has said nothing that is meant for anyone else. As for the children, we respect them, their convictions, their freedom and the freedom of God.

Without comment, after Mass, he read this testimony (which at least allowed for the possibility – however remote – that the children's experience was a genuine one). He had preached about St Peter, and the necessity of believing without the aid of miraculous signs. Then he drove off to see his mother in hospital, and to spend the rest of the day with his brother's family. It was late at night when he returned to Medjugorje.

He was told that as the children were getting ready for Mass that day, the police had arrived and taken them to Mostar in an ambulance. In another attempt to have them declared insane, they were examined by Dr Džuda, a professional psychiatrist in the neuropsychiatric department of Mostar hospital. "She tried to make out we were some kind of weirdos," reported Vicka furiously. "She said we'd imagined everything or that we were addicts or just having people on. She attacked me for being dressed in the latest style!"[3]

At one stage they were taken down to the mortuary where the interrogation continued. A gun was held to Vicka's head. "Put it away," she apparently said. "The economy's in a bad enough state without you wasting ammunition like that." In the end, according to the incorrigible Vicka, Dr Džuda threw up her hands and said: "It's the people who brought you here who must be insane. There's nothing wrong with you." They were sent home, but Darinka Glamuzina, a woman doctor with the Čitluk ambulance corps, and an atheist, was told to follow them up the hill that evening.

This psychiatric investigation upset the children. Fra Tomislav Vlašić, who came to Medjugorje that day for the first time, but who would become a central figure in the drama, found Jakov calm enough, but Mirjana badly shaken. "She said it had been like being in prison or shut up with mad people. When I asked her if she'd go to the hill again, she said she very much doubted it: "If they question me once more, I'll have a nervous breakdown."

But Mirjana *did* return to the hill, and when Fra Tomislav taxed her with being inconsistent she replied: "When it came to the point, nothing and no one could have stopped me. The question of whether or not I should go simply didn't arise."

The crowd that night was larger than ever. "One on top of the other," said Vicka. "You couldn't stand upright anywhere. Our menfolk had to make a path for us again." People – Muslims and Orthodox among them – were now coming in not just from the surrounding villages, but from other parts of the republic, from southern Croatia, western Serbia and even from as far away as Belgrade. Many of them walked barefoot. They prayed, sang, waited. Some had stayed two or three days in the village, trying to speak to the visionaries. Vicka had solved the problem of communication by climbing on to her balcony and addressing the crowds in a voice like a loud-hailer: "I told them how the apparitions had started, what the Madonna looks like, what she wants and so on."

This time there was a message for everybody present. "There is only one God, one faith," the vision said. "Believe in God with all your might, trust in Him."

"Shall we be able to bear the harassment?" asked the children.

"You will bear it, do not be afraid."

"And what shall we pray?" they asked. Until this time they had been following the suggestion of Mirjana's grandmother and reciting seven Our Fathers, seven Hail Marys and seven Glorias. The Madonna told them to continue with these prayers, and add a Credo.

Dr Darinka Glamuzina, sent by the Communist authorities, was standing close by. Could she be allowed to touch the Lady, the children asked. "There have always been Judases in the world. Let her come." Guided by Vicka, Dr Glamuzina touched the unseen Lady on the left shoulder, and later publicly admitted that she felt a violent tremor along the whole length of her arm. When she eventually stumbled down the hill, she was in a state of shock. What is certain is that she categorically refused ever again to go up the hill. Dr Ante Vujević, who had examined the children earlier in Čitluk, may have experienced something similar, for, although he wouldn't commit himself on the subject of the apparitions, he announced that he could no longer be described as an unbeliever.

Someone in the crowd held out a small boy, Danijel Šetka, mute and spastic from birth, a suspected epileptic. His parents had left no stone unturned in their desperate search for a cure; but in vain. On the previous day, they had arrived in Medjugorje to beg the children to intercede for their son. Could the child be cured, the children hesitantly asked? "If his parents believe firmly, then he will be healed," replied the Lady. "Go in peace of God."

On the way home to Mostar, the family stopped in Čitluk for something to eat. His mother takes up the story: "Danijel could neither speak nor walk, but somehow he'd become stronger since we visited the site where the Madonna appeared. Suddenly, as we sat at the restaurant table, Danijel raised his hand, banged the table, and said, 'I want a drink.' . . . I immediately shouted, 'He's been cured.'"[4]

After that, Danijel's mother – his father was a migrant worker in Germany – took the boy several times to Medjugorje, and each time he made more progress both in speech and movement. Three years later, his mother claimed that, "not only can he climb steps like a normal child, he can race down them too! His right hand is not yet as good as his left, and his speech is not quite as clear as it should be, but still . . . ! For the record, Danijel enjoys kicking a football around."

For the villagers of Medjugorje, the day was not yet over. In a Communist system such as prevails in Yugoslavia, every citizen is automatically enrolled in the Socialist Alliance, which has a branch in every village. An emergency meeting of the Bijakovići commune had been summoned for that evening. Instructions were explicit: obstruct the gatherings on the hill at all costs. "If you must do these things, do them in church," they said. ("As if that wasn't what we'd been telling them ourselves," complained Zrinko. "The church was standing there empty while they were up on the hill trampling the brambles underfoot.") In the face of official fury, which they well knew meant a threat to their jobs, the people remained silent; they dared not be openly defiant. From now on, they would have to make at least a show of co-operating with the authorities.

The fact was that the local Čitluk commune (which incorporated several of the smaller village communities), knew that it had badly over-reacted. In declaring these events to be dangerous and seditious, and in comparing them to the Albanian demonstrations in Kosovo, they had wanted to frighten the people, but had ended up frightening themselves – and alerting politicians at federal and republican level as well. Anxious voices were protesting from Belgrade and Sarajevo about subversion. It was rumoured that the Croatian flag had been raised, that cries of, "Rise, Croatia," had been heard, and nationalistic songs been sung. In official eyes, the Medjugorje children must be a new breed of terrorist intent on overthrowing the State and masterminded by cunning Ustaše priests. The Čitluk Communists found themselves in the uncomfortable and thankless position of pig-in-the-middle, under orders to prevent the situation getting out of hand; but with no clear ideas about what they should do.

They couldn't, however, prevent the children having the last word that night. As Vicka later told Fra Jozo: "We were shouting at the top of our voices from Marinko's terrace, telling the crowds everything Our Lady had said to us, over and over again. They wouldn't leave us alone till long past eleven. They just wouldn't go home."

4

The Hill

Always the same hills crowd the horizon,
Remote witnesses of the still scene.
And in the foreground the tall Cross,
Sombre, untenanted, aches for the body
That is back in the cradle of a maid's arms.
R. S. Thomas

Early next morning, Fra Jozo summoned the children again to his office.
While he was interviewing them individually, two other Franciscans
arrived: Fra Tomislav Pervan and Fra Ivan Dugandžić, the provincial
novice master. Fra Jozo was not altogether pleased by the intrusion; he
preferred to sort any problems out for himself. Refusing to let the visitors
sit in on the interviews, he left them in the waiting-room with the
children's parents. When he re-emerged, it was to find both Vicka's and
Jakov's mothers in tears, and Fra Tomislav shouting angrily that the
children were possessed by the Devil. Jozo and Fra Ivan tried to comfort
the distraught women. "You can't blame the mothers for what their
children are supposed to be seeing," Jozo protested to Pervan. "They're
not exactly delighted about what's happening."

Undeterred, Tomislav Pervan went on to suggest exorcism, an idea that
Fra Jozo dismissed as too alarming for all concerned and unlikely to bring
them any nearer to the truth. Indeed, Zlata, Vicka's mother, was already
wailing: "When you were away yesterday, Father Jozo, the police took the
children to Mostar. And now *we* are being threatened. Oh, why did it have
to happen to *my* child? There's no peace in our house any more."

Fra Jozo's mind was reeling. His interviews with the children had left
him dissatisfied – they seemed so immature and superficial – and he
needed time to think:

They said they'd seen Our Lady and they all agreed about what she looked
like. But when they came to repeat what she'd said, they were terribly
vague. In answer to my questions, they would say, "Oh, we were just going
to ask her that when she disappeared." They said, "She wants us to have
peace in the world," but they wouldn't be more explicit than that. I asked,

"Well, what are we supposed to do to find that peace?" but they had no idea. They were so ignorant and shallow, and I was terribly afraid that it was all just a joke with them. How could these children possibly have seen the Blessed Virgin? It was unthinkable that anyone could have seen her and not be radically changed by the experience. There was tension among them too. They argued a lot and disagreed among themselves about what had happened. Vicka and Mirjana seemed to be jostling for position as leader. I was very much aware of it, and was careful to treat them all exactly alike.

He did not, however, speak his thoughts aloud. "Go home now, and pray," he urged the children and their parents. As for the two priests, "Go back to the novitiate," he told them wearily, "and pray that the Holy Spirit will grant us wisdom." The future of the Church was at stake, he assured them. "Just think how awful it will be if one day newspaper headlines proclaim that twenty, thirty, maybe even fifty thousand people have been the victims of a hoax on our bleak and barren hillside."

That morning, in the long, musty cellar where the grapes were stored and which doubled up as a catechetical centre, Fra Jozo and Fra Zrinko were teaching catechism. During the break, the two priests were standing outside the church talking when an official car drew up and its driver handed over an envelope addressed to "Friar Number 1 and Friar Number 2". It contained a summons to attend a meeting of the Čitluk League of Communists that afternoon. "You'd better be there," said the driver ominously, when the priests protested that they had another catechism class in the afternoon.*

At the League of Communists headquarters in Čitluk, a special emergency session was in progress, with state representatives present, and a general air of crisis prevailing. The priests walked into a wall of hostility. The gatherings on the hill were politically dangerous, averred the chairman; they threatened the peace of the entire region. "What if a bomb should go off up there?" he asked angrily. "They're already asking questions in Sarajevo and Belgrade, and we haven't got any answers." He made it quite clear that he held Jozo responsible, and ordered him to put an immediate end to the dangerous charade, remove the children from the hill and disperse the crowds. He himself had already taken a few precautionary measures: ordering the villagers to cause as much obstruction on the hill as possible, and having Marinko Ivanković brought in for questioning.

Hearing this, Jozo retorted that that was a sure way of alienating the whole community and of ensuring that lips remained permanently sealed. If the thing was a hoax, then sooner or later it would fall apart of itself; but

* As the law in Yugoslavia does not allow Catholic schools to exist, the children receive all their religious instruction from their parish priests.

if the Communists went on behaving like bully-boys, and charging innocent people with conspiracy, they would never get at the truth. He launched into a lecture on this theme, but the Communists cut him short: "Damn you, we didn't come here to be preached at; we're supposed to be hacking out some kind of agreement."

"What kind of agreement?" asked Zrinko dourly. "We're not gods who can tell God what to do. If this is from God, neither you nor we, nobody, will be able to stop its course. And if it's the work of the Devil, then we'll be the ones to suffer, not you people in the socio-political organisations. You'll be able to cheer."

When a woman on the committee informed them that revelation had ended with the death of Jesus Christ, the priests thanked her for such concern for theology but insisted that there always had been and always would be miracles. In this case, however, they were ready to admit themselves as confused as everybody else and Zrinko asked for more investigations to take place. "Neither we as priests nor you as politicians can judge whether the children are sane or not, drugged or not, lying or not, being manipulated or not. We are all laymen in this matter," he said. (Next day at a community meeting in Medjugorje, his words would be unblushingly turned against him: "Father Zrinko says the children are mad, drugged, lying and being manipulated.")

Finally, in a statement that took the priests' breath away, the chairman suggested that if only the crowds would move into the church, the situation could be controlled. "They can pray all day long, and all night too if they want, so long as they don't do it on the hill. The law makes no provision for worshipping on a hill."

Thus did the Communists give their sideways blessing to getting the crowds into church. "They all but pushed them there," says Jozo, relishing the memory. "The state authorities played quite a prophetic role in the drama, much as Herod and Pilate once played their part in making the old prophecies come true. The hill worried me every bit as much as it worried them. I was sure that only in church could that gathering find its true fulfilment: only through the Mass, the sacraments, penance and prayer."

Unknown to the priests, the authorities had already banned the children from the hill: "Even if *you* don't mind making idiots of yourselves, you've no right to make fools of everybody else," they were told. "Stop this nonsense. The people are abandoning their work-places to follow you; no one's doing any work any more."

As a way of ensuring that the children did not go to the hill that night, two women social workers with the republican Council in Sarajevo had been ordered to take them for a sight-seeing tour. Ljubica Vasilj and Milica Ivanković were local girls, well known to the children and their families. So when they arrived in Bijakovići at about two on Tuesday, 30th June, and suggested taking the children out of harm's way, no objections were raised at all. The five children themselves (Ivan was not with them) were delighted at the prospect of an afternoon's entertainment which would take their minds off the horrors of the psychiatric department.

The two girls drove them first to Čitluk, then to Žitomislić and Počitelj, a picturesque old fortified town built up the side of a steep escarpment overhanging the Neretva river: a tourist haunt, famed for its mosques and minarets, and for the figs, tangerines and lemons which grow in profusion alongside the oleanders and cherry trees. From there, they drove to Čapljina, county town of Southern Hercegovina, where the girls bought them cakes and soft drinks. Then to the unforgettably dramatic waterfalls of Kravice; and on to Ljubuški – with its pre-Roman (Illyrian) remains and its fifteenth-century fort from which there is a superb view over most of Hercegovina and Dalmatia.

By now the children had understood the real reason for the outing. It was early evening when they started back for Bijakovići, already too late for them to reach the Podbrdo hillside in time. By six-thirty they had reached a place called Cerno, on the other side of the Crnica hill, and the children asked if they could get out. Ignoring the request, the social workers turned up the volume on the car radio. But the children persisted, saying that they'd jump out of the moving car if necessary; and the women reluctantly came to a halt. Some fifty metres off the road, on the right-hand side, the children suddenly fell to their knees on the stony ground. From the direction of Podbrdo where the children could see the crowds already waiting, a light began to roll towards them. "We were praying our usual prayers," Ivanka later told Fra Jozo. "Then I looked up the hill and saw the light coming down towards us. Those two women saw it too. I asked them and they said they had seen it. I kept on looking at the light, and then out of it came the Madonna."

"They've forbidden us to go to the hill any more," Mirjana told the vision. "Will it upset you if we wait for you in the church?" The Madonna, she said, seemed to hesitate before nodding agreement. Promising to come again at the same time the next evening, she left them. As she disappeared from sight in the direction of Podbrdo, the light reappeared high up on the hill.

Unnerved by this experience – both girls had been terrified by the strange and brilliant light – the two social workers drove the children back to Medjugorje, where they went straight to see Jozo, just back from the gruelling commune meeting in Čitluk. He questioned the whole group at great length (the tape of this interview still exists), thoroughly bewildered by this latest development, impressed in spite of himself by the stunned expression on the face of the two state employees: "They were far more eloquent witnesses than the children themselves."

The question now was whether the children should go up to the waiting crowds. Mirjana was keen, the others less so. Ivanka feared being crushed by the crowds, while Vicka was more afraid of the police. "They told us not to go near the hill until everybody had gone home," she said. The argument grew heated, Mirjana insisting that something was calling her to the hill, Vicka reminding everyone about the threats made by the police. Mirjana felt sorry for those who had come and been disappointed; she wanted to tell them to come to the church the following night.

"I know a lot of those people have only come out of curiosity or to jeer," she said, "but if we move into the church, then they'll just go home." Vicka agreed, but flatly refused to go back to the hill.

"And what will those people say," objected Mirjana. "They'll say we've run away. They'll claim we've been frauds all along."

"Rubbish," snorted Vicka. "They know we're not telling lies. When I go home, at ten o'clock, I'll tell everybody I see what's happened."

But when they did eventually return home to their distraught families, it was to find that Marinko had been taken to Čitluk for questioning by the police – and they went straight out again. Persuading another friend with a car to take them to Čitluk, they marched into the police station, to protest Marinko's innocence – "The man wouldn't so much as tread on an ant," argued Vicka – only to learn that he'd already been released and sent home. "We sure blasted the mayor and those who were there," she said afterwards. "We brought out everything we could think of. Arrest us if you want, we told them, but leave Marinko alone." The police had plenty of questions for the children, however, and subjected them to a barrage of threats and abuse. It was two o'clock in the morning when they were bundled unceremoniously into a car and taken back home.

On Wednesday, 1st July, the villagers were summoned to a meeting in the Medjugorje school with the state security police (SUP). It was announced that the children were to be banned from both the hill and the church. The parents were threatened that if they allowed the children to go to the hill again, they might find them declared mentally unsound and debarred from all further education. They themselves came in for the sort of character assassination to which the regime frequently resorted:

> We are dealing here with problem families. Zlata [Vicka's mother], for example, has eight children, her husband is in Germany and sends no money home for the family. She can't cope with the children, and they run wild on the streets. Marija Pavlović's father is mentally disturbed and an alcoholic. Jakov Čolo's parents are divorced.

And so on. The villagers for the most part remained silent, though the parents stoutly defended their children. "Those poor parents were terribly badly treated," Fra Jozo recalled later. "They were really heroic – buffeted this way and that by us priests, by the Communists and by the sensation-seekers. I think the parents were the real martyrs of these days."

The harassment did not seem to disturb the children greatly. "The interrogations didn't scare us," says Marija:

> We felt quite strong. Our Lady helped us through. Somehow, the more problems we had, the better we coped. We spent all day talking to pilgrims, and every evening praying; so at most we got two or three hours' sleep. Yet in those days we seemed to be living under a special grace. Several times they tried to persuade us to tell lies. And they would trick us. When they wanted to take us away for a medical examination, they'd come to our homes and say they had a warrant. But they had no such thing, they just knew we'd take their word for it. It wasn't till much later that we realised we could have refused to go with them.

That afternoon, two members of the regional police from Mostar came in a police van to Bijakovići to see the children, and showed no inclination to go away again. At six-fifteen, the time for going to the hill, the policemen attempted to cajole the children, rather as the two social workers had done on the previous day. Perhaps they would like a ride, they suggested, to go somewhere and have something to eat and drink?

As the children (all but Mirjana and Ivan who were not in the village that day) began to leave, still arguing, they were pushed into the police van. Jakov's mother managed to drag him out, as the van drove off with Vicka, Marija and Ivanka inside, away from Bijakovići and Podbrdo. The policemen drove past the church and over the bridge, until, as the children were by now beating a tattoo on the windows, they finally stopped the van.

"So," Fra Janko Bubalo asked Vicka, "you didn't see the Virgin that day?"

"Indeed we did," she replied. "And how! I'll never forget it."

Janko Bubalo:	Where did you see her?
Vicka:	Right there in the police van.
Janko Bubalo:	Was it moving?
Vicka:	I don't know.
Janko Bubalo:	What do you mean, you don't know?
Vicka:	It's quite simple . . . When the Virgin appeared, there was no sign of the van or of anyone . . . Just as, when we see the Virgin in that little room, we're not aware of anyone or anything.
Janko Bubalo:	Had you prayed for her to appear?

Vicka:	No, we weren't even thinking about it then. She just came.
Janko Bubalo:	Were you frightened?
Vicka:	Well, *I* wasn't, I hadn't time to be afraid. But Marija and Ivanka were, they were rigid with fear. That's why those two policemen with us said they were witches.
Janko Bubalo:	How long did the Virgin stay with you?
Vicka:	Not long. She told us not to be afraid, smiled at us and left.[1]

In all probability unnerved at the sight of the children's faces, the policemen returned them hastily to the church, and drove away. The children, according to Vicka, "stayed round the church for a bit, then walked over to the Parish House, before taking the short cut home across the fields . . . We arrived somewhere around sunset." For the second night running, the people waiting on Podbrdo had waited in vain.

Next day, 2nd July, at midday the police again arrived in Bijakovići to stalk the children; but, more wary now, their intended prey slipped out of their houses to hide. "We really didn't know where to hide," Vicka told Fra Janko Bubalo. "In the end we went towards the church, not via the road, but through our tobacco fields and vineyards, so that they wouldn't spot us. The church was locked . . . We thought, 'Oh God, where can we go now?' But, as luck would have it, one of the friars was praying in the church and . . ."

Against his better judgement, Fra Jozo Zovko was beginning to believe in the children's story. Perhaps the stunned looked on the social workers' faces had unsettled him. Those two girls had been pawns in the authorities' game, but they had had enough. Both were intent on resigning from the government service, and refusing any further part in the affair. (In fact, one went to work in Sarajevo, and the other migrated to Germany.)

At six o'clock on Wednesday evening, Jozo had celebrated Mass and since the children did not come to the hill, the people had streamed down towards the church. The police tried to frighten them away, for, in spite of the Čitluk Communists' rash words, the church suddenly seemed just as menacing as the hill. But there was safety in numbers, and the crowds would not be browbeaten. "I wouldn't have believed the church could hold so many people," said Jozo. "I was scarcely able to push my way through to the altar, and when I got there and began to say Mass, I had no room to lift up my arms to give a blessing."

Jozo had his opportunity now to beg the people to stop being inquisitive hangers-on and to advocate caution. "God is with us here and now, not up there in the brambles," he assured them. If God had indeed sent them a sign from heaven – and they could not yet be sure of that – such a sign had tremendous implications for their own lives. They could not remain as idle sight-seers. "I wanted to convey God's eternal appeal to men to change their lives."

On the afternoon of 2nd July, Jozo's moment of truth was at hand. It was he who, as Vicka said, happened to be in the church, brooding miserably on the tens of thousands still flocking nightly to the hill and terribly aware of the responsibility weighing on him; of the unanswered questions in his heart. He had no inkling that the next few minutes would be a turning point in his life and in the story of Medjugorje:

> I was in the third pew in the church, on the left hand side, where Our Lady's statue now stands. I had my breviary and a Bible in front of me. I picked up the Bible and opened it at random at the passage in Exodus which describes Moses before the Red Sea crossing. I tried to develop the perfect trust in God that Moses had felt. "God," I said, "you appeared to Abraham and to Moses, you spoke to them and guided them. Guide me now. I don't know where this mighty river comes from nor where it is going to."
>
> It was a prayer of despair. And God responded to it. Of that I am certain. I was quite alone in the church. Suddenly I heard a voice just like my own, say, "Go outside now and protect the children." Without a second's hesitation, I put the Bible down, genuflected and went out through the main door of the church. While my hand was still on the door-handle, the children rushed up on my left, grabbed hold of me and said, "Please help us, the police are after us."

"Quick, come with me," he said, and led them across to the presbytery:

> I wondered where to put them. There was an empty room which was used as a library. I said, "Stay here, say your prayers, and don't make a sound." I went outside, locking the door behind me. As I came down the steps, a man was running past. "Have you seen the children?" he asked. "Yes," I said. But he ran on, still looking for them. I returned to the church and resumed my prayers. And I thanked the Lord.

That afternoon, the children saw their apparition in the clergy house: "We began to pray," said Vicka, "and in a moment the Virgin appeared to us. She prayed a bit with us and sang a bit. She said we'd come through all right and not to be afraid."

It was the first of many visions in that little presbytery room, one of which Jozo was to see for himself, although, as he told journalist Gitta Sereny, "It was not really for me. There was a need and this was the response. I was only the tool."[2]

From that moment in the church, Jozo's doubts had disappeared. The rumour that the children had been hauled off by the police yet again, and for the third time would not be on the hill, had already spread far and wide. At the same time it was somehow known that, as on the previous night, there would be a service in the church at six, preceded by the Rosary at five. By early afternoon they began arriving from all directions, and long before five the church was filled to bursting point.

Jozo preached about Moses leading the Children of Israel out of Egypt and across the Red Sea; of their long, forty-year journey through the desert, accompanied always by sure signs of God's love. He spoke of Mary: "The first believer who completely obeyed God and His call was Our Lady . . . Mary, as the first Christian, is here today with me, your priest, and with you, as faithful Christians." But it was with Christ, not with Mary, that the matter rested. And here the young priest's eloquence may have had the informers in his midst reaching for their notebooks. They had already been alerted by his reference to the forty years in the wilderness, precisely the duration of the Communist regime in Yugoslavia:

> This should be the era of Christ, the Christian era. There is no place for atheism, no place for superstition, in a man who trusts the word of God . . . My dear brothers and sisters, this is the festival of our faith, the night in which we are to make our Red Sea crossing – into the freedom of God's kingdom where no fears will enslave us, because there is no power stronger than our God.

At this point he swung towards them and appealed:

> And now, to end with, I beg you to start fasting, to fast tomorrow, to fast the day after tomorrow, taking only bread and water, so that God may reveal Himself to us and tell us what we are to do. There is no heaven so closed that prayer, fasting and penance may not find a way into it. Are you with me in this?

Jozo, a man of immense magnetism, inspired the congregation, which was swept off its feet with enthusiasm; "Yes" was shouted in unison. As a Communist civil servant told the priest afterwards, "Father, if you'd asked us to fast for a whole month, we'd have done it."

When Jozo announced that, in spite of the authorities' ban, the children would come into the church, their excitement knew no bounds and people began clambering over the seats to get a better view. They were restrained only by Jozo's threatening not to bring the children if they didn't behave.

A defiant Vicka was the first to speak, telling the crowd that the Madonna had appeared to them that very evening in the clergy house: "Many have been cursing because she's not appeared to them, but how could she appear to people who curse God and plot against the lives of their fellow-men. We've been harassed and threatened, but we're not afraid." Her honesty was evident, her anger at the way they were being treated no less so. Mirjana then took over, and asked everyone to recite seven Our Fathers, seven Hail Marys, seven Glorias – and the Creed. People were talking about the cure of little Danijel Šetka, she said, but if there were more faith, there would be more healing. She added that there was no further reason for them to come again to the church – or to the hill. "If there should be any messages for you, we'll let you know."

For that rather high-handed and confident announcement there was a curious explanation. By this time, the children had read the book on apparitions lent to them by Jozo and had become fascinated by the story of Bernadette Soubirous of Lourdes, to whom, in 1858, the Blessed Virgin had appeared eighteen times. Presuming, in their ignorance, that eighteen was a standard figure, they had counted up their own apparitions and concluded that the last one would occur on Friday. "That's what happened in Lourdes, so that's what'll happen here," Mirjana confidently told Fra Jozo. Although it seemed to many in the church that night as though God were calling them to change their lives, there were some who objected – and many more who would later do so – that Fra Jozo had just succeeded in imposing his own interpretation of the apparitions. The suggestion about fasting had come from him, not from the Virgin Mary. To such objectors Fra Jozo retorted that the sole source and guarantee of all messages from on high is Jesus Christ; that the gift of God's Spirit is always the same, through whatever medium it is transmitted; that whatever messages were being received they were merely "different dimensions of the one and only source of life". If the messages of Medjugorje are authentic, he claims, they can be attributed to no one but Christ. "If this is God's call to conversion and penance, then no one can meet God here except through conversion and penance."

Prayer, penance, conversion, reconciliation, then. The great themes of the New Testament were what Medjugorje was about. "In the hearts that were moved that night," suggests Fra Svetozar Kraljević, "the Gospel was coming to life in all its fullness . . . The Church must always go the way of the Gospel . . . Wherever Mary comes, she comes with her Son, Jesus, giving glory to God and peace to man. Mary has nothing to offer but her Son."

Contrary to the children's expectations, however, the apparitions did not end on the Friday. So sure were they of the approaching end that they did not even meet on the Saturday evening. Ivan was at home stringing tobacco leaves for drying, Vicka was picking flowers to take to the hill. In the act of picking them, her hands went stiff, and she dropped to her knees. Marija walked into a room at home, and "all of a sudden, there was the Madonna, and I fell to my knees". Her brother, Ante, who was with her, rushed out of the room, leaving her alone to pray.

And that was the beginning of the apparitions' semi-clandestine phase. From now on, they would take place in random locations, wherever the children happened to be: in a neighbour's house, out of doors, in the clergy house, and only sometimes in the church.

All six of them saw the Madonna that night. On the Sunday, therefore, "we got together and she came to us. We decided that we weren't going to be the same as Lourdes after all."

5

Growth of a Legend

Oh, he realised full well that for the humble soul . . . there was no
greater need and comfort than to find some holy shrine or person, to
fall down . . . and worship: "if there is sin, injustice and temptation
among us, then there is at any rate someone somewhere on earth who
is holier and superior, he has the Truth, he knows the Truth, which
means that it is not dead on earth and will therefore come to us too one
day and rule over all the earth as it was promised".

Dostoievsky, *The Brothers Karamazov*

Although it was little more than a week since the apparitions had started,
the preliminary skirmishing was already over and all-out war was about to
be declared by the regime. A symbolic day was chosen for the declaration,
4th July, Fighters' Day, which commemorated the fortieth anniversary of
the 1941 Partisan Uprising. Addressing a crowd of several hundred
thousand in Tjentište in Bosnia, Brando Mikulić, a senior Party official
from Sarajevo, fired the opening salvo. In Medjugorje, he claimed, in the
very area where the most atrocious crimes of the war had been committed,
"clerico-nationalists" were touting a ludicrous story about the Virgin
Mary "to intimidate uneducated people and try to fool them; that is, to
manipulate them politically and make them serve those who work against
the interests of our nations and nationalities".[1]

In all probability, many of the men and women in that assembly were
hearing the name Medjugorje for the first time. But before the day was out
it was on its way to becoming a household word; the presence of television
and radio reporters, journalists and foreign observers guaranteed maximum coverage for the speech. The Sarajevo TV report was picked up by
international news agencies, and before long journalists from Germany
and other surrounding countries were arriving in Sarajevo demanding to
know what was going on. The report was, of course, heavily propagandist,
its sole aim being to point up the politico-nationalistic meaning of the
Medjugorje events. As Fra Jozo complained, it "tried to offload on
Medjugorje all the guilt for wartime atrocities that even we older ones
hadn't heard of; and as for the children, they weren't even born".[2]

Taking the hint, a local Čitluk official began speaking of "the Ustaša

60

Madonna". Open season had evidently been declared on Medjugorje. The press were baying for blood; particularly Fra Jozo's. The secular press cast him as a sinister Machiavellian figure capable of all kinds of villainy. He was described by some as a nuclear scientist, by others as a professional psychologist. "The Virgin Plays Hide and Seek" shrilled a headline in *Vjesnik*, the leading Croatian daily, the report censoring the Virgin for, at the very least, causing a great deal of unrest. Satirists had a field-day: a savage cartoon showed an Ustaše terrorist Madonna towering over a group of children, with a large knife between her teeth and a caption proclaiming, "The True Face of the Blessed Mother".

Such free publicity merely brought the crowds to Medjugorje in even greater numbers. "I can see from your licence plates that you have come from every part of Yugoslavia," Jozo welcomed the newcomers to the evening Mass on 11th July. "As a journalist has just remarked: 'Your telephone exchange may have been out of action, yet it took only twenty-four hours for news to spread over the entire country and maybe all over Europe.' If we had trailed a huge streamer from a helicopter inviting you into the church, nobody would have taken a bit of notice. But when the Lord has work to be done, he has no need of advertising techniques." He marvelled at what had made them come to this dusty backwater – "this primitive village with its jagged rocks, its piercing thorns, and its stupefying heat". Their reward, he told them, would be their cleansed and reawakened souls.

That evening Fra Jozo sailed dangerously close to the wind in a country that was celebrating the fortieth anniversary of a successful Communist uprising, as he asked: "Did not Christ come to liberate you and me and all of us who have been in slavery for forty years, so that this evening or tomorrow we may kneel before him and say: 'Break these chains, break these shackles, break the fetters which bind my life with the evil of sin. You alone have the key'?"

He called for courage in the face of their common peril: "Is this a time for the Catholic Church in Croatia, in Hercegovina, to be afraid? Is it Good Friday we are experiencing – or is it Easter?"

In the prayer for peace which followed the Mass came a litany of Catholic grievances: "We dare not have large families, in case we are not able to feed them. We dare not get married because people will laugh at us, and because we'll be worse off financially."

And perhaps, most dangerous of all: "We are afraid, Lord Jesus, of letting it be known that we go to church. We are afraid to send our children to catechism lessons."

But there was little sign of that fear in Medjugorje, as thousands made their confessions who had not been near a church for decades. "These people are in search of values which the state is unable to give them," a journalist from Zagreb admitted to Jozo. "I'm an atheist, but you have somehow brought me to the threshold of belief." One old man who came to confession after a fifty-year absence claimed to feel "like a new man". Jozo was more delighted by this "than if Križevac had suddenly been moved to Mostarsko Blato, or a new spring had broken out at the bottom of the parched hill". The Communists, he said with a smile, had taken pains to warn him: "If ever you find a spring up there, don't go claiming it as a miracle. The geologists have always said there's water hidden somewhere there."

In any case, there were miracles enough. Old Jozo Vasilj was both blind and paralysed. "I'll soon tell you if it really is the Madonna," he said when he heard of the apparitions. Persuading a reluctant neighbour to fetch him a handful of earth and some wild thyme from the site of the first apparition, he mixed them with water and smeared the paste over his face. Then after washing his face with ordinary water and reciting the Creed with great fervour, he told his wife he could see her. At first she would not believe him, but when he said that she ought to be ashamed of herself, a woman of her age going round with bare legs, she knew that he was telling the truth. The old man then plastered the same mud over his left arm which for eight years had been covered from shoulder to hand with bleeding sores. He wrapped a towel round the arm and again recited the Creed. Next morning the sores had completely disappeared.

Matija Skuban, a paraplegic pilgrim from West Germany, reported that "during prayer on 20th July 1981 in the church at Medjugorje, I felt a strong current flow through my entire body and especially in my paralysed left leg. I got up and went to communion without help." There were reports of all kinds of minor ailments – back aches, rashes, nervous disorders – disappearing after a visit to Medjugorje. A nun who for several years had suffered from severe pain in the back and from eczema of the ears was completely cured of both conditions; and a blind Orthodox Christian telephoned the presbytery to say that though he was still blind, Medjugorje had filled him with a peace and joy greater than he had ever known.

Pavle Pavlović, a Sarajevo journalist, had been to see the old man and to visit the children. His reasonably objective piece in the Communist weekly *Arena*[3] had sparked off considerable interest among other journalists. The fame of Medjugorje was thus being spread by the Communists themselves. Soon after the *Arena* report, a pilgrimage arrived from Macedonia, the pilgrims having read of the miraculous signs and healings that were happening in Medjugorje. Many of the journalists were simply hanging around waiting for something sensational to happen, trying to trick the villagers into false statements. "They pestered us all," recalls Fra Jozo, "priests, visionaries and parents":

They believed nothing themselves, they were completely ignorant about religion and they despised all believers. They had no understanding of what was going on; but that didn't stop them writing knowledgeably about it. Some poured scorn on Medjugorje without ever having set foot in the place. They had their orders – to slander and defame, to crush, but never in any circumstances to inform.

Nevertheless, even some of these went away impressed and, though they were not free to say so in their papers, they tried to limit the damage to a minimum.

Change was coming over Medjugorje itself. A visiting priest remarked in astonishment that he had seen villagers who had not spoken to each other for years working together in the fields. It seemed as though the place were becoming a real community, with the old people being cared for as never before, and with former enemies forgetting old quarrels and helping each other to clear land and build houses. Fra Jozo was visited by a worker from a Čitluk building co-operative. "Father, we have made a vow that from now on anyone who curses God in our work-place must pay a fine. Here's the money we've collected so far." This change wrought by the visions was likened by Gitta Sereny to the historical watershed between BC and AD:

> "Before", there was competition between the farmers and between the villages; "after", there is none. "Before", they worked from sunrise till late in the evening; "after", they stop work in mid-afternoon to rest and prepare for nightly Mass. "We used to think we had to work all hours to get done," said one farmer. "now we stop early and it still gets done." He laughed. "And we don't swear any more, nor get drunk. How can we – and why should we – if the *Gospa* comes to our village each day?"

Late on the night of 14th July, the children secretly returned to the hill. Their friend and neighbour, Marinko Ivanković,[4] describes what happened next:

> Twenty days after Our Lady had first appeared, she told the children to go to the hill at 11 o'clock at night. About fifty neighbours went along too, and we all began praying. All at once seven or eight of us began shouting, "Look at that light." It came from the sky, as if the sky had opened up about ten metres, and it came towards us. It stopped over the hole in the ground (he pointed to where the people had been digging up the earth). There was a wooden cross in the hole and the light seemed to stream from it. It was as if a balloon of light had burst and there were thousands of tiny stars everywhere. We were just bathed in light. We knelt down, some of the children with us began crying, but we said, "Hush, Our Lady is here with

us" and we began praying aloud. We prayed for about forty minutes altogether. We were all crying. As long as I live I shall never forget that night.

After forty minutes the Madonna apparently joined in our prayer, and she told the children we could touch her if we wanted to. *We* couldn't see her, so we surged forward. Some touched her and said their hands went numb. But then it seems that someone stepped on her veil, and she disappeared. Then over there, over the cross on Križevac, we saw two Madonna-like shapes. One of them was glowing like white fire. I ran home for my camera and when I came back up again it was still glowing. I took a picture but there was no sign of the glowing shape on the photograph; only the other shape was visible.

Vicka described the light as "a shining balloon. It came down quickly and burst above the ground. A thousand star-like bursts emptied out of it."[5] Although people from the surrounding villages had seen the light and many of them had come rushing to the hill, the Čitluk authorities had missed it. But the Communists were increasingly alarmed by the number of young people who were going regularly to the hill. In a frantic effort to woo them back, they began laying on special forms of evening entertainment: dances, films, football matches. Few came. It was baffling, not least because even some Party members were succumbing. Those in power felt the ground move ominously beneath their feet. At a meeting of the Socialist Alliance in Čitluk, members were ordered to state whether they had been to the hill. Eleven who admitted to going there regularly were expelled from the Party; forty-eight more, who said they had been there only once, were given more minor punishments – and a caution against repeating the offence.

One night at the end of July, the word *mir*, the Croatian word for peace, appeared written in the sky over Križevac. Many saw it, Fra Jozo among them. "Let the earth quake, let signs appear in the sky," he preached on the Friday evening. "They are signs that God has not abandoned His people. The Church here is a small island in an atheist and materialist society. Mary is trying through these children to tell us not to be afraid."

On 2nd August the sun appeared to turn on its axis, to come close and then retreat, a "dance of the sun" such as was described during the apparitions at Fatima in 1917.

I was with a large group of people outside the church [related a taxi-driver], and suddenly I noticed the sun doing strange things . . . it began to swing to and fro . . . Finally a ray of light separated itself from the sun and travelled like the rays of a rainbow towards the place where the Virgin had first appeared. It then rested on the church tower, on which a clear image of the Virgin appeared.

About 150 people watched transfixed, staring into the sun without damage to their eyes. According to another signed statement, they

> saw figures around the sun, in the shape of a cross. The strange phenomena caused many to cry, or pray or even run away. Then six small hearts appeared in the sky, centred round a large heart. A white cloud covered the hill and the site of the first apparition and the sun returned to its normal place.

In Turcinović, near Medjugorje, the entire village had gathered for the funeral of a ninety-year-old woman. Just as the procession began to leave the dead woman's house, everyone caught sight of the sun performing antics. They dropped to their knees, and stayed there praying for about ten minutes.

A visiting priest, Fra Umberto Lončar, was not among the sky-watchers that day, and poured considerable scorn on these tales of dancing suns. When he himself saw something similar next day, he brushed off the experience, saying that it was doubtless due to unusual meteorological conditions or anomalies in the temperature. On Tuesday, 4th August, however, on a clear and cloudless evening, Lončar was forced to eat his words. Though he refused to look at the sun, in case the glare should affect his vision, nevertheless:

> At six-twenty exactly I saw a huge red and violet cloud over Cerno. The cloud was massive and was moving in my direction at unusual – tremendous – speed, then hovered over the hill of Križevac for a minute or two, moved eastward and seemed to sink into the earth. Because of the hills and trees between me and the cloud, I couldn't see what was happening, so I ran to the upper floor of the rectory to get a better view. After the cloud disappeared from sight, I descended to the terrace between the rectory and the church. Precisely at 6.40, the red and violet figure of a magnificent lady arose from the hill of Crnica. The red and violet faded in intensity as she ascended in the sky; then she disappeared. The last thing I saw was a brilliant white scarf that dangled from her feet and swung in the air. The vision . . . lasted about thirty seconds in all.[6]

And here is Iva Vasilj again:

> I had gone to our tobacco fields at sunset to pick the leaves, and a neighbour of mine was pasturing her sheep there and doing her knitting as she watched them. Suddenly a really cold wind got up, and, as we looked up, the sun was dancing, and the head and shoulders of a woman came out of it and went towards Križevac. There were balloons coming out of the sun, red, purple and blue. I was paralysed with fright. The neighbour's fifteen sheep were so frightened that they huddled stiffly together. When the

neighbour and I had recovered the use of our legs, we ran home. I told my husband, Pero, and my daughter, and they laughed at me and said I'd been seeing things. I burst into tears. Just then, Pero's mother came up and said, "God help us, but Iva's telling the truth. I saw it too."

Since the children were still banned from going to the hill, they had been having their nightly visions in their own homes, or in the fields, even in cow-sheds, as far away as possible from the watchful eye of the militia. At times the children had to make a several-kilometre detour in order to break free of police surveillance. Within the village or outside it, they were constantly followed. After Mass that evening (2nd August), a number of villagers gathered with the visionaries after Mass to pray and sing in the Gumno threshing-field between Bijakovići and the church. Marinko Ivanković recounts:

> All together we recited the seven Our Fathers, Hail Marys, Glorias and the Creed. Then the children again told us that we could touch Our Lady if we wished . . . [As the Lady departed] Marija gave a sudden cry and I ran to her to ask what was wrong. "Oh, Marinko," she said, "she has gone black all over . . . There were atheists here who touched her, and as they did so, her robe grew darker and darker till it was quite black."

Appalled by this visible evidence of the power of sin, Marinko didn't hesitate. "Everyone to confession in the morning," he shouted at the top of his voice. Later, Marinko stayed behind to talk with Marija. When she was changing into her jeans after Mass, she told him, the Lady had appeared to her. "This very evening," she said, "the Virgin told me that Satan is making determined attempts to get control of events here. He is leaving no stone unturned to insert himself into our midst." It was a re-statement of an age-old theme of Christian apocalyptic – the forces of evil arrayed against those of good; the whole world a battleground for the cosmic struggle. The children were now claiming that secrets concerning the future of the world had been entrusted to them by the Lady. As yet they would reveal these to nobody, not even to their families; but one of the secrets was known to concern a sign that the Lady had promised to leave at the site of the first apparition, to convince unbelievers. In Mirjana's words,[7] "the unbelievers will run to the hill and pray and be forgiven".

Next day the number of penitents in the church at Medjugorje redoubled. The priests who heard their confessions were astounded at the number. A few days later, there were even more, after the Madonna had summoned the visionaries to the hill, in the early hours of the morning, to demand "repentance for sins".

6

Arrest

What must come to pass, *should* come to pass. Within the limits of that *must*, therefore, you are invulnerable.

Dag Hammarskjoeld, *Markings*

Bishop Pavao Žanić of Mostar was to become the most implacable adversary of the Medjugorje events, but he was ready to admit that on first hearing of the apparitions, he had wept for joy.

Without delay he sent an emissary to talk to Fra Jozo and see how the land lay. At that stage, Jozo was still doubting the children's story, still unable to discern the "finger of God" (a phrase used at Lourdes), in these events; the sight of so many thousands, priests among them, "stumbling headlong to the hill" saddened him.

On 21st July the bishop came in person to speak to the children, putting them on oath to tell the truth – and recording the conversations. Though he would later claim to have had doubts about the children right from the start, and that these conversations did nothing to allay those doubts, his own words at the time belie him. In fact, he went so far as to state firmly: "These children are not telling lies."

In those first weeks, Bishop Žanić visited Medjugorje five times. Jozo was slightly irritated by the bishop's sporadic forays into the beleaguered parish, whence he retreated to the sanctuary of his episcopal palace, leaving Jozo himself permanently in the front line. Nevertheless, he invited the bishop to say Mass and preach on 25th July, the feast of St James, the patronal saint of the Medjugorje church. Žanić preached on the subject of the apparitions.

Referring first to the Christian duty to forgive the secular press for their offensive behaviour – "though if *we* spoke and wrote in that way about atheism we'd be accused of not believing in brotherly love" – he went on to affirm his faith in the children's honesty:

> Six simple children like these would have told all in half an hour if anybody had been manipulating them. I assure you that none of the priests has done any such thing. The accusation is insulting and must be firmly rejected. Furthermore, I am convinced the children are not lying. They are saying

only what they most profoundly believe. Whether, however, their experience is subjective or supernatural is hard to determine . . . Our Lady has said nothing new here. Indeed, there is nothing new for her to say. Wherever she appears in the world, it is only to bring us back again, to warn us to turn back to her son, Jesus Christ, to his gospel and to his Church . . . Lourdes is dear to us, Fatima is dear to us, the presence of Our Lady in the Church is dear to us, but our one solid foundation is Jesus Christ.

One thing is certain: something has stirred in people's hearts. Confession, prayer, reconciliation between enemies – that is a most positive step forward. All the rest we must leave to Our Lady, to Jesus and the Church, which one day will most certainly give its opinion on the matter.

Fra Jozo warned the bishop to tread carefully and not commit himself too soon. "I sensed that he was the sort of man who makes his mind up very quickly and then refuses to change it. That could lead to trouble with the regime." It could also lead to a great deal of trouble within the Church, when the bishop's certainties underwent a radical transformation. For the time was not far distant when he would dismiss both the children and the Franciscans as liars and cheats.

High-level pressure was being brought by the regime on Bishop Žanić to put a stop to the events or at least to disown them. He refused. The diocese issued a statement protesting against the "unacceptable and offensive" press reportage and rejecting all the charges made. The only question was whether the children's experience was subjective or supernatural, it said. The statement ended with those words of Gamaliel (Acts 5:38–39), which Zrinko had quoted to the Čitluk Communists: "If this enterprise, this movement of theirs, is of human origin, it will break up of its own accord; but if it does in fact come from God, you will not only be unable to destroy them, but you might find yourselves fighting against God."

Much water would have passed under the bridge and the political temperature have risen by several degrees when the statement came to be published on 16th August. It would simply, in government eyes, be the last straw.

Harassment was being stepped up; the Medjugorje priests were constantly being summoned for interrogation. The Communists had started a rumour that the Franciscans had hatched the plot in order to get money for building an extension on to the church; and although this was a familiar Communist tactic, a few half-believed the rumour. In that atmosphere nobody knew what to believe. A young seminarian from Zagreb told the children that all kinds of wild stories were circulating about them in that city, and they were being accused of preaching sedition. In Mostar it was much the same. Marija told of travelling unrecognised by bus from Mostar to Medjugorje one Saturday morning with a friend. "We listened to what the people were saying, and it was incredible rubbish."

Informers were everywhere. "They followed the parents, the pilgrims, the priests who came to help us out," said Fra Jozo. "They were keen to find out who we were in contact with, to see whom we met and when. And at the same time they did their utmost to obstruct our movements." One girl came to Jozo in great distress to ask forgiveness for her brother, a young man who had been ordered against his will to spy on the priest. "I sent him my good wishes," Jozo said, "and assured him he was committing no sin if he was acting under pressure."

Two delegations arrived from the Čitluk authorities, demanding that the church be closed down. Jozo refused, and one morning in July drove to Sarajevo to argue the matter at a higher level, with Franjo Folj, a member of the Executive Council of the Commission for Religious Affairs. Folj made sympathetic noises, agreeing that it would be a pity to close down the church, particularly in view of the potential effect of such a move on Yugoslavia's reputation abroad. Of *course* another solution must be found, he assured the priest.

After Mass that evening, Jozo had scarcely time to tell the people what Folj had said before rushing off to attend a community meeting in the school hall. Mate Bencun, the local Party chairman (whose wife was a devout Catholic and entertained pilgrims in her house), opened the proceedings and introduced Jure Jerkić, chairman of the Commission for Religious Affairs in Čitluk. Mr Jerkić offered a confused jumble of charges: that the gatherings on the hill were nationalistic, hostile to the State and masterminded by an "enemy of the people"; that they had been condemned by the Church; that Jesus Himself had said there would be no more miracles after his death; that these were nothing but old wives' tales; and that (a very real grievance, this) crops were being trampled underfoot, no work was being done, roads were being destroyed and the local water supply used up for the benefit of the pilgrims.

Once again Jozo stood accused, Jerkić claiming that even a fellow-Franciscan, Fra Ante Leko, had denounced him as the puppet-master directing operations. In fact, as the Communists well knew, Father Leko's actual words (at a Franciscan assembly) had been: "Well, if someone *is* behind all this, the obvious person would be the parish priest; but we all know it couldn't be him." Mr Jerkić had selected his illustration with a classic disregard for objective (i.e. "bourgeois") truth.

The discussion threatened to get out of hand. When comment was invited, a puzzled young man from Mostar took the floor:

Comrades [he said], when I finished my army service two weeks ago, I received two good service awards. You're trying to tell us that anyone who

69

goes to the hill is an enemy of the people. But I'm a believer and I've been there. How can I be an enemy of the people when the Army has just presented me with two good service awards? Besides, how can a religious activity be hostile to the state? Answer me that one.

Consternation reigned until, to the organisers' relief, it was discovered that since the young man was from Mostar he had no legal right to be at the Medjugorje meeting. He was expelled on a point of order.

The villagers present were urged to voice their opposition to the hill and its disgraceful goings-on; but their response was half-hearted at best. "I am in favour of the Madonna," one of them said doggedly, "and I want our church to have the most beautiful statue of her, sky-high, chiselled out of marble. What I don't see is why we need bother to go up the hill. Put a statue like that in the church and we'll pray there."

Most remained prudently silent. Fra Jozo then spoke up, throwing Mr Jerkić's charges back in his face. Who, he asked, had told him that the Church had condemned the apparitions? Had he ever read the last part of St Mark's Gospel where Jesus spoke of the miracles His followers would perform? How could he justify calling these events seditious – had anyone been seen carrying banners, shouting slogans or singing revolutionary songs? Reluctantly Jerkić admitted that so far there had been nothing of the kind.

It is Fra Jozo's belief that this meeting, no doubt intended to strike fear into the inhabitants of Bijakovići and Medjugorje, had entirely the opposite effect. Suddenly it was obvious that the authorities had no case – and that they knew it. It put fresh heart into their troubled audience.

But in a more threatening way, too, the meeting had been crucial. Aware that their credibility was crumbling, the authorities became more dangerous and unreasonable. Fra Jozo was under no illusions about what might happen:

> We all recognised that night that we must go out and bear testimony to these events. I knew that my own witness must be a radical one, and that it would probably land me in prison. Fra Tomislav Vlašić had just arrived on a visit from Čapljina. "Tomislav," I said to him, "I shall be going away soon. Be ready to take my place."

Towards the end of July, a group of young people noisily ascended the hill, singing patriotic Croatian songs and shouting anti-regime slogans. There was a strong whiff of deliberate provocation in the air. The villagers scented trouble.

On 7th August Jozo gave his usual talk after the evening Mass. Referring to the crowds coming down the hill clutching a clod of earth or a handful of weeds, he warned:

You are wrong if you think that peace will come into your lives with that clod of earth, those few leaves of thyme. God wants only one thing from you – your heart . . . We have all resolved to renew ourselves. Each of us is part of the world, and we want our own part to be a more fruitful one. That is the message of Mary's apparitions, be converted, trust the Gospel, make peace with one another and with God.

In apocalyptic vein he added:

Great alarm is being felt at your coming here. Satan and the forces of darkness are alarmed; those who have turned their backs on God are alarmed. We have become a sign of the Church's reawakening to its mission.

At about 10 p.m. on 11th August Jozo was called to Party headquarters in Čitluk and ordered once again to stop the faithful going up the hill and to abolish the evening Mass. He replied that he would do what he could about the hill, but would go on saying the Mass as long as the people kept coming. Angrily they produced "incriminating" documents of a political kind, allegedly found on the hill. "We know you're the man behind all this," they shouted. "We have witnesses. We can put you behind bars." "You've absolutely no justification for doing so," retorted the priest, "and how can there be witnesses to something that didn't happen? A witness is *not* someone who's ready to swear to whatever you tell him, even when it's a lie." Furiously they dismissed him.

Next day, police came to inspect the hill and question anybody they found there. Ivan Ivanković, who had been one of the original group on Podbrdo the first day, was one of those arrested. As night fell, a round-the-clock police guard was put on the hill at all points of access. The visionaries did not know where to go. "But," said Vicka, "the Virgin is cleverer than us. We gathered at the regular time behind a house and began to pray. She appeared immediately. She prayed with us and gave us courage, then said her farewells and departed."

Despite the guard, the children continued going to the hill: "Something irresistible drew us there. We would gather in the neighbourhood, chat, joke a bit, sing a bit . . . then, all of a sudden – let's go, and off we went. There would be anything from ten to fifty of us, and nobody ever caught us."[1]

Two days later (13th August) two special squads of armed police with dogs came to Medjugorje from Sarajevo. They came expecting to find an armed mob, and they found people on their knees praying, with rosaries in their hands and not a weapon in sight. An officer made a spot-check, to make sure. Buying a water-melon, he asked innocently for a knife. Of *eighty-two* people asked, not one could oblige. "These people aren't armed with so much as a fruit-knife," he reported disgustedly, "let alone anything more lethal."

Nevertheless access to the church was placed under police guard. No cars were allowed into Medjugorje that afternoon or evening. Sixty-one-year-old Fra Ferdo Vlašić, temporarily helping out in the parish while Fra Zrinko was on holiday, made a protest to the police, and was arrested. (Both he and Ivan Ivanković were held in prison in Mostar for two months, the ominous word "clerico-nationalist" appearing on the priest's indictment.)

On the sixteenth, Mgr Žanić's courageous declaration of support was published in *Glas Koncila*, the Zagreb fortnightly and main Croatian-language Catholic publication in Yugoslavia. The statement was regarded as deliberately provocative. Nemesis would surely follow.

"*Will* they send you to prison?" a friend had asked Jozo the previous day.

"I think they probably will," replied Jozo. "Don't worry, I shall welcome it."

"My going to prison was no accident," he said much later, "but it had nothing to do with my being stubborn or wanting to provoke the authorities. It was the logical result of the choices which at some stage of his life every Christian has to make."

At seven in the morning of 17th August, Fra Zrinko knocked on the bathroom door to tell Jozo that two agents of the Mostar Ministry of the Interior had come for him. "Let them wait," said Jozo calmly. Five minutes later he emerged from the bathroom to find a plain-clothes man in the corridor; and as he went into the bedroom, the man opened the door a crack to keep him in view. Jozo dressed and shaved, aware of the man's eyes on him:

> When I'd finished dressing he said: "You're to come with us." I told him I'd wear my Franciscan habit, but he didn't think that would be suitable. "All right," I said. "It doesn't matter." I put on my civilian suit and asked if he wanted coffee. "No, thank you, I've already had one," he said, "but you can have one if you want." I picked up my papers and said goodbye to everyone as I left the house. I dared not shake hands with them all personally, it would have been too upsetting for all of us.
>
> Outside, a policeman was standing on the small staircase, with handcuffs attached to his belt. "Shall we put these on him?" he asked, but the other man said no. Down below I could see someone with a TV camera filming us. Another policeman was at the wheel of a VW Golf. I got in the back with the first policeman beside me, and two others in front. We drove off at a dizzying speed as far as the crossroads where a Black Maria was parked. A policeman got out of it and opened up the rear doors for me to get in, then

he locked them behind me. I was driven to Mostar, and then, through a tunnel to – where or what the building was I still don't know – and I was put in cell number eighty-three.

A girl who had witnessed Fra Ferdo, and now Fra Jozo, taken away and saw the frightened faces of those left behind, felt impelled as never before to pray specially for them:

> Until that day I had prayed mechanically, but I suddenly found myself praying from the heart. I felt no hatred. I tried to thank God for all that was happening. I saw those priests now as being just like everybody else. We were all in this together and had to support each other with our prayers.

An extensive search of parish premises was instigated. The five Franciscan nuns from the nearby convent who assisted the priests in parish work were subjected to a humiliating body search by a policewoman brought along for the purpose. The sisters were alleged to have some secret electronic device for "projecting" the vision in front of the children – at, of course, the instigation of Fra Jozo. The police took away the collection boxes from the church (with money amounting to about $4,000 which was later returned); and, more significantly, removed documents, letters, books and the cassettes on which the earliest interviews with the children had been recorded. "But no matter how hard they tried," said Fra Zrinko,

> our enemies did not succeed in depriving our people of Mass, not even for a single day. Everybody thought there would be no Mass that night, and, humanly speaking it was impossible: Fra Jozo had been arrested, we were in quarantine and not allowed to leave the house, barricades had been erected and were being manned by three guards. No one was allowed to go near the church. Yet Mass started with only ten minutes' delay, and they did, after all, let the people in at six o'clock. Mass was celebrated by a priest I didn't even know, Fr Stanko Dodig, a Capuchin friar, a local man. He had been preaching in Sarajevo, and had dropped by to visit his mother.

The village was in a state of shock, as grief mingled with dismay and despair. Some were so distressed that though they felt no urge to pray, they came to the church just the same. In the parish ledgers the following account appears:

> When the bell rang for Mass, the church filled up in dead silence. The people were looking at the set faces of the priests and nuns, the scattered altar cloths, overturned vases, wide-open cupboards all around. When Fra Zrinko came to the altar to address the people, he could hardly speak: "This is the hardest day of my life," he said, and everyone began crying. During Mass they tried to sing, but they gagged on the words. The sisters

73

said they couldn't bring themselves to say the Glorious Mysteries of the Rosary, and said the Sorrowful ones instead.

At the end of Mass, in the middle of the seven Our Fathers, the visionaries stopped dead, and hurried to the side room opposite the sacristy. There was a hush, prayerful and expectant, and all eyes were fixed on the door where the children were. Then Jakov came to the microphone: "Our Lady called us into that room, where she was already waiting for us. She told us to tell you: 'Don't be afraid. I want you to be happy and to let joy show on your faces. *I* shall look after Father Jozo.'"

There was a great burst of clapping, followed by a long silence as everyone knelt in prayer. "We had felt a terrible sadness," said Marija:

> At first the priests hadn't believed us, and wouldn't even speak to us. Then, when Fra Jozo did come to believe us, they took him away. He was one of us, he'd accepted us, and we lost him. We accepted the sacrifice, but it was terribly hard.

It was, as Jozo described it some years later, "a day which brought a new understanding into our relationships with each other. Priests and people alike, we became aware of our mutual dependence and mutual responsibility. The dynamic was so powerful that, despite the suffering, we were immeasurably richer for the experience."

That night Sarajevo TV gave its own explanation of the day's events, quoting a press release issued at a meeting of the Čitluk commune:

> We decided that it was necessary to underline that what the priests, Jozo Zovko of Medjugorje, and his colleagues, Ferdo Vlašić, Pavao Zanić, Bishop of Mostar, and other extremists intend and desire is nothing less than to restore the terrorist Ustaša organisation. All of this constitutes the very gravest abuse of religious freedom.

Bishop Žanić protested in a letter to the Federal President on 1st September. Speaking for himself and the other accused priests, he expressed himself saddened by: "these irresponsible calumnies and these attacks whose bad taste will in no way facilitate a calm appraisal of the events which have been taking place in Medjugorje. Such behaviour violates fundamental human and civic rights."

In the "quarantine" where he awaited his trial, Jozo's guards were at first rough and unfriendly. He was allowed no newspapers, so had no knowledge of the outside world, nor of the lies being written about him. Everything was taken from him, as though he were a regular criminal. But as time passed, and Jozo refused to be intimidated, the guards' attitude changed to one of respect and even affection. They would offer him cigarettes, and perform small kindnesses for him. When, two months later, in October, he was put on trial in Mostar, many of his jailers told him they hoped for an acquittal.

The charges against him were three: that in his sermons, in this fortieth anniversary year of the Communist Revolution in Yugoslavia, he had repeatedly referred to the Israelites' forty years in the desert; and had claimed, moreover, that believers were afraid to be married in church, have their children baptised or sent for religious instruction, in case it cost them their jobs. Believers do not go far in public life; all the best jobs are denied them. As a British journalist recently said: "Being a Christian in Yugoslavia will not get you shot . . . Nevertheless it means that you do not advance in the state bureaucracy, army, police, law, medicine, journalism or industry."[2]

Secondly, Fra Jozo had claimed that it was sometimes necessary to shed one's blood for one's beliefs. And thirdly, his enthusiastic comment that events in Medjugorje were awakening the whole Church throughout Croatia and Hercegovina, was dismissed as double-speak for: "the Church in Croatia and Hercegovina is flexing its muscles and becoming aware of its power".

Filip Simić, Secretary of the republican Commission for Religious Affairs in Sarajevo, is in no doubt that Fra Jozo was a young, irrepressible hothead who could not resist making verbal attacks on the Communist system: "But as his insinuations directly undermined the country's constitutional and legal system and abused the religious feelings of the people for political purposes, it follows that we had to charge him . . . although nobody was very happy about doing this."[3]

Simić still believes that there was a master-mind at work in Medjugorje. He cites in evidence the suspicious activities of certain Croatian émigrés:

> It is a known fact that certain forces hostile to this country attempted to use this religious gathering, to exploit the apparitions for their own political ends. There *were* slogans like "Croats, arise", there *were* Nazi symbols up there on the hill . . . Certain church people were writing articles to suggest that the Madonna was appearing in Yugoslavia just because the Communists are in power here . . . When people begin assembling in large numbers and claim that the Virgin Mary has come to bring liberation to one or the other of the nationalities in our country, it is difficult for a Yugoslav citizen who has suffered greatly through political division and strife, to believe that there is no political message here.[4]

This point of view would prevail in the court proceedings. It was heightened by awareness of events in nearby Poland, where Solidarity, supported by the powerful Catholic Church, was beginning to look and

75

sound like an alternative government. Since the Croats regarded their fellow-Catholic Slavs in Poland with both admiration and love, it was feared that they might be tempted to follow their example. So Fra Jozo became one of the first scapegoats to suffer for his country's general nervousness; and his punishment would be exemplary.

It was no time for weakness on the part of the authorities. Though few local people could be prevailed on to testify against Fra Jozo, a few false witnesses *were* brought along to swear that the priest had intended to overthrow the Communist constitution – though, in the event, some of these decided not to perjure themselves. Only eighteen witnesses were found for the prosecution, and one statement from an absent witness was read out in court. But 330 people who had volunteered to speak on Jozo's behalf were refused permission to do so. Nor would the prosecution allow theological experts to explain the biblical meaning of those fateful words: "forty years". A request by the defence for taped recordings of Fra Jozo's offending sermons to be played in full was likewise refused.

On 22nd October the court sentenced Fra Jozo to three and a half years' imprisonment – but in a display of reasonableness, ordered the police to return the money taken from the church collecting boxes on 7th August.

Fra Ferdo Vlašić, who edited *Our Hearths*, a Franciscan publication widely read by the migrant Croat workers in the West, was accused of having written articles in favour of Medjugorje and prejudicial to the State in this magazine. He and thirty-year-old Fra Jozo Krizić, an assistant on the magazine, were tried in Mostar at the same time as Fra Jozo. Fra Ferdo was additionally charged with receiving books about Cardinal Stepinac from abroad, and with publishing a picture of a Croat Franciscan poet who lived in exile in Switzerland. Jozo Krizić was said to have preached to Croatian exiles in Canada in 1979.[5] Fra Ferdo was sentenced on 11th November to eight years' and Jozo Krizić a little later to five and a half years' imprisonment. Both men were banned from publishing their magazine for a full three years after their release from prison. The incredible harshness of the three sentences amply illustrates the authorities' jitters in the face of possible agitation on the part of the volatile Croats.

Jozo's fellow-prisoners had been led to expect a dyed-in-the-wool villain, one who had "exploited and robbed, gathered arsenals of weapons, planned an uprising" – to say nothing of murdering and throwing innocent people into a pit when he was as yet unborn. They were immensely curious to see this monster of iniquity. Unaware of the reputation that had preceded him, Jozo behaved with his usual quiet courtesy, and the curiosity soon melted away. A few dared to seek him out and talk, but most were afraid to do so: "Our every move was watched, mine and Fra Ferdo's, and for those who hoped to get their sentences commuted it wasn't advisable to be seen talking to us."

Jozo himself was none too sure either of his fellow-prisoners or of their motives in approaching him. He was assigned to a room of about eighty to one hundred people:

> criminals of all kinds: thieves, murderers, embezzlers, men who'd raped their own children, and so on. The drug addicts and rapists were the most tragic figures, and one could only feel sad for them. They were zombies, living dead, barely recognisable as the human beings they had once been. They knew what they were, and made no attempt to deny what they'd done.

However hard he tried, whatever overtures he made, Jozo was unable to reach such as these; and his inability to communicate with them made him wretched. With the two priests (Jozo Krizić had joined them) it was a different story, and a warm friendship sprang up between them: "It's a togetherness you could experience nowhere else. The bonds forged in prison are unique: you feel that you live in your brother and he in you." Of events outside they knew only what the official press chose to tell; they were allowed neither breviary nor books, though other professional men were at least allowed the books relevant to their own calling. For six months Father Krizić was ill, but no doctor was allowed to see him. During the day they all worked long hours as machine operators in a furniture factory, where the noise of the drills left Jozo Krizić with permanently impaired hearing.

They saw no cause for complaint. It was right, they agreed, that the visible representatives of Christ should suffer for their beliefs; after all, it was the persecutions and martyrdoms of the early Christian era that had attracted so many men and women into the Church. "Let me add only this," says Jozo, "in prison the heavy locks were not proof against God's power. No one can take faith away, nor deny the action of grace. You cannot truly imprison anyone who believes. At the very moment when he has lost everything, he finds his greatest strength."

A Place of Pilgrimage

Although a pilgrim is an ordinary person, he is proceeding through extraordinary space, *en route* to his roots. One cannot book a pilgrimage through a travel agency – only the ticket.

James Roose-Evans, *Inner Journey, Outer Journey*

The children were deeply distressed by Fra Jozo's arrest and sentence, but they were not left long without a spiritual adviser. On 18th August, the day after Fra Jozo was arrested, Tomislav Vlašić (no relation to Fra Ferdo) came to Medjugorje in his place. Father Vlašić had been working in Čapljina, about forty-eight kilometres away, when the apparitions started, but since his first visit on 29th June had been a crucial part of the happenings there. He, perhaps, had a strange feeling of inevitability, of a prophecy fulfilled. For in May, just one month before that fateful June, at a conference for leaders of the Charismatic Renewal in Rome, Sister Briege McKenna, an internationally-known healer with psychic powers, claimed to have seen in a vision a twin-towered church with Vlašić seated in the centre of a huge crowd, rivers of life-giving water flowing from the chair on which he sat. At the same meeting, Fr Emiliano Tardif also delivered a divinely-inspired message to Tomislav Vlašić. "Do not be afraid," ran this message. "I am sending my mother to you." ("One has to wonder," Bishop Žanić would later acidly remark, "who on earth is this man who can send the Blessed Mother wherever he wants.") The words evoked a *frisson*, since a few years earlier the Italian visionary, Padre Pio, had told a group of pilgrims from the Mostar diocese: "The Blessed Virgin will soon be visiting your homeland." Perhaps this prophecy had inspired the picture that hung above the main door in the church at Medjugorje. Painted in 1974 by a parishioner, it showed the Virgin Mary in white robe, blue girdle, white veil and blue cloak standing above Medjugorje, arms outstretched in blessing. Below her, on the left, was the church and, recognisable in the background, the hill of Križevac.

The parish of Medjugorje had been set up as long ago as 1599, but in the seventeenth century it had ceased to exist. The Catholic villagers, like so many others of their kind, crippled by Turkish taxes and weary of being discriminated against, fled to the Dalmatian coast. The village was reborn at some time in the eighteenth century, when the situation had become more stable; and the new parish of Brotnjo was organised. Medjugorje remained part of this Brotnjo parish until 1892, after Hercegovina had come under the control of the Austro-Hungarian Empire. A church was built in 1897 but on such shaky foundations that forty years later it was badly damaged by an earth-tremor and a new one had to be built. (The remains of the old one were not actually demolished until 1977.)

Building a new church was no simple matter where hot-blooded and tricky Balkan peasants were involved. The thirties were a time of bitter feuding among the villages of the parish; of a corrosive mutual envy which found expression in hatred, curses and violence. The prospect of a new church would not distract them from their rivalry: it would merely sharpen it.

The trouble began over where the church was actually to be sited. The old church had been built on land belonging to Bijakovići, on one side of the road that separated that village from Medjugorje. The Medjugorjans wanted the new church to be on *their* side of the road. But as the school was already on Medjugorje territory, the Bijakovićians wanted to retain the original site. The passions generated by the dispute were powerful and violent. One old man in the village claims to remember that in 1933 there was a gun battle between rival factions, and three people were killed. The majority, however, firmly deny that there were any deaths.

It took five years for a compromise solution to be reached. It was decided to build the church 200 metres away from the old one, in a field, a no-man's-land well away from any houses. For, quite obviously, had the church been sited within the boundaries of either one village, no one from the other one would have set foot in it. While passions still simmered, plans were drawn up, materials assembled. And in 1937 building commenced. But the outbreak of war made it impossible to proceed; and in the ensuing chaos and disruption of all civilised life, the building materials were destroyed or confiscated.

Not until over twenty years later, when the dust of war and revolution had settled, could a new start be made. Although, unlike many other atheistic regimes, the Yugoslav Communist government never tried to stamp out religion altogether, merely to limit its scope and make sure that it didn't spill over into politics, in the early years of the revolution the pressures brought to bear on the Church were intolerable. Only in the late fifties, when relations with the Vatican improved, were these pressures relaxed in any way, and the Church allowed a measure of autonomy. Since the law held that Church and State were completely separate, religious communities (whether Orthodox, Catholic or Muslim) were permitted by law to spend their money as they wished provided they stayed within that law. In Hercegovina alone, thirty-two new Catholic churches were built, or old ones restored, in the next thirty years.

While the new church was being built, the people attended Mass in three small chapels – at Vionica, Šurmanći and Miletina. By the time the church of Medjugorje was finally completed in 1969, passion had been largely succeeded by indifference. "It needed more hard work and sacrifice than they were prepared to give it," said one former parish priest. "To them the church was far from being a sacred place for which they were willing to give their last penny." But another priest disagreed: "The people had to work in the fields all day and couldn't spend all their time in church," he said. "But they were one of the best parishes you could find anywhere. They built that church out of faith. The families all prayed together at home." Nevertheless, it was only thanks to contributions from émigrés abroad that the church was able to be finished. The locals grumbled that, with its huge floor area, it was far too big for their needs: "What do we want a church like an airport for?" It seemed doomed to become something of a white elephant.

Yet within days of the apparitions starting, the church of St James at Medjugorje was already too small. Built for 600, it was being used for many thousands. (The majority had to sit or stand outside, whatever the weather.) The church, naturally enough, gave its name to the apparitions – the world at large knows this place by the collective name of Medjugorje, even though the visionaries are all from Bijakovići and the earliest apparitions all took place there. In the not-so-distant past, that would have been enough to trigger a furious outburst of jealous quarrelling. But not any more. Such was the overpowering effect of the apparitions and the Lady's impassioned appeal for peace and reconciliation, that there was not so much as a ripple of protest. Mindful of the area's blood-stained past – the in-fighting over the church being as nothing compared to the terrible wartime massacres – one Franciscan, Fra Ivan Dugandžić, was moved to tell a BBC interviewer: "In this context, I have from the very first seen what is happening here as a call to replace senseless hatred by peace, to bring about brotherhood and understanding between all people."

"Why do you think the Lady wants to be called the Queen of Peace?" Mirjana was once asked.[1] "Because the situation in the world is so dreadful," she replied. "Wars everywhere, tensions. We need peace – a just and true peace – more than anything else. But first, we must establish peace in our own hearts . . . the rest will follow." The world had lost its way, Ivanka said,[2] and the Lady had come to the rescue: "Merely by coming, she's put the process in motion. People have been converted, and begun to believe, to pray a little. Our Lady says that with prayer and fasting, wars *can* be averted. Because she is the Queen of Peace, I think she will be able to reconcile the world to itself."

In September 1981, some two months after the first apparitions, Orthodox and Muslim pilgrims began coming to Medjugorje. This would be roughly analogous to Northern Ireland Paisleyites visiting the shrine of Knock. The gaping divide between Serbian Orthodox Christians and Roman Catholics was every bit as fraught with danger as that dividing Catholics and Protestants in Northern Ireland. Or Christians and Muslims, in the Lebanon. The mutual hatred was everywhere the same. So it was almost shocking to devout Catholics when the Madonna was reported as saying: "You must respect each man's beliefs. No one should despise another for his convictions. God is one and indivisible. It is not God but believers who have caused the dreadful divisions in the world." To Mirjana she pointed out that devout Catholics seemed to go out of their way to avoid contact with Orthodox and Muslims; yet nobody who refused to take other believers seriously was worthy of the name of Christian. By way of underlining this difficult message, the Lady had singled out one of Mirjana's neighbours in Sarajevo, a Muslim woman called Pasha, for special praise. "She is a true believer, a saintly woman. You should try to be more like her."

One day a gipsy child of Orthodox parents was cured on the hill, and a priest, in Marija's hearing, expressed amazed disgust. "How can you say such things?" Marija rounded on him. "How can a priest, of all people, react in such a way?" It seems that the Lady also commented: "Tell that priest and the others like him that it is they who are perpetuating the divisions in the world. Muslims, Orthodox, Catholics, to my Son and myself all are one. You are all my children."

It was a message that would bear constant repetition. For the mutual mistrust between Catholic and Orthodox was the age-old hatred of Croat for Serb, Serb for Croat; and behind the attitude of both to the Muslim hung the shadow of the Bogomils and of more than four centuries of Turkish oppression. Where there were so many old scores to settle, forgiveness was hard and could not be legislated for. "In today's Yugoslavia," said a young Croat girl, "Catholics, Orthodox and Muslims are ordered to get on with each other, and so, on the surface, they do. But in their hearts they don't want to." Fierce, implacable reminders of past hatreds echo from those awesome clusters of Bogomil tombs that survive in large numbers around Medjugorje, partly perhaps because of the legend that to tamper with them is to invite divine retribution. And at the entrance to the church belonging to the Orthodox monastery at nearby Žitomislić (whose beautiful name means "dreaming of wheat") a more recent past is starkly recalled. A commemorative plaque dated 21st June 1981 (just three days before the apparitions began) marks the fortieth anniversary of the day when the entire community of that monastery was taken out by the Ustaše and buried alive.

"We must find a way of coming closer to the Orthodox communities," reflected a Franciscan. "But, not surprisingly, they find it difficult to trust us. Perhaps the young will find a way. They are not burdened by so many terrible memories."

Mistrust was greatest of all in the rural areas, the battleground over which the bloodthirsty civil war had raged. But in Medjugorje a start, albeit a slow one, was being made. People there were working their way, however painfully, towards a change of heart. As Tomislav Vlašić urged in a sermon:

> Let us open the door wide so that God may, through His mother, enter our hearts. If we are blasphemers, let's stop blaspheming. If we are scandal-mongers, let's stop spreading rumours. If we're liars, let's stop lying. And if we hate, let us stop hating. All of you, just for a moment, stop and take a good hard look at your lives.

To those who had come to the church that night in hopes of a miracle, he threw out a challenge:

> Allow yourselves to be healed by God's holy word. Perhaps you have come here to pray for Our Lady to cure your big toe. But it is your hearts that are sick, and your big toe will not get better till your hearts are cured. It is your lives that need healing . . .

Tomislav Vlašić would later be accused by his bishop of being the unscrupulous manipulator of the Medjugorje events. An old church quarrel would fuel that harsh assessment. But to a lay observer, Vlašić, "warm, kind and forceful", with a more commanding presence than Jozo Zovko, seems merely to have carried on where the latter left off, allowing the people to gather as before and refusing to discontinue the evening Masses. He was careful not to be used as a political pawn either by the Communist authorities or by Croat nationalists. He did not exaggerate the role of the Madonna. As Vicka had told him, she was someone who prayed to God, not one who bestowed favours. His focal point was the Gospel, and "the Gospel loses its force if it is allowed to become political". Nor would he permit the commercialisation of Medjugorje: it must not be allowed to go the way of certain other pilgrimage centres, where the money-makers had been let loose; hotels, wine-bars, shops and cinemas had changed the character of the original place; and where the central spiritual message was all but lost in a welter of cheap and tawdry religious tat.

In this he was at one with the regional authorities who had no intention of allowing Medjugorje to develop in that way. Although service buses continued to operate, coach-hire firms had been forbidden to take anyone there at all; and a ban was placed on building extra accommodation – or even a few basic facilities – for the increasing number of tourist/pilgrims. With the only public convenience a hole in the ground watered by a spring, and with no shelter of any kind against extremes of weather, Medjugorje offered little in the way of twentieth-century comforts.

But nothing seemed to deter the people from coming. They came by car, by public transport or on foot. Long-distance coaches were coming in, not only from other regions of Yugoslavia – and with many Orthodox and Muslims among them now – but also from Italy, where priests connected with the radical youth movement *Comunione e Liberazione* had begun organising pilgrimages. Hard on their heels came groups from Austria, Germany and Switzerland. They were given a warm welcome by the villagers. "They came morning and night," said Vicka, "and hospitality was always offered them. Not only a bed to sleep in, but supper and breakfast too. And of course there were all the cold drinks. One man was handing out grapes and water-melons to thirsty passers-by."

Potential pilgrims from abroad were warned against admitting their destination, for once it was discovered that they were Medjugorje-bound, many were being instantly turned around and put on the next plane home. Though it was a little easier to slip in by road or rail, even here the border guards were on red alert and it was advisable to conceal one's true aims. Even where this hurdle was successfully negotiated, hire-car firms, travel agencies and hotel managers might yet betray the unwary pilgrim, who would then be deported. Robert Faricy, an American Jesuit who first travelled to Medjugorje from Italy in the autumn of 1981, has written of the spy-thriller atmosphere in which the visit took place. Arriving in Split, he searched for a priest-friend to direct him to Medjugorje:

Eventually I find the priest but he tells me I cannot go to Medjugorje alone. It is too far and there is no public transport. Then he turns on the radio. "They watch us and listen to us all the time," he explains; the radio will cover our voices. Then he tells me that if I were to go to Medjugorje alone I would be spotted as a foreigner before I even arrived. Once the authorities discovered my destination, I'd be escorted to the nearest border.[3]

All through that late summer and autumn, as a guard continued to be posted on the hill of Podbrdo, the children scattered to five or six different locations for their nightly apparitions. The Madonna appeared to them in a glade of trees; and also in various houses in Bijakovići, the exact venue a closely-guarded secret to prevent reprisals against the host. On one of these occasions (19th October) the children reported having seen the imprisoned Fra Jozo in a vision; he had told them to have no fears on his behalf: "I shall doubtless be condemned; but I would willingly die for my faith."

At some time in October, Fra Ivica Vego, a young Franciscan from Mostar, asked Marija to put three questions to the Madonna: about Poland; about the Hercegovina problem (see Chapter 9); and about the East-West struggle. She replied that in Poland great conflicts would soon take place, but that right would prevail in the end. (Indeed, the imposition of martial law, or, as the Poles preferred to call it, General Jaruzelski's war against the Polish nation, was a mere two months away. But few people would claim now that, since the crushing of Solidarity, right has been seen to prevail in that unhappy land.) In the "Hercegovina issue", much prayer and patience were needed, the Lady advised. But it was her reply to the third question that was the strangest. The Russians, she prophesied, would come to glorify (literally, "make manifest") God to the world; while the West, though it had attained an undeniable technological mastery, had lost God in the process.

The Children

This quest may be attempted by the weak with as much hope as the strong. Yet such is oft the course of deeds that move the wheels of the world: small hands do them because they must, while the eyes of the great are elsewhere.

J. R. R. Tolkien, *Lord of the Rings*

The six youngsters at the centre of these events were ordinary children, most of them hitherto unremarkable for piety or good works. They claimed the Madonna had chosen them simply because of their ordinariness:

We're neither good nor bad [said Mirjana], just like everyone else. When the apparitions began, my grandmother said: "Why should the Madonna appear to the likes of you, when you go around with boys?" I said: "Well, she knows what we're like, and she doesn't want us to pretend to be something we're not."[1]

They were very different in temperament, social background and mental capacity – their intelligence ranging from slightly above to way below average. They had no common interest, no obvious leader. Only when the six had begun to see the apparitions together did they become and remain a group, in the real sense of the word.

Marija Pavlović, the most serene of them all, was a girl of deep spirituality but no academic gifts. She was learning hairdressing at her middle technical school. Although she would have preferred floristry, that would have meant attending school far away in Sarajevo. Both she and Ivanka Ivanković, a typical late twentieth-century teenager, fond of colourful clothes, cosmetics and boys, had failed their first-year exams and were due to repeat a year.[2]

Vicka Ivanković was quite unlike either of these two, being a cheerful, smiling extrovert, a chatterbox, bossy, energetic, unlettered and outspoken. Rough around the edges, Vicka was no respecter of authority, whatever its source. To a priest making a query about the messages, "Are you sure?", she replied testily, "Of course we're sure; we were there, weren't we?" Another priest who once taught her catechism describes her as "incapable of telling a lie", and recalls with some amusement that the whole family – grandmother in the lead – could be heard all over the village loudly reciting their night prayers. In a sense, the apparitions saga had begun with Vicka. Two months before the drama began, she and her sisters had been preparing to set off at first light to gather firewood, when they had noticed in the trailer-cart two antique rosaries of strange design. The cross of one of these was nearly ten centimetres long and was decorated with carved Stations of the Cross. Since nobody had seen the rosaries before – Vicka's mother later asked everyone in the village – Vicka had one day asked the Madonna about them. They had been put there, she was told, as an invitation to prayer.

In September 1981, before the beginning of the school year (she was at a textile school), Vicka went to repeat the maths exam she had failed that summer. As she told Fra Janko Bubalo, an instructor had stopped her:[3] "I was wearing a cross and chain round my neck. [He] stopped me at the door and told me I must remove the chain before going in to do the exam. I refused, and he sent me away."

The instructor had read about Vicka and seen her picture in *Arena*. "You took your exam with your Virgin Mary," he sneered, "goodbye."

"I caught the bus and went home singing," recalled Vicka.

But that was not the end of the matter. When term began, she received a letter offering to reinstate her in the school. She ignored it. By that time, the Madonna had asked her to stay at home and look after Jakov, the youngest of the group, and the only one still at primary school in Medjugorje. So Vicka resigned herself to the monotonous daily routine of the peasant woman: "I do whatever the time of year calls for. I dig, weed with the tiller, pick tobacco, firewood."

Vicka, remaining in the village, would be the one constant fixed point in the fluctuating saga of Medjugorje, always at hand, as the others were not, to bear witness to the extraordinary events.

Ivan Dragicević could not have provided a greater contrast to Vicka. He was serious and shy, as introverted as she was outgoing. And – until the apparitions began – not at all pious. On 22nd August he had entered the junior seminary at Visoko, in hopes of becoming a Franciscan, though it was unlikely that he would ever pass the necessary examinations.

Only Mirjana Dragicević and little Jakov Čolo could be called clever. Mirjana, blonde and pretty, hoped to go to university in Sarajevo after completing her high-school studies. As for Jakov, he was a normal, mischievous boy. "He was young for his age," said one of the Franciscans, "and seemed just an empty-headed kid, mad on pop music and football." Yet after the apparitions started, said Fra Svetozar Kraljević, of all the six Jakov was the most regular in attendance at the evening Mass. "Jakov becomes transfigured when he talks about the Madonna," he said. Jakov was not above asking the Madonna to forecast a win for the Zagreb Dynamos. (She merely smiled in response.) Once, he said, the Madonna had told him he ought to be nicer to the other children at school. He ought to love them all, she said. "Well," he protested, "I do. But some of them are so boring." The Madonna told him to put up with the boredom as a penance.

Jakov lived with his mother in a little, tumbledown hovel in great poverty. (Ivan, who lived nearby, lived in a very much larger and grander house.) His father, a migrant worker in Austria, virtually ignored the family's existence, leaving them to survive as best they could. A priest from Zagreb, who called to see Jakov, tried discreetly to slip a sum of money under the tablecloth. Jakov spotted him and insisted on giving the money back. Never, under any circumstances, would the children accept money from well-wishers. "From the way they act," said Fra Slavko Barbarić, who would later become their spiritual director, "one would conclude that *whatever* it is they are seeing is a supreme authority for them. It enables them to bear whatever is in store for them and yet remain serene. They feel no enmity towards those who persecute them and never encourage others to feel enmity. They always and only ask for peace, reconciliation and prayer."

As time went by, however, the children ceased to talk freely about the Madonna's messages. It became clear that each of them had been selected for a specific role. Vicka would receive apocalyptic messages about the fate of the world; to Mirjana was given an understanding about the state of the Church; while Marija was made responsible for particular messages to pilgrims, priests, the bishop, and even the Pope. For Ivan, Ivanka and Jakov, a lower-key role was reserved.

The guard at the foot of Podbrdo was still in place. On 28th October, a spectacular fire broke out at the site of the first apparition, and a crowd of several hundreds watched it blaze fiercely for about fifteen minutes. When police and firemen investigated the area of the fire, they found nothing: no brazier, no smouldering embers, not even a sign of ash. "It was just a small herald of the great sign that is to come," the Madonna told the children that evening.

Even this failed to impress the taciturn Fra Zrinko. He had seen the fire and taken it for an ordinary bonfire started by irresponsible hotheads. Even when he heard that no sign of the fire remained, he still refused to attach any significance to it. "I admit it's a sign of sorts," he said grudgingly. "But as far as I'm concerned, that kind of sign is worthless."

But there were plenty of other signs around. On Thursday, 15th

September, Anka Pehar, who had gone outside to bring in her washing, was startled to see a funnel-shaped light above the hill of Crnica:

> Then I saw in this light Our Lady with her arms spread wide. She floated in the air going in the direction of the church. I called my daughter . . . and my grandmother . . . and two friends joined us . . . We all saw it. We were kneeling and praying. Our Lady was surrounded by light, but the brightest rays came from behind her head and shoulders. All this lasted about an hour.

At five o'clock on 22nd October, Fra Janko Bubalo was in the presbytery waiting for the time of Mass, when he heard a commotion outside. Looking out of the window, he saw the two nuns who looked after the house and church kneeling on the damp ground with their arms spread wide:

> With them were about seventy men and women, all on their knees, forming a line that extended right to the church. No one seemed worried about the rain. No umbrellas. Everyone was praying . . . some were crying, some singing hymns. All eyes were turned to the cross on Križevac hill.
> I too looked towards the cross, but it had disappeared. In its place was a strange light, pale pink, unlike anything in real life.
> I was moved. Since I do not have good eyesight, I asked for a pair of binoculars . . . Then I saw, in place of the cross, the silhouette of a woman with outstretched arms. Her head reached a bit above the vertical beam of the cross. Her feet were hidden in a luminous cloud near the base of the cross.
> I was filled with a great joy. There were four or five priests with me. We all saw the same thing. So did others in the village. Everyone looking just then at the cross on Križevac saw it.[4]

And so on. These recitals disgusted Fra Zrinko who had hoped that the search for the sensational was dying down:

> After the first two or three months, hardly anyone was bothering about the hill, though there were always a few gullible souls who were in Medjugorje for the first time and had heard about the cross performing its antics. They would stand there staring at the cross in hopes of seeing it spin. Then, "Oh, just look at the cross, it's spinning," they'd say in amazement. Well, of course it was spinning, given the time they'd been gazing at it. I used to upset them by saying: "It's your heads that are spinning, not the cross."
> And when I used to see people turning round to gaze in the direction of the hill during Mass, I'd shout, "Look, there she is, right behind you. She's here in the church. What do you want to be gazing up there for?"

The Communist authorities, aware of all these signs and disturbed by the way they were proliferating, were doing their best to persuade people to deny having seen them. Ivan Ivanković , in prison after his arrest in August, was told to deny having seen anything. When he refused, he was sent for psychiatric tests in Čitluk and Mostar; but in each place, doctors pronounced him healthy. The children claimed that one night, in a vision, they had seen the head and shoulders of Ivan in his prison cell. "Why do we see only his head?" they asked. "Because Ivan is being witness to the truth," the Madonna told them.

But hill or no hill, it was in the church that the pilgrims were seeking God. Visiting Medjugorje for the first time, incognito, in December, the Archbishop of Split, Frane Franić, was "deeply gratified":

> It was dark when I entered the church, which was full of people, and outside the church were cars with licence plates from many cities. A Franciscan priest preached about faith as being trust. He spoke about the miracles and what they really point to. It was obvious that he himself believed in miracles . . . and was inclined to accept the reported happenings at Medjugorje. Everyone listened attentively, including the numerous young people there.

With Christmas drawing near, the problem of accommodating the vast numbers expected at Midnight Mass was daunting. (Despite the fact that, in Communist Yugoslavia, Christmas Eve and Christmas day are normal working – and school – days.) "Then God solved the problem with some heavy rain," recalls Zrinko cheerfully. "Those who came had to wade knee-deep through water on the asphalt road. And those who couldn't squeeze into the church simply went home again."

When Fra Zrinko was promoted to senior chaplain, the authorities were pleased. They knew Zrinko's sarcastic tongue at first hand and hoped he would take a firm hand with the villagers and pilgrims. The villagers were less delighted. As senior chaplain, he would be in charge of visiting all the families of the parish, a prospect that did not appeal. And the priest lived up to his reputation among them. Though not in any way disposed to play the authorities' game, he tried, as always, to curb the people's wilder flights of fancy. It was the only way he knew of keeping order:

> People simply couldn't be allowed to do whatever they pleased. That's why I bullied and shouted at them. I knew it was unpleasant behaviour, especially from a priest, but it was the best I could manage. I was rude to them all: male, female, young, old, cleric, lay. I even snapped at the elderly friars.

The authorities came in for their fair share of attack, Zrinko asking in a loud voice, whenever he spotted plain-clothes police in his congregation,

"What are you here for? Have you taken up mysticism and superstition?" Sometimes he made a mistake and railed in this way at innocent pilgrims. "I could never be sure who was here for the right reasons and who for the wrong," he admits, "but I did expose many an informer and give him the sharp end of my tongue. I wanted them to know I knew who they were."

Zrinko was fighting on three fronts at once: against the villagers, the authorities, and the zealous pilgrims. When the latter tried to ask him about the apparitions, he would tell them to stop wasting his time, and would stump off into his garden. "There at least I can do something useful," he would declare. "Let them believe what they want, so long as they don't expect me to believe it too."

Caught between their wariness of the choleric priest and their fear of the authorities, the children found the pressures almost unendurable. If this had really been a hoax, the price for going on with it would have been too high. When a group of theological students from Zagreb visited Medjugorje in February, one of them said that, if it had been him, he'd have run away long since. "Me, too," retorted Vicka, "but for the finger of God." All of them felt impelled to stay where they were, witnessing to the Madonna's presence and to her message. It was, they said, as though some special grace enabled them to endure all the harassment and the endless demands on their time.

As winter came on, the bitter January cold forced the children to abandon the fields and come into the church for their apparitions. Between 24th June 1981 when the apparitions had started and 20th February 1982, there were only five occasions when the Madonna had not appeared when expected. (Ivan, during his first days in the seminary, had gone a whole week without seeing her.) But from the time they came into the church, there were no such disappointments. The little room immediately opposite the sacristy became known (and is still known, though the locale has changed) as "the chapel of the apparitions".

A routine was now established. After saying the Rosary with the people at about five-twenty, they would rise and go into the small chapel, often accompanied by up to ten visiting priests, scientists, doctors or foreigners with a special interest in the apparitions. They would then begin immediately to say the seven Our Fathers, Hail Marys and Glorias. At about the second or third Our Father, they would fall to their knees, eyes mysteriously converging on the spot where, unseen by everyone else present, the Madonna emerged from the light. They described her as more real than anything they had ever known, a three-dimensional, flesh-and-blood woman with whom they prayed, talked or sang. When she was there, they were aware of nothing else; all their senses were concentrated on her. They believed that they were speaking quite normally, and were surprised to learn that their lips moved only silently.

These visions would last anything from two to fifteen minutes, though just occasionally one would last as long as forty-five. When it was over, they would return to the body of the church and join in prayer with everybody else.

As time went by, Zrinko came to accept that the "finger of God" *was* in the Medjugorje events. It was something quite simple that finally convinced him, not the fact that on the second day of Jozo's trial he himself had seen a brilliant whiteness around the cross of Križevac, but a woman waiting for him to hear her confession very early one morning:

> She gave me a written testimony, so I am at liberty to disclose what she said. It was like this. She was barren and longed to have a child. She prayed, fasted, went on pilgrimages, but to no avail. When she heard of the visions, she cursed Our Lady, saying, "If she existed at all, she'd have heard my prayers." But the next Sunday she went to Mass and when she arrived at the church she could barely summon the courage to go in. When she caught sight of Our Lady's statue she was seized by such a dreadful anguish of spirit that she had to be helped out of the church. Her husband took her home in a state of great distress. In the middle of the night, she wanted to go back to the church and make her confession; but her husband wouldn't hear of her "bothering the friars" at such an ungodly hour. But by dawn she was outside the church. It was this woman's breakdown that brought light into my own darkness, and made me realise that God must have some hand in the situation, regardless of any doubts I might have. It was a moral sign, far clearer to me than the light around the cross or the fire on the hill.

He never, however, managed to come to terms with the children, though he could not deny that they were being used as instruments of the divine will:

> The essential question for me was this: had those children really received a sign from God through Our Lady? Had she really spoken to them, even if only with a single sentence: Go and tell those people down there to stop quarrelling, to make peace with each other and with God, because it's high time they did so? If she had, then that was enough for me.

If God was at work in Medjugorje in a special way, how could he, Zrinko, refuse to co-operate, however powerful his reservations?

> I recognised that the children were a bridge, and that without such a bridge it wasn't possible to get to the other side of the river. But somehow I could never bring myself to take much of an interest in that bridge. I still find my reluctance surprising, but there it is.

His main concern was that Medjugorje should become a place of pilgrimage, a true spiritual oasis, not a day out for the inquisitive.

And in this he succeeded, forcing people to be less credulous and more discerning. He was never one to interpret literally the demands of the place. Since a bread-and-water fast (which the Virgin had urged) upset his stomach, he preferred to take nothing at all on fast-days, apart from the occasional cup of sugarless tea:

> I leave myself free to interpret the appeals in my own way. For me the messages are not an absolute command but an expression of God's liberating love. It is the spirit of the messages which is important – the expression of God's love for us.

Years later, it would seem to him that there was a pattern in all this:

> We used to worry about what would happen. But looking back, it's as though a director had taken up his position behind the stage, watching the events unfold, arranging everything. We might eat our hearts out with worry but everything would turn out exactly as it should. For me that was the real sign of "God's finger", because, when all is said and done, we humans are not all that clever.

He was even prepared to include the Communists in the divine strategy:

> All our meetings took a strange turn which always surprised us. Actually, all the actors in this drama – the SUP, the League of Communists, the socio-political organisations and we priests – were acting somehow against our own wishes, plans, ideas. It was always like that. No matter how hard we pulled in one direction, events had a will of their own. One day I told the state officials that it was as though we'd all been hitched to a cart and told to pull it, one of us as an ass, another as a horse, a third as coachman . . . Or, put it like this, it was as though we were all of us in a boat being ferried and rowed across a river. All of us, without exception.[5]

He would go so far as saying:

> I used to resent that guard who barred access to cars and people. But the time came when I felt I ought to invite all the police and the whole Socialist Alliance of Čitluk to a great barbecue feast because . . . well, what a mess we'd have been in but for them. Just imagine the traffic jams if they'd let all the cars in. What a circus we'd have had to contend with if they'd not stopped the people going up the hill. So, I believe that God used them all – the Party bosses, the local Communists, the police, the bishop, the priests and friars who were with us and those who forbade their people to come near us – just to make this possible.

But as long as he remained in Medjugorje, life seemed to Zrinko to be one huge insurmountable problem. Finally, he could stand it no longer. Exhausted by work, worry and the sheer impossibility of coping with the flood of pilgrims, he petitioned the Franciscan Provincial to take him away. Much to his own surprise, when the time came for him to leave, "something happened to me that had never happened before when I left a parish: my eyes were full of tears."

By then it was August 1982, and in June, Medjugorje had celebrated the first anniversary of the apparitions. On 24–25th June it was estimated that 50,000 pilgrims packed the church and its surrounding terrain. The church was wired for sound so that even those outside would miss nothing. And although it was unscheduled, Masses were said in Italian and Slovene as well as the local Croatian. As coach-hire firms were still unable to provide transport, some groups of young people had walked as much as sixty to eighty kilometres; and over thirty buses had brought thirsty and sweating pilgrims from even further afield. Drinking water was provided in cisterns and tanks. AKSA, the Catholic news agency in Zagreb, reported that the police controlled the incoming traffic, but made no attempt to interfere.[6] Other reports said that some tourist coaches were searched and the driver of one of them arrested. The visionaries themselves were once again investigated by the police.

Strange happenings were again reported during that anniversary period. Fra Rudolf Kadleb of Zagreb testified:

> After Mass on 26th June, just after six in the morning as we came out of the sacristy door, all the pilgrims (about eighty of us) watched the uncommon manifestations occurring at the cross. A shining white cloud descended on the Križevac hill. The cross itself disappeared completely. In the cloud, the silhouette of a person in white in a long white garment could be seen. The person could be seen through the transparent shining cloud, but it could not be clearly seen who it was. Suddenly, a completely round white circle, like a large white host, with a small white cross above it, appeared. A woman standing next to me who photographed the spectacle of the white cloud developed a good, sharp photo without the cross. The spectacle was viewed by all the people present on the hill . . . as well as from all the places in the area of the church, the roads and fields of Medjugorje, on 24th, 25th, 26th June from six-thirty in the morning until seven.

With numbers like this, and phenomena such as these being reported, it seemed that Medjugorje had already developed a momentum that nothing would be able to stop.

The Bishop and the Friars

We all carry within us our places of exile, our crimes and our ravages.
But our task is not to unleash them on the world: it is to fight them in
ourselves and in others.

Albert Camus, *The Rebel*

But if the events of Medjugorje had ever been clear and simple, they were
certainly so no longer. Hostility now enveloped them, not only from the
authorities but perhaps even more so from the bishop. Despite his own
earlier championship of the children, by the end of 1981, Bishop Žanić
was asserting that he had always doubted their truthfulness. He had, he
claimed, merely been reserving judgement. If the apparitions were
genuine, they might be God's way of "encouraging the disobedient ones
to return to obedience".

Who on earth were these "disobedient ones"?

To understand that loaded reference, we must plunge once again into
history and uncover the roots of the complex "Hercegovina problem" that
has long bedevilled relations between the bishop and the Franciscan
friars. It is not an edifying story, and nobody comes out of it very well; but
the interests of truth demand that it be told.

The friars' roots in the Bosnian soil go back to the era of the Crusades.
A handful of them had begun missionary work there shortly after the king
of Hungary's Crusade against the Bogomil heretics in 1203. But Bogomilism was well-entrenched in Bosnia, and all through the thirteenth
century the Catholic Church was in decline there; the clergy had long
since fled. The Franciscans, vying for converts with the white-robed
Dominicans, had little success. Nevertheless, with their simplicity and
homeliness they were preferred to the Dominicans who had come from
Catholic Hungary and showed too ardent an enthusiasm for the In-
quisition. The preference, however, was academic, since Bogomilism
continued to flourish.

When the itinerant friars returned in 1339 to this "land infested with
heretics", they had the good fortune to convert its king. This gave them
the foothold they had long been waiting for; and they were allowed to
establish themselves. Though Bogomilism did not markedly decline,

about 500,000 Bosnians were converted to the Catholic faith, and in 1378, in the absence of any regular clergy in Bosnia, Pope Urban V permitted the Franciscans to act as priests.[1] Ten years later, his successor, Urban VI, gave them the right to build churches and set up parishes; and by 1385 they were established throughout Bosnia in thirty-six monasteries. (They did not appear in Hercegovina till early in the fifteenth century, when monasteries were built at Konjic, Mostar and Ljubuški.) In 1444, Pope Eugenius IV decreed that the spiritual care of Bosnia and Hercegovina belonged to the Franciscans alone, although certain Catholic Bosnian nobles were allowed to bring secular priests into the churches on their estates.[2]

When the Ottoman Turks conquered Bosnia in 1463, a wholesale Islamisation took place. The Bogomil nobles, to protect their lands and privileges, converted *en masse* to Islam and began to persecute their former Catholic tormentors with great ferocity. Roman Catholicism was outlawed, churches were burned down and once again the secular clergy fled to Dalmatia. But although the Bogomils hated the Franciscans out of enmity towards the Pope, the friars received a guarantee from Sultan Mohammed II in Constantinople that their work could continue. A decree of 1515 granted them exemption from the crippling taxes imposed on the Christian community.

Officially, then, the Franciscans were not persecuted. Reality, however, proved different. Bosnian culture and civilisation had come to an end, submerged in an Islamic tidal wave. Local feudal lords who would not accept Islam were stripped of all they possessed and returned to the level of the peasantry. Though many Catholics did submit, a few became outlaws, seeking refuge in the forests and mountains. Where they went, the Franciscans went too. From now onwards their mission would be to keep the faith alive among those whom the Turks had dispossessed, wherever they might be found. Sporting Turkish-style moustaches and wearing civilian clothes as a camouflage, they became all things to the people they served, acting as bishops, priests, doctors, teachers and general protectors against a tyrannical power.

Recruited largely from among the peasants, the Bosnian Franciscans obeyed their founder's command to devote themselves to the welfare of the poor. "In this slave state, non-Muslims had no right of any kind," says an ex-history teacher from Mostar:[3]

> The people owned nothing but a stone house with a straw roof and a hole to let the light through. All the land belonged to the Muslim nobles. If you were a peasant, you belonged to your master body and soul and he could do what he liked with you; you just farmed the land and gave him most of what you produced.

Can you imagine what it would have been like if the Franciscans had not been there to protect them? The Franciscans were the only shepherds during Turkish rule.

Turkish rule in Bosnia was a strange mixture of the liberal and the despotic, depending on the whims and caprices of the local rulers, usually fanatical Bogomil converts, who interpreted the laws as they chose. The Franciscans were at their mercy. They still had a few monasteries, but many of them, including the one near Mostar, had been burned down by the Muslims and the friars were scattered over the countryside. They travelled about with little portable altars, saying Mass for the people, giving them the sacraments, teaching them to read and write, using their knowledge of herbs to cure their ills. It was a very *ad hoc* form of Christianity.

The people in their turn protected the friars. When the Turkish police found a Franciscan in somebody's house, he was claimed as an uncle of the family. They were, in fact, popularly referred to as "the uncles" rather than as the brothers which the word "friar" denotes. But the subterfuges did not always work:

> Many of them were caught and put to death by a particularly horrible method: the Turks stuck a sharpened pole into the rectum and pushed it through the body to the top of the spine. The victim could remain alive for several days like this. Sometimes they varied the method and skinned the Franciscans alive.[4]

Franciscan martyrologies give the names of friars killed in this way, and of many others who were tortured, hanged, stoned and cudgelled to death. On a wall in the restored Franciscan monastery of Mostar hangs a picture of two friars with stones tied to their legs, about to be flung from the Mostar bridge into the Neretva far below: "The people have never forgotten those things," said a Croatian girl. "An intimacy was forged between the peasants and the Franciscans that no stranger could ever understand. Even today the word 'Franciscan' is synonymous with 'priest'. No other will do."

Although the material fortunes of the Franciscans must have improved during the seventeenth century, since a Roman prelate wrote to Pope Innocent XI in 1680 complaining of the friars' wealth, the end of that century brought another change for the worse. After its resounding defeat at Vienna in 1683, the power of the Ottoman Empire slowly but inexorably began to wane, as that of the Austrians rose. Fearful that the Franciscans would turn for help to Catholic Austria, the Turks once again began slaughtering them and pillaging their monasteries.[5]

After the occupation of Bosnia and Hercegovina by the powerful Austro-Hungary in 1878 (see Chapter 2), it became apparent that, whatever the Turks might have expected, the Austrians in fact resented and feared the close links between the Franciscans and the people, and were determined to drive a wedge between them. Complaints began arriving at the Holy See in Rome that the Franciscans were half-educated semi-literates, unsuited to be in charge of their parishes, incompetent and intolerant. For its own good reasons, Austro-Hungary wanted to phase out the recalcitrant friars, replacing them by more malleable secular clergy.

Pope Leo XIII could see what the Austrians were up to, and at first pleaded the cause of the Franciscans.[6] But the Austrians were determined; and they had considerable support within the Church as a whole. In this battle of wills, it was the Pope who gave way. Although, to the Austrians' annoyance, he adamantly refused to expel the Franciscans, he allowed Jesuits and secular clergy to be brought in and agreed that new seminaries should be set up for the training of indigenous secular priests. On 5th July 1881, in the teeth of dogged Franciscan opposition, Pope Leo announced the formation of a regular hierarchy for Bosnia and Hercegovina, with an archbishopric at Sarajevo and diocesan sees at Banja Luka and Mostar. He added the pious but forlorn hope that the running of the parishes within the area would be shared equally between Franciscans and the secular clergy, and that all would work amicably together "in the vineyard of the Lord". He should have known better.

Pope Leo was weary of this particular problem, and was in no mind to make any more concessions to the Austrians. When the Austrian Archbishop Stadler claimed an immediate right to the Franciscans' parishes, Leo told him curtly that he had no rights over any parishes that were expressly linked to monasteries; and that he could not take over even independent parishes until the Franciscans had been allowed to state their own case for retaining them. The Franciscans did so, generously (in their estimation) offering to release thirty-two of their parishes, twenty-four immediately and eight later. Stadler refused angrily, insisting on a fifty-fifty division.

In Bosnia he had his way. In Hercegovina he did not. In May 1885 the wily Franciscans of the Hercegovina Province came up with a proposal. They offered to hand over the parishes on the left bank of the Neretva to the local bishop, while keeping those on the right bank, which included Mostar, Ljubuški and Duvno, together with the right to any new churches that might be built there. The fact that there were many *more* parishes on the right bank seemed to them eminently fair, a matter of simple justice.

Rome, predictably enough, ignored the suggestion; so three years later the Franciscans tried once more. Again there was no reply. But in 1899 the Holy See agreed to accept the friars' proposals, and the Franciscans virtuously handed over twenty parishes on the left bank of the Neretva. Unfortunately, there was no one to man them. Only nineteen secular priests had as yet been trained, and only four of them were in the Mostar diocese. So, amid popular rejoicing, the Franciscans were invited back. It was an outcome they had almost certainly foreseen.

After the First World War and the decisive rout of the Austro-Hungarian Empire, there was a great need for new parishes, but still no more than a handful of secular priests to put in charge. The bishop found himself in a cleft stick – what alternative did he have to asking the Franciscans to do the job? The friars joyfully consented but wanted cast-iron guarantees that these new parishes would be theirs in perpetuity. In 1923 Rome gave them a written agreement to that effect.

And there the matter rested for almost twenty years, until in 1942 a secular priest was appointed Bishop of Mostar, an area governed for centuries by the Franciscans. Bishop Petar Čule immediately asked Rome for help in removing at least some of his parishes from Franciscan control. But in 1942, in the middle of a bloody European war, the point was academic. With the support of large numbers of the Catholic population, Ante Pavelić and his Ustaše controlled Bosnia-Hercegovina, and not a few Franciscans had given their allegiance to that fearsome regime. "The Franciscans went over the top," comments a Croat exile who was opposed to the Pavelić regime:

> but they were still regarded, even then, as the people's priests. Remember they were mostly from peasant families themselves and had all the traditional peasant prejudices. Retribution overtook them afterwards, though. Many Franciscans, the innocent along with the guilty, were massacred in their own monasteries by the Partisans. In Listica and Čitluk, for example. We don't know the full story: it was the victors who wrote post-war history and the victors hated the Catholic Church.

In the persecution that followed the revolution, there was no lack of vocations to the priesthood. With more secular clergy available, the required transfer of parishes was made in some parts of Hercegovina. But in the diocese of Mostar the tensions remained. "The mutual animosity was unbelievable," commented an observer. "The Franciscans simply didn't want to go. After all, they *had* been there for more than four centuries." All Bishop Čule's attempts to replace them met with a blank refusal and determined popular resistance to back it up.

In 1966 the situation began to assume intractable proportions. Declaring angrily that the 1923 agreement (which had given permanent rights of tenure to the Franciscans) was not worth the paper it was written on, Bishop Čule appealed over the heads of the Franciscans to Rome, insisting that he urgently needed at least a hundred new priests. In vain did the Franciscans protest that this was a domestic dispute which in no way concerned Rome.[7]

Rome stepped into this over-heated arena and ordered the combatants to make peace. The Provincial (head) of the Hercegovina Franciscans offered to hand over five parishes of the fourteen the bishop was demanding, on condition that the remaining nine would remain in the hands of the Franciscans who had built them. In November 1967, he was ordered to vacate these five parishes within six months.

As the take-over was put into effect, however, the people put up a fierce resistance. In Serbo-Croatian the word used to describe a secular Catholic priest is the same as that used for an Orthodox priest: "pope". To Croat Catholics, the diocesans were not real priests at all, since real priests were Franciscans. When they marched on the bishop's residence to tell him so, the bishop called the police. The Franciscans begged for more time, to give the people a chance to accommodate to the change; but their request met a wall of silence. They had to go.

They went. But from only one of the five parishes was their departure peaceful. In the other four, there was rioting: stones were thrown, physical violence offered to the newcomers. In the parish of Gruda, the parishioners actually walled the church up, refusing to allow access to the unfortunate secular priest when he arrived. As to whether such disturbance of the peace was spontaneous or orchestrated, opinions still differ, though at the time the majority were convinced that the Franciscans had stirred up the riots.

Bishop Čule was furious and banned the guilty parishes from having a priest at all. They were to have no Masses, no sermons, no baptisms, no teaching of the catechism. In imposing this medieval-style interdict, Čule had the enthusiastic support of his new auxiliary bishop, Pavao Žanić, freshly seconded to Mostar from his home area of Split.

From September 1970 there was some dialogue in Zagreb between the Franciscans and the bishop's representatives led by Žanić. At their last meeting, both sides submitted proposals about the required fifty-fifty division of the parishes. For their part, the Franciscans agreed in principle to the division but asked for it to be made on the basis of the whole of Hercegovina, not of Mostar alone, where they had a seventy-five–twenty-five share. They also asked that when the final division was made, it should be a permanent one. Žanić (and the Holy See) ignored these provisos, insisting that Mostar and only Mostar was under discussion. A decree, *Romanis Pontificibus*, promulgated in Rome in 1974, allowed for the creation of more diocesan parishes in Mostar, and implied that the Franciscans had agreed to this development. The friars sent off an indignant letter to the Pope denying any such agreement, but once again their pleas were ignored. Instead, they were ordered to leave seven of their parishes instantly, and prepare to leave thirteen more. This they categorically refused to do, claiming that such a transfer would do serious spiritual damage to their congregations. This stubborn intransigence was too much for Rome, which proceeded to abolish the Hercegovina Franciscan Province, suspend its entire leadership and make the friars directly responsible to their Father General in Rome. In 1978, a Franciscan from Croatia was appointed by Rome to act as a liaison between Hercegovina and Rome. "The only response to all our pleading," complained the Franciscans, "was punishment and humiliation. Our Superiors were removed, our Province was persecuted. We lost the right to ordain our own novices; and in all respects our jurisdiction was undermined."[8] The Roman decree had falsified the facts, they claimed, adding with some bitterness, "It is hard to believe that this was the work of Rome. It seems to us that the real author was someone much nearer to home."

Such unworthy suspicions seemed to be justified in 1980, when Bishop Žanić at last showed his hand. In that year, Bishop Čule resigned and Žanić became full bishop of Mostar. On 31st August 1980, in a Franciscan church, he dropped a carefully manufactured bombshell. The diocese was to be divided into two, with a new cathedral parish replacing the old Franciscan one. It was a master-stroke. In a single move he had neatly commandeered three-quarters of the city's churches and cut the ground from under the Franciscans' feet. It seemed like game, set and match to Bishop Žanić who proceeded to tell the people that the Franciscans had agreed to the division, and to tell the friars to get out of his new cathedral parish.

Before announcing this master-plan from a Franciscan pulpit, Bishop Žanić had told the resident parish priest what to expect. The horrified Franciscan replied that Žanić's proposed division bore no resemblance to what had actually been agreed. "We most emphatically did not agree," he said, "to the unconditional surrender of three-quarters of our Mostar parish. We stipulated certain conditions. And since these conditions were not accepted, the agreement was null and void."[9] This priest was present in the church when Žanić exploded his fire-cracker. In the electric silence that followed, he stood up and read aloud to the stunned congregation the text of the 1973 Zagreb talks, underlining the extent to which Bishop Žanić had "misrepresented the Franciscan proposals and falsified the details".

Uproar ensued – a spontaneous outpouring of rage and dismay. Bishop Žanić accused the priest of inciting the people against him, and within days had suspended him from his priestly functions. In Mostar, history began to repeat itself, and the people prepared for a siege.

Once again stones were thrown and church doors were walled up. "You must understand," says a Croatian émigré, "the Franciscans are in the bloodstream of the Croatian people. Yet one cannot deny they can be unscrupulous. They're extremely good organisers, and they're determined not to be pushed out."

But Bishop Žanić's determination was the equal of the friars'. The new men were installed according to plan. Nevertheless, the people stubbornly continued to seek out the Franciscans, persuading them to say Mass in chapels and private houses within the new parish. Much of the Franciscans' own opposition was covert, but some few threw caution to the winds. The exasperated Žanić expelled two of the more obstreperous and recalcitrant, the young priests Ivica Vego and Ivan Prusina. Once again leading Franciscans were summoned to Rome and rapped over the knuckles for insubordination.

An extremely lucky accident saved them. Two weeks later, the apparitions in Medjugorje began – in a Franciscan parish in the diocese of Mostar. "How very convenient for them," wryly remarked an American Franciscan visiting Rome.[10] And as Žanić continued to fulminate against the "lawless behaviour" of the two "stubborn and contumacious" friars, the latter received incessant warnings from Rome. Finally, in January 1982, their Superior General in Rome expelled them from the Order and suspended them from their priestly functions. But Fathers Vego and Prusina went on living in the Franciscan monastery in Mostar and acting as though nothing had happened.

This, then, had been the bishop's dilemma from the time he first heard of the apparitions. Were they a Communist conspiracy to discredit the Church, or a last-ditch effort by desperate and determined friars to hang on to their power-base? Yet, in those early days, he was far from excluding a third possibility: that the apparitions were what they claimed to be.

The Madonna was not allowed to remain outside the dispute. Even on his first visit to Medjugorje, the bishop had asked if she had commented on the Hercegovina problem. The children, more or less ignorant of the facts, said she had promised that with prayer and patience it would soon be sorted out. All succeeding requests for information met with the same vague reply. But when in August the two offending friars began going to Medjugorje, the Lady's pronouncements became more partial. She no longer spoke of a speedy solution but – though it is hard to believe – on thirteen separate occasions she declared, in answer to the children's questions, that the bishop had acted too hastily and that the two friars were innocent. She even appeared to grow weary of the topic: "You think of nothing else but those two friars," she apparently remonstrated with Vicka one day.

On 10th January 1982, the bishop, increasingly fearful for the Church's reputation in the face of the growing wildness of the claims for Medjugorje – all that talk of dancing suns and other "absurdities"; to say nothing of the forty-seven "copycat" apparitions which had been reported from various parts of Hercegovina – set up a four-man Commission to sift the evidence for and against the apparitions. The four theologians, who included just one Franciscan, Fra Ivan Dugandžić, announced that they would be going to Medjugorje to investigate the apparitions and interview everybody concerned. Meanwhile the Catholic press was asked to stop writing about Medjugorje.

Four days after this, Vicka, Marija and Jakov came to see the bishop in Mostar. Without preamble, Vicka, never noted for her tact, passed on the Lady's criticism that he had been over-hasty in suspending the two friars. She did not enlarge on the theme, since Father Vlašić had already advised her to be careful how she answered questions. "Tell them the Lady's messages," he had told her, "but do not report all her replies to individual questions. The meaning of these messages may well be obscured by certain problems."[11] So, after delivering herself of her brief message, Vicka became evasive. "I hear the Madonna gave you a message for those two priests," pressed the bishop. "Which two priests?" asked Vicka, wide-eyed.

The bishop had in fact already been informed by the Franciscan Provincial Superior that though the two priests had now been expelled by Rome, they were refusing to leave Mostar because the Madonna had said they were innocent and should stay where they were.

Vicka returned on 3rd April saying that the Lady had scolded her for telling the bishop less than the whole truth. "She told us all about these friars . . . and says they're completely innocent. She said it three times." Žanić was furious. "Go away," he shouted at Vicka, reportedly adding, "And when your Lady finally reveals her true colours and curses God, be sure and let me know." To him it was unthinkable that the Blessed Virgin should enter the lists on the side of two unfrocked friars against the lawful bishop of the diocese. It was further proof, if any were needed, that the whole thing was a pack of lies:

> The real aim of this group of Franciscans is to point out to the simple people and the foreign pilgrims, with the authority of Our Lady, that they are in the right while the Bishop and the legitimate Superiors of their Province and their Order are in the wrong concerning the famous problem of the division of parishes. The sad case of the two ex-chaplains of Mostar, expelled from the Order for their misdemeanours and then defended by "Our Lady of Medjugorje" despite the decrees of the Holy See and of the Franciscan Order, is clear proof that they are manipulating the affair.[12]

When the Commission met for the second time on 10th May 1982, Bishop Žanić brought up another of his grievances, the non-arrival of the so-called "great sign". Such a sign seems to have been a central feature of most apparitions this century – at Fatima in Portugal and Garabandal in Spain, for example – always promised but never as yet materialising. The Madonna of Medjugorje has promised that a visible sign will be left for all to see on the hillside at Podbrdo or Križevac, as incontrovertible proof to unbelievers that she has been there. The children claim to have seen the sign in a vision, and that it is "very beautiful, permanent and indestructible". Miracles of healing will accompany its appearance. Five of the children know the date on which the sign is to appear – Marija alone does not – and all of them stress that in the intervening time, people must make every effort to strengthen their faith. "As for you," the Lady told the children, "you do not need a sign; you must *be* a sign." In the spring of 1983 she was urging, "Hasten your conversion. Do not wait for the sign, for by then it will be too late for non-believers to change. For those who already believe, now is the time for them to deepen their faith."

The sign is an integral part of the ten secrets being imparted to each of the children. These secrets refer to the future of the world and are linked together in a chain. Three secrets are known by all six children and will be revealed only on instructions from the Madonna. "First of all, three of the secrets will be revealed," promises Mirjana. "Then the people will be convinced that the Madonna was truly here. Afterwards they will be able to understand the sign. They will run to the hill and pray and be forgiven."

But in spite of such a specific assurance, the Madonna appeared to be in no hurry to produce that irrefutable proof which the pilgrims awaited with as much dread as hope.

10

Apocalypse

> Though the West is still nominally Christian, we have come to be governed, in practice, by the unholy triumdivate of Pluto, god of wealth; Apollo, god of science; and Mercury, god of thieves. To make matters worse, dissension and jealousy rage openly between these three, with Mercury and Pluto blackguarding each other, while Apollo wields the atomic bomb as though it were a thunderbolt. For, since the Age of Reason was heralded by his eighteenth-century philosophers, he has seated himself on the vacant throne of Zeus.
>
> Robert Graves, *The White Goddess*, 1948

The secrets represent the strange – to many people, repellent – apocalyptic aspect of Medjugorje. With its emphasis on the cosmic struggle between Good and Evil, God and Satan, apocalyptic has always held an important place in the Christian world-view, though in the later twentieth century it has come to be unacceptable to all but a very few Catholics and some of the more extremist evangelical sects.

The Madonna has apparently told Mirjana that the twentieth century is under the influence of a Satan seeking to destroy the world. In an interview with Tomislav Vlašić in January 1983, she said:

> The Virgin told me God and the Devil conversed, and the Devil said that people believe in God only when life is good for them. When things go badly, they cease to believe in God. Then people blame God, or act as if He doesn't exist. God, therefore, allowed the Devil one century in which to exercise dominion over the world; and the Devil chose the twentieth century. Today, as we can see all around us, everyone is dissatisfied, people cannot stand one another. Look at the number of divorces and abortions. All this, the Madonna said, is the work of the Devil.[1]

The implications are horrific. But Fra Slavko Barbarić, the visionaries' spiritual adviser, sees no reason for panic: "The Madonna has not come to announce catastrophes but to show us how to avoid them. We didn't need an apparition to convince us that nuclear war is a possibility. If a house is on fire, it doesn't burn down because the mother shouts 'Fire'. On the contrary – the mother is trying to save the house from destruction." On 21st July 1982, the Lady told the children: "The world has forgotten the value of prayer and fasting. But with prayer and fasting, there need be no more wars."

All six children claim to have seen Heaven, and four of them to have been taken to visit Hell. Two of the girls were frightened and begged the Lady to excuse them from this vision. Jakov, too, was scared. Gitta Sereny reports a conversation with Vicka on the subject:

> When the *Gospa* said she was taking them to see Heaven and Hell, Jakov said, no, he didn't really want to go – he was his mother's only child, how could he go? Vicka laughed at the memory: "He said *I* could go, it was different for my parents, they had eight children!" But, said Vicka, the Madonna took me by the right hand and Jakov by the left and stood between us, with her face towards us, and we immediately began to lift upwards . . .
>
> Vicka described Paradise as a huge endless tunnel with an unearthly kind of light, countless people in light-coloured robes walking and talking. "It's so beautiful your heart stands still when you look at it." She described the people in Hell going naked into a great fire. "When they come out," she said, "you couldn't tell whether they were men or women, for they had blackened skin like animals."
>
> Most curious of all was her description of Purgatory, some sort of dark chasm, a dark space between Heaven and Hell, where they saw no people, only grey ash. No walls or floors but, "you can hear people knocking, as though they want to get out. The *Gospa* said, 'Pray for them'."[2]

Fra Svetozar Kraljević relates that on that occasion (November 1981) Vicka and Jakov simply vanished for twenty minutes:

> Jakov's mother searched for him because she had seen him in the house shortly before he disappeared . . . neither Vicka nor Jakov could be found. The moment they returned, Jakov told his mother what had happened and where they had been, and both of them told her they had seen Heaven and Hell and had passed through Purgatory.[3]

Mirjana, who claims to have been told that only a few go to Heaven, asked the Lady how a God of Love could be so lacking in mercy. People choose Hell for themselves, the Lady replied: "They rage against God and they suffer, but still they refuse to call on God. They have already become part of Hell while they are still alive." In June (1982) Mirjana would claim to have seen Satan:

> As usual I had locked myself into my room alone and was waiting for the Madonna. I knelt down . . . and suddenly there was a flash of light and Satan appeared . . . He was horrible . . . black all over . . . terrifying. I felt weak and fainted. When I came to, he was still standing there, laughing . . .

He told me I would be very beautiful and very happy in love and life, and so on, but that I would have no need of the Madonna or of my faith. "She has brought you nothing but suffering and hardships," he said. He, on the other hand, could give me everything I wanted. Then something inside me shouted, No! No! No! I began to shake and to feel sick. Then he disappeared and the Madonna came and immediately my strength returned, as though she had given it back to me. I felt normal again. "That was a painful trial," she said, "but I promise it will not happen again."

"Satan has become aggressive," Mirjana would also aver, "because he sees that he is losing his power. He is breaking up marriages, causing quarrels among priests, obsessing people, even killing them. You must protect yourselves by prayer and fasting."

Vicka's notes as early as 27th August 1981 prophesy that the sign will come "soon", and that meanwhile everyone must be patient. Again and again in the months that followed, she expressed this same hope; but nothing happened. Bishop Žanić, his patience wearing thin, and intent on proving that the "sign" was a product of the children's over-fertile imagination, despatched two of his Commission members to Medjugorje to ask the children for a written statement (in duplicate) about the sign. The children replied that Tomislav Vlašić, who was becoming a considerable thorn in the bishop's side (forewarned by Ivan Dugandžić, the Franciscan on the Commission of Inquiry), had told them to ask the Lady's permission first. They had done so and been refused.

Jakov had already shown himself adept at avoiding unwanted interviews with journalists. "He's the strongest-minded of us all," Vicka had told a friend who doubted the wisdom of entrusting vital secrets to Jakov. The boy was about to be put to a stringent test. "Why not just write down the secrets, put them in an envelope and leave them with us?" the two theologians cajoled him. Jakov was a match for them. "Yes, and I could just as easily write them down, put them in an envelope and leave them at home," he replied. Marija, Vicka and Ivanka were equally unyielding. Baffled, the two Commissioners went instead to Sarajevo to ask Mirjana, but she too refused. (The others had tipped her off by telephone, the bishop claimed angrily.) But at last the scales tipped in the bishop's favour. On 9th May, the Commissioners went in search of Ivan in the seminary at Visoko. Nobody could give Ivan any advance warning, said the bishop triumphantly, since the seminary telephone was controlled by the local authorities. So poor demoralised Ivan, confronted by visiting Commissioners and his own intimidating Prefect of Studies, "described everything, without the least hesitation".[4]

There is, to say the least, some confusion about Ivan's action; and he has not helped matters by going to pieces and contradicting his own testimony. Probably the boy panicked; and there was nobody at hand to help him out of his difficulty. Ivan was miserable at the seminary, not least because his fellow-students made fun of him and poured scorn on the apparitions, which had continued after his first week there. The Commissioners found him in a state of utter wretchedness and self-doubt: he had just – to nobody's surprise – failed his first exams, and his future was very uncertain. The bishop claims that when ordered to divulge the secret of "the sign", the boy did so. But Ivan tells a different story – or, rather, two different stories at two different times. At first, he told the Franciscans that he simply wrote "nothing at all" on the paper he was given. Later, in 1985, when the Commissioners opened the envelope, he admitted that he had written "something", but that it had nothing to do with the sign. The *affaire Ivan* inevitably reduced the boy's credibility, an outcome no doubt desired by the bishop and from which he would make considerable capital in the months ahead.

Rome, meanwhile, was urging caution. On 2nd June, Bishop Žanić went there to present an up-to-date report on Medjugorje to the Vatican. Rather to his dismay, he was asked to soft-pedal his opposition, to let events take their own course. It was hardly the outright support he had counted upon.

On 12th September, 70,000 pilgrims climbed Križevac for a Mass in honour of the Holy Cross, a traditional annual festival. Twelve thousand were at the six o'clock Mass in (or outside) the church. By 29th November, Mirjana and Ivanka had both received nine of the ten secrets and in the following week Vicka received her eighth. Those who were in a position to observe the visionaries during the apparitions noted that at certain times (it was, in fact, when the secrets were being imparted), their faces grew sad or even frightened, in contrast to their usual joyous expression.

On Christmas Day 1982, Mirjana was told the tenth and last secret. Interviewed some months later by Tomislav Vlašić, she was deeply pessimistic. The world would be given three warnings, in the form of three dire events, before the visible sign would appear; and three days before the first warning, Mirjana would announce its imminence to a priest of her choice. The short intervals between the three warnings would be, she said, "a period of grace", but if, once the great sign appeared, the world did not turn to God, the punishment would come. There was no use expecting the whole world to be converted, she conceded, but prayer could alleviate the extent of its punishment. The seventh secret had already been annulled. But:

> The eighth secret is worse than the seven before it. I begged for it to be made less severe. Every day I beseeched the Madonna to get it mitigated, and at last she said that if everyone prayed it might be averted. But then she told me the ninth secret and it was even worse. As for the tenth, it is terrible, and nothing can alter it. It will happen.

"Can we prepare for it in any way?" asked Father Vlašić.

> Yes, the Madonna said that people must prepare themselves spiritually . . .
> and not panic . . . They should accept God now so that they will not be
> afraid . . . If they commit their lives to God, he will accept them . . .

With that Christmas Day visitation Mirjana's regular visions came to an
end. "She [the Lady] said that she had stayed with us for longer than
necessary, because this is the last time Jesus or herself will appear on
earth," Mirjana told Vlašić in an interview on 10th January. When Vlašić
asked her to be more specific, she could only repeat: "The Madonna said
these are the last apparitions on earth. I don't know what she meant."
Mirjana was more concerned with her own desolation at the sudden and
unexpected loss: "She told me . . . that from now on I must live like
everybody else – although she promised to visit me every year on my
birthday":

> After she left, I just sat there like a statue, feeling very strange and thinking
> to myself: "This can't be happening: she will come back. I will go on
> praying at the same hour and she will come." I was very restless and insisted
> on being left alone. I locked myself into my room and thought: "She *will*
> come, she *won't* come." I didn't know what to think, what to do. How could
> I live without her? What would become of me? I prayed long and hard, as
> though I were in a trance. I kept asking myself why this had to happen, why
> she wasn't there any more. Oh, it was terrible.
> At school they all thought I'd gone mad and laughed at me. I didn't want
> to talk to anyone . . . for these last fourteen days I've just wanted to sit by
> myself. In class I wasn't aware of what was going on, and if the teacher
> asked me a question I couldn't answer. If he asked why I wasn't listening,
> why I was behaving so strangely, I burst into tears, for no reason at all . . .
> Gradually it's getting a bit easier but it's still difficult . . . There's a terrible
> pain in my heart.
> But now, if my school classes are in the morning, I go into my room each
> afternoon, at the time she used to come. I say the Rosary and I pray for at
> least an hour, sometimes two, depending on the time I have. I pray that God
> will give me the strength of spirit to think and act normally again.

Four days after Mirjana virtually left the Medjugorje scene, two other
young girls made an entrance. From 29th December, ten-year-old Jelena
Vasilj claimed to be seeing a vision of Our Lady, "all in white", the edges
of her gown lined with gold. Her friend Marijana Vasilj* began to receive
the same gift on the following Good Friday. They saw the vision, but were

---

*No relation. Almost every family in Medjugorje seems to be called Vasilj. They are
distinguished from each other only by the use in brackets, of their father's Christian name.

unable to touch her. As Jelena told Fra Slavko Barbarić: "I hear her voice
. . . somehow in the heart and in the head. I feel it like a fire in my heart . . .
It's not a picture that I see. I see Our Lady . . . but . . . I don't see her as I
see other people. I can't see her at all if I have not spent at least fifteen
minutes in prayer."[5]

At the request of the Lady, the girls formed a prayer group for about
fifteen young people of the village. They met every afternoon at four for an
hour; and from June onwards also formed part of a larger group (about
sixty people, run by Tomislav Vlašić) which met three evenings a week in
the basement of the parish house. Of this latter group Father Vlašić said:
"The Madonna asked for boys and girls who were willing to give their
lives to God to join the group. She gave us a month in which to make up
our minds. Our group was born on 24th June 1983. Our rules are that we
pray every day for at least three hours and fast twice a week on bread and
water."[6]

One day, said Jelena, as they were saying the Rosary together, the Lady
interrupted them. "That's not praying," she said.

"We thought we must have left something out," said Jelena, "but it
wasn't anything like that. In trying to find out what she meant, we started
to read the Gospels and meditate on them before praying aloud. Then the
voice came again, saying: 'That's better. Read the Gospels, and you will
understand everything.'"

"Why ask so many questions? Everything is there in the Gospels." It
was the vision's frequent cry. She did not, it was clear, want people to pray
to her, but was pointing them in the direction of Christ. She stressed the
need to love one's enemies, to bear no ill-feeling, but only to love and
bless. She asked the young people in the group to follow her guidance for
four years and during that period to make no decision about their future.
Not even about entering a convent? asked Jelena. "Not even that," came
the reply. "You do not have to belong to this prayer group. But if you do,
those are my conditions. The most essential thing is for you to learn about
prayer; and then you will be able to make a wise choice."

If Jelena had hoped to become a visionary on the pattern of the original
six, she was to be disappointed. When she asked if she too could learn the
secrets, the answer was a firm refusal: "That gift is not for you. What the
other six have told you is the truth. Your part is to believe it, like everyone
else." She and Marijana had to be content with their own given role: "I do
not intend to reveal any secrets through you," Gospa told them, "but
rather to guide you on the path of consecration to God."

Jelena has reservations about the effectiveness of the larger group. "We
in the little group are like sisters," she once told Fra Slavko. "In the large
group, they're more self-conscious . . . no one wants to speak up . . .
they're more shut in."

But, whatever the difference in style, both groups have one and the same aim: "To be closer to God; to learn to serve Him better." "My life hasn't changed much outwardly," reflects Jelena, "it's just that I live more consciously now. It's my spiritual life that has changed. I feel God to be so much closer." One day she had a vision of a richly glowing ruby which suddenly splintered into a thousand pieces. It was an image of a human heart, she was told, radiant when it belongs to God, but fractured when it does not. "I have come to tell the world that God is Truth," the vision assured her. "He exists, and only in Him can true happiness and fulfilment be found. I come to this place as Queen of Peace to tell the world to look for the only peace that can save it . . . you must pray, pray, pray. Prayer is the only way to peace."

Unlike Mirjana, Jelena is encouragingly optimistic: destruction is assured only if the world refuses to turn back to God. "So is it possible for humanity to be saved?" asked Vlašić.

"Oh yes, in spite of everything, it *will* be saved."

Vicka reported that since 7th January 1983 the Virgin Mary had been telling the story of her life to the five remaining visionaries.[7] (These appearances would last for Jakov till April, for Ivanka till 22nd May, for Marija till 17th July and for Vicka herself until 10th April 1985.) For Vicka the narration lasted 825 days. "Did the Madonna give details about her parents, her native village, her childhood friends?" asked a journalist. "Oh yes," smiled Vicka, "and she showed it to us in moving pictures."[8] Vicka transcribed the "Life" into three large exercise books which were carefully hidden from view and shown to nobody. The question of whether or not Vicka had, in addition to these, secret notebooks in which she recorded what was said during the apparitions, would soon be triggering off a spectacular and unpleasant new row.

It came about this way. Towards the end of January 1983, Fr Radogost Grafenauer, a Jesuit from Slovenia, came to stay with Bishop Žanić in Mostar, and spent three days reading the evidence about Medjugorje. Unimpressed, he decided not to bother visiting the place, but to return home immediately.

Bishop Žanić, however, persuaded him to go to the village, if only to find out what the Franciscans were up to. Father Grafenauer duly proceeded to Medjugorje, and, much to his own surprise and the bishop's disgust, after two weeks there underwent a change of heart. The bishop maintained that he was "got at" by Tomislav Vlašić, and that as soon as the friars realised what a valuable conquest they had made, they allowed him a privileged look at Vicka Ivanković's "secret diary" and at the detailed chronicle of events kept by Vlašić.

According to Father Grafenauer, however, all he saw were five sheets of paper, four of them in Vicka's handwriting, the other in Mirjana's. He denied and continues to deny the existence of a secret diary. Whatever it was that he saw, it is undeniable that he returned from Medjugorje (16th February 1983) with his own verbatim copies of various messages said to have been transmitted by the Lady for the bishop, by way of Vicka. Messages concerning the two expelled Franciscans which could and did raise Bishop Žanić's blood pressure several degrees:

> Saturday, 19th December 1981. Our Lady said that the guiltiest person in this affair is Bishop Žanić. She said that Fra Ivica Vego is not guilty . . .
>
> Sunday, 3rd January. All of us asked Our Lady about Ivica Vego. She answered: "Ivica isn't guilty. If he is expelled by the friars, he must be brave! I say every day, Peace, Peace, and there is more and more trouble. Ivica is not guilty. Let him stay where he is . . . The Bishop isn't attempting to resolve the friction so he is guilty. But he won't always be bishop . . .
>
> Monday, 26th April 1982. The Bishop has none of the real love of God for those two. Let Ivica and Ivan stop worrying about the bishop, since he has saddled them with a great weight in order to shift it from his own shoulders. He has begun with the younger friars and intends to feel his way forward a little at a time. I know this has all been a big shock for them, but they mustn't worry. They should try and forget about it, and learn how to suffer in silence for justice. What the Bishop is doing is not in accordance with God's will. Innocent, blameless young men, and punished in this way. God would never want such a thing.[9]

By this token, the Mother of God was taking sides and branding the bishop of the diocese as a guilty man. The messages bore all the hallmarks of Vicka's choleric and uncontrolled temperament, and the outraged bishop set off in pursuit of the "secret diary", the existence of which the Franciscans firmly denied. There were, they said: one notebook belonging to Vicka's sister, Ana, describing the events of 25th June to 5th July, with written comments by Vicka herself; a second notebook belonging to two other sisters of Vicka, Mirjana and Zdenka, briefly recording the apparitions of 18th October to 14th January (1982); and a third, in Vicka's own hand relating to those of 6th February to 25th March 1982. To write anything at all at the end of such long and exhausting days was too arduous for Vicka; and after 25th March 1982 even her random jottings ceased, despite urgings from the friars who wanted her to continue.

Ignoring all this, the bishop ordered the offending "diary" to be handed over to him without delay. The friars remained silent, but on 1st May Vicka wrote: "I have recently discovered that typed extracts from my diary have been distributed – my diary is private and written exclusively for myself from the very start of the apparition of the Blessed Virgin Mary at Crnica in the parish of Medjugorje." A confirmation, surely, that the diary did exist, even if, as Father Vlašić would claim, the letter was written by a priest and Vicka had merely signed it.

It is all extremely confusing; and it is hard not to agree with Bishop Žanić that if the diary is said to exist at one minute and not to exist at the next, then someone somewhere is telling less than the truth. But all Žanić's determined efforts to lay hands on the "original" document were in vain. He was by now completely convinced that Vicka's missing "diary" held the key to what was happening in Medjugorje, that it contained irrefutable proof of Franciscan complicity and guilt. Though the apparitions had pre-dated the latest crisis over the two expelled friars, and the Lady had delivered her most important messages before it blew up, nothing could have persuaded the bishop that his feud with the Franciscans did not lie behind these "imagined" apparitions. In his famous position paper of 1984, he made himself quite clear:

> The sole unique feature of the Medjugorje apparitions lies in the declaration that the local bishop is responsible for all the problems caused by the disobedient friars; and in the claim that the two chaplains, though expelled from their Order and suspended *a divinis* are innocent.[10]

The Franciscans shrugged off the bishop's attitude as paranoia. "He's furious," they said, "because so many people are being converted in Medjugorje, and he has no control over the situation."

On 16th November 1983, the bishop went in person to Medjugorje and demanded to see the diary. Unsurprisingly, he did not succeed, but he did come away with four volumes of Father Vlašić's written chronicles. A careful search revealed that, in spite of vigorous editing, a surprising entry still remained:

> 16th March 1982. Today I spoke with Vicka for slightly longer than usual. Since she hasn't brought her diary of the apparitions to me for quite some time, I felt it necessary to question her for longer ... She records everything in her diary in chronological order ...

That did seem fairly conclusive, and Žanić believed himself triumphantly vindicated. But it may well have been a question of semantics, of when is a diary not a diary? That Vicka kept some kind of record is not open to doubt; but what the bishop had in mind was something much more sinister. As he wrote to Father Grafenauer, "The friars have hidden it, and now they say it doesn't exist. They're afraid of something."

If Father Vlašić *was* afraid, he hid it well. He was prepared solemnly to swear that the diary did not exist, and did so on the bishop's own crucifix on 14th December:

I have never seen the secret diary which the bishop talks about, nor am I aware that a diary of Vicka's exists. I have done my best to find out from her if it does exist, and from my conversations with her I am convinced it does not. During all this time I suggested to Vicka that she should write such a diary, but from what I can gather she did not do so.

To the bishop, this simply meant that the treacherous Vlašić had added perjury to all his other crimes.

"Do you, in fact, have a secret (a fourth) notebook which you don't want anyone to know about?" Fra Janko Bubalo asked Vicka in 1986.[11] "No," she replied. "I have no secret notebook except the one where I record the story of the Virgin's Life. I will, if you wish, swear to that on oath."

The bishop had cast restraint to the winds. In an interview given to the Italian journal, *Il Sabato* (17th September 1983), he came full circle and disowned his former words. "These events may indeed be of diabolic origin," he proclaimed. "Those children are little liars."

He was further incensed to receive a "threatening" letter in June from Ivan. The latter, who was no longer in the Visoko seminary but at home awaiting his call-up papers, claimed that the Lady had given himself, Marija and Jakov the following message:

> Tell the bishop that I beg him most earnestly to endorse the events in the parish of Medjugorje before it is too late. I want him to approach those events with great understanding, love and a deep sense of responsibility. I don't want him to cause friction among the priests or to draw public attention to their negative attitudes. The Holy Father has told all the bishops to carry out their diocesan duties and do their best to smooth out all disputes and problems. The bishop is father-in-chief to all the Hercegovina parishes, and head of the Church in that province. For this reason, I beg him to accept what is happening there.

The sting of this message from the Lady was in the tail, and to the irate bishop it seemed like undisguised blackmail:

> I am sending him the last warning but one. If he doesn't accept these events and behave accordingly, he will hear my judgement and that of Jesus, my Son. If he does not heed my message, then he is not walking the Way of my Son.

Not for one moment convinced that the letter had been composed by the slow-witted Ivan, Bishop Žanić sent it off to Rome, as further evidence of Franciscan duplicity. Over the next few weeks, he received milder, more tactfully worded versions of the message from Ivan himself, from Jakov, and from Marija, through whom the Lady said:

I have sent the bishop many messages. But he has not wanted to receive them. I have also sent you. Yet he is still not prepared to listen to the Queen of Peace, because his heart is full of anxiety, an anxiety that will not leave him alone.

The matter had burst the bounds of its own importance. An affair that should have been no more than an irritating side-issue had turned into a creeping cancer that threatened to destroy the integrity of the Medjugorje events. This clerical in-fighting was, in the words of one commentator:

a bad thing for the bishop, for the Franciscans and for Our Lady herself. Her message is one of reconciliation. In the village of Medjugorje and apart from this one issue, reconciliation has not been an empty word. However, Medjugorje will not be credible so long as the apparitions have not brought the Bishop and the Franciscans to a reconciliation.[12]

"Love your enemies and bless them," the Madonna had, by way of Jelena, urged the people in June. But in this particular dispute passions on both sides were running too high for such counsels of perfection to prevail. Reconciliation did not seem to be on anyone's agenda.

11

"Pray to be Healed"

Then I must know that still
I am in the hands of the unknown God.
He is breaking me down to his own oblivion
to send me forth on a new morning, a new man.
                                    D. H. Lawrence

The majority of pilgrims, however, neither knew nor cared about such things. Medjugorje's fame was spreading, not least because of the cures that were constantly being claimed. By mid-August 1982, 140 had been notified.

Damir Corić, who suffered from internal hydrocephaly, had undergone three drainage operations in the Zagreb Surgical Clinic. Each time the operation had resulted in a cerebral haemorrhage which had necessitated further surgery. The likelihood of more haemorrhages was great, and Damir's prognosis was gloomy in the extreme. Meanwhile, he had lost a great deal of weight and was very weak. At Medjugorje, during the summer of 1981, Vicka prayed for him. Damir Corić was cured – and rapidly regained his former weight and strength.

Mirko Brcić of Banja Luka had been treated in various hospitals for an open sore under one knee. But the wound had continued to fester until finally the bone was exposed. At that point, the doctors decided to amputate; whereupon Mirko's family went on pilgrimage to Medjugorje, praying and fasting. On the day before the amputation was to take place, the wound suddenly began to close up, and the astounded doctors cancelled the operation. Within a few days the leg was completely healed.

Cvija Kuzman from Stolac had suffered for eleven years from degenerative arthritis, passing from one hospital to another, able to walk but with arms and legs swollen and painful. In August 1981 she had brought back some soil from Medjugorje and made a paste of it. Her daughter applied the paste, reciting seven Our Fathers, Hail Marys and Glorias. Mrs Kuzman was instantly healed.

A Croat nun, Sister Blaženka, described the cure of a six-month-old baby covered all over with eczema:

The parents consulted numerous doctors and specialists, but in vain. They were told that the affliction would disappear when the child was two, but that they must on no account wash it with water. The mother went to Medjugorje, gathered a few herbs . . . boiled them in water and washed the child with the infusion. Next day the scales had disappeared – only dark patches remained. Within twenty-four hours these too had disappeared.[1]

In gratitude the baby's family made a pilgrimage on foot to Medjugorje, a distance of sixty-three kilometres.

Ulcers, spinal disorders, cancers were also reported cured, though most of the healings were gradual rather than sudden. Few medical dossiers came with the reports and verification was difficult. According to the children, the Madonna's constant reply to all requests for healing was: "*I* cannot heal; only God can do that. But pray to be healed and *I* shall pray along with you. Have faith, fast and do penance and I shall intercede for you."

Most of those claiming to have been cured came from Yugoslavia. As a visiting journalist pointed out:[2] "Sick foreigners would not go to a place without even lavatories, let alone hospitals and wheel-chair attendants." And this was almost to understate the awfulness: the only facilities available were three stinking holes in the ground housed within three small huts with doors that did not shut. A sojourn in Medjugorje could not fail to be penitential. For a start, the place was difficult of access: the only approach road was across a ramshackle bridge in a state of terminal decay. There were no hotels, banks, or shops; not even one selling postcards. The only exception was a fruit-seller who came at dawn and stayed till nightfall. All plans for a new car park had been ruthlessly vetoed by the authorities and Tomislav Pervan (who in August 1982 had come to take Fra Zrinko's place) was fined for spreading gravel over the existing parking area – and also for installing air-conditioning in the over-crowded church.

In February 1983, Jozo Zovko had been released from prison,* and the next day came to Medjugorje to say a Mass of thanksgiving. "It was thanks to your prayers that I was set free," he told the crowded congregation. But he was not allowed to work anywhere near Medjugorje, and in April was assigned to a parish near Imotski, from where he was soon transferred even further away, first to Bukovica and then to the parish of St Elijah in Tihaljina.

In April 1983, a police helicopter flew low over a group of young

---

*After 40,000 people signed a petition for Fra Jozo's release – a fact liable to make the authorities even more nervous of him – the three-year sentence was eventually halved, and Fra Jozo was released in February 1983, on condition that he did not return to serve in Medjugorje.

pilgrims on the hill of apparitions. The group was later arrested and interrogated by the police for ten hours, threatened and abused. A young girl who made the sign of the cross at the police station was struck on the face.

Local transport firms were still forbidden to provide coaches. Other regions were more amenable. Pilgrims, mainly from Slovenia, were arriving at the approximate rate of one coach-load a month. In June 1983, at the time of the second anniversary, while helicopters clattered overhead and militia vans were ostentatiously parked all over the place, about 3,000 cars came in, and roughly 15,000 pilgrims arrived on foot. Anything from 30,000 to 50,000 in all. Wilder claims of 200,000 may be dismissed – as the bishop contemptuously dismissed them – as wishful thinking on the part of the Franciscans. (It was said that the Lady, on being asked to adjudicate, had suggested 110,000!) That day the Madonna told the children:

> The sign *will* come, but you must not spend too much time looking for it. My urgent message to you is: Be converted. Pass this message to all my children wherever they are. There is no trouble I will not take, no suffering I will not bear, to save them. I shall beg my Son not to punish the world, but I implore you, be converted, change your lives. You cannot begin to imagine what lies ahead . . . so, I beg you again, be converted!

Of those who came to Medjugorje for the third anniversary, not a few were less inspired by piety than by curiosity and the hope of being witness to something sensational. "A lot of them weren't interested in praying," reported an irritated teenage pilgrim. "What they enjoyed doing most was looking at the sun and applauding the visionaries whenever they appeared."

But a well-known American Pentecostal leader, David du Plessis, came away with a quite different impression. Having expected to find unrestrained Mary-worship, he had been amazed to discover the emphasis being placed on Jesus and the New Testament. "The whole place," he concluded, "is charged with the love of God. You can feel it and you can see it. I told myself that if there had been anything wrong with what was happening here, there would not be the manifestations of the Holy Spirit that I could clearly observe."[3] "There is a rare kind of unison about the prayers and hymns," another observer noted, "real attentiveness to the lengthy sermons, tolerance for cold stone floors for hour after hour, long lines of penitents waiting for confession at the head of each aisle and at many other points in the church. I felt personally that I was in the midst of people who were truly raising their minds and hearts to God."[1]

Every evening now there were doctors in the church, observing the children's behaviour during ecstasy. In August 1983, Dr Philippe Madre, founder and director of a research clinic which investigates the links between somatic, psychological and supernatural forces, pronounced the children to be mentally and physically healthy. His stay, however, was cut drastically short. When he and two Canadian priests, Fr Emiliano Tardif and Fr Pierre Rancourt, arrived from France to give a much-publicised course on Charismatic Renewal, the police watched warily. On the first day, Father Tardif, who had powers of healing – a "magician", sniffed Bishop Žanić – was said to have cured up to twenty people of sclerosis, of cancer, of paralysis, and on the next day went on to cure twenty more. But by early afternoon of the second day, the police swooped and all three men found themselves in a prison cell for the night. The following morning they were invited to leave the country and forbidden to return within twelve months.

The Abbé René Laurentin, a noted French Mariologist and world authority on the phenomena of apparitions, was a little more fortunate, although on arrival at the airport in December he was subjected to a thorough search of his person and his papers. Laurentin was preparing an adaptation of a French translation of *The Apparitions of the Virgin at Medjugorje* by Fra Ljudevit Rupčić, a Franciscan from Sarajevo. Deciding that it was high time to go and see for himself, he had come to spend Christmas 1983 in Medjugorje.

He was not disappointed. That first evening he was swept up into the prayer of the huge congregation that had stood or sat for hours on end in a freezing church. (One pilgrim claimed that the experience of kneeling on tiles in Medjugorje in mid-November had given an entirely new dimension to the word "cold".) "It is not a sentimental prayer," wrote Laurentin:

> There are no starry-eyed gazes, no tense atmosphere or surface emotion. The prayer which continues in the parish church is peasant prayer, pure and hard like the rocks of the mountain where the apparitions began. The voices are rough without any intonation. They recite the prayer in strong, well-carved syllables, almost hammered out. It is really from the soil, as though from a rock, that this prayer goes up to heaven. It goes up not like smoke but like a flame. It is not complicated, exaggerated or affected. It is impressive. It seizes you not at an emotional level but in a much deeper area of your being. It is that place where man discovers himself to be indwelt by God.[4]

As a distinguished foreign visitor, Laurentin was one of the handful of people allowed into the apparitions room with the children, so he was in a position to observe:

They prayed out loud along with everyone else. A few moments later (the length of an Our Father) their faces lit up and at the same time, with alacrity and in perfect unison, they knelt down, each in his own way. They looked up, all in the same direction. Their gaze was full of love and satisfaction, but their expression was restrained; their faces were without notable expression though they were relaxed and happy. Only Vicka (the extrovert) blossomed with many smiles and nods of agreement, speaking a great deal, as one could make out from her lips though her words were inaudible. Little Jakov tilted his head a little more than the others because he is much smaller than they. His gaze showed a particular intensity, I was going to say avidity. Marija's gentle smile was transparent. Ivan's face (the most introverted) stayed the same. It is clear, however, that he also was absorbed, filled with what he beheld. Less than two minutes later, their prayer began again out loud. They all began together, and this was all the more striking because they began with the third word of the Our Father: ". . . who art in heaven." No one heard the Virgin who intoned the prayer. A minute later, when the prayer was over, they got up. The end of the apparition did not leave them either sad or disappointed. They remained joyful and deeply satisfied. They went back into the church and knelt down behind the altar.[5]

Meanwhile, one of the Franciscans had been demonstrating the children's immunity to external stimuli by pinching Vicka's arm hard, then lifting Jakov right off the ground. Neither visionary reacted at all; they were seemingly unaware of anything being done to them.

The children were all that Laurentin had hoped. "They bear witness simply and joyfully," he said. "They are neither too forward nor too timid. They have seen something. They still see something. They are happy. Their life is growing with God, and there is light in it."

There was the ever-smiling Vicka who had nevertheless been seriously ill for over a year, apparently suffering from an inoperable brain cyst which caused atrocious headaches and necessitated frequent medical treatment; Ivan, solitary and withdrawn, yet gradually emerging from his shell; Jakov, brimming with health and high spirits. Yet of them all it was Marija who stood out, disarming in her simplicity and glowing goodness. "I think we are the happiest people on earth," she told Laurentin. Marija in her own person epitomised all that was good about Medjugorje, she was the answer to all the questions. If the witness of the young visionaries was unfailingly impressive, he concluded, it was because "that which they are speaks more loudly than that which they do".

"What does the Virgin want? What is her basic message," Laurentin asked Jelena Vasilj. "Peace", she replied. "It is for this that the Holy Spirit came down on earth . . . But the peace must come from us. We have to build it inside ourselves, so that others will believe us."

Recalling that he was to go next day to meet Bishop Žanić in Mostar, the

Frenchman asked if the Madonna had anything to say on that score. "No comment," replied Jelena firmly. "Our Lady desires peace above all things."

12

When the Wind Blows

'Nothing dies harder than a theological difference.'
Ronald A. Knox

"When the wind blows, know that I am with you, the wind is my sign," the
Madonna told the children one stormy, ice-bound night, when, for once,
there were barely 250 pilgrims in the church. But a more deadly and
destructive wind, from which the Madonna seemed wholly absent, was
blowing through the corridors of Bishop Žanić's episcopal palace in
Mostar.

"The propaganda for Medjugorje is appalling," the bishop wrote
anxiously to a French priest early in 1984. "We are preparing for war."
In a postscript he added: "René Laurentin seems besotted with the
place."[1]

When Laurentin came to Medjugorje in December 1983, he had gone
to Mostar to speak to the bishop. The two men had taken each other's
measure. They had not as yet locked horns and each was treading warily
with the other. Why did the bishop not believe in the apparitions, asked
Laurentin courteously. Because of Vicka's hidden diary, came the swift
reply; because of the "Virgin's" incomprehensible support for the two
expelled Franciscans; because the visionaries kept contradicting their
own stories about why they had gone up Podbrdo that first day: to round
up sheep, to smoke, to pick flowers; and finally, but perhaps most
importantly of all, because of the "lies" of Tomislav Vlašić.

Alarmed by the anger in the bishop's voice, Laurentin begged him not
to give voice to accusations which could only scandalise the pilgrims.
Bishop Žanić professed to misinterpret this advice as cowardly and
hypocritical. "On hearing my views," he would later write (referring to
himself in the third person singular):

> René Laurentin advised the bishop not to publish them because it would be
> damaging with regard to the numerous conversions among the pilgrims.
> This advice scandalised the bishop. He wondered if such an attitude was
> compatible with scientific investigation worthy of a famous Mariologist.[2]

Laurentin, however, was not so easily dismissed:

> This is a total misrepresentation of my remarks. I pointed out to the bishop the disadvantage of displaying before the public the sordid quarrels which distress the diocese, on the principle that one washes one's dirty linen *within* the family. But especially I urged him not to publish "inexactitudes". Out of courtesy I did not use the words "lies", "calumnies" or "slanders", hoping that he would better understand mollifying words. But I urged him not to publish so many false accusations against Tomislav Vlašić.[3]

It was true. Bishop Žanić was not hesitating to share his low opinion of Tomislav Vlašić with whoever cared to listen. This was particularly distressing to the Slovenian Jesuit, Father Grafenauer, who could now see what a hornet's nest he had unwittingly stirred up. Writing to a Franciscan friend in October, he expressed his growing dismay:

> You know what he [the bishop] has been telling everyone about this diary and how he has publicly put Fra Tomislav to shame . . . He [the bishop] says that Vicka showed [the diary] to me. He considers me a witness against Vlašić. I have heard all this from Mate Zovkić who sent me the bishop's circular letter. I immediately let the bishop know, through Zovkić, that I had not seen Vicka's diary. He cannot consider me a witness against Tomislav in this affair . . . In this letter I explained to the bishop in what way I had spoken about and written about Vicka's diary. The bishop did not take into account my extracts from Tomislav's chronicle, because he doesn't believe in the chronicle. He only believes in the diary . . . Even though I communicated [this] to the bishop . . . he has not withdrawn what he originally declared. And he continues to write in foreign newspapers and refer to me as a witness as regards Vicka's diary.[4]

When the book *Is the Virgin Mary Appearing at Medjugorje?* co-written by Laurentin and a Croat Franciscan, Ljudevit Rupčić, was published in France in the spring of 1984, thousands of French pilgrims – from France, Belgium and French-speaking Canada – were inspired to set out for Medjugorje. Sackloads of letters descended on Laurentin (more than he'd ever received in response to all his other books put together), mainly from people who were returning to the faith after an absence of many years. The apparitions, he wrote, had reawakened faith and hope on a global scale: "Many people recognised their own plight in that cry of alarm and Our Lady's urgent warning that the world has given itself over to sin and placed itself in mortal peril. The remedy comes from God. It is not magic; it lies in prayer, conversion and fasting." Hundreds of invitations poured in for him to speak about Medjugorje, and, however large the hall in which he spoke, it was always too small to accommodate his listeners. "We should not," he said, "have needed a sign from Heaven to remind us that God exists, that Christ is at our disposal in the Eucharist, that the Virgin is always with us in the Communion of Saints. But we had grown deaf, and that is why a sign was necessary – to bring us back to long-forgotten truths."

Nevertheless, despite his personal conviction, he was bracing himself against the storm to come, against the hostility from both right and left in whose flak he was sure to be caught. Within the Church itself, there were those, on the left, who were allergic to the mere mention of apparitions, dismissing them as hallucinations, a projection of the subjective unconscious; while the traditionalists on the right would condemn and reject the ecumenical message of Medjugorje, the new ecumenism which Archbishop Frane Franić of Split praised as one of Medjugorje's principal fruits. His observation, that "Our Lady is bringing us closer together, uniting us with our brothers from the Orthodox Church, the Muslims and even our Marxist brothers", was calculated to send a shudder down many a conservative Catholic's spine, but warmly endorsed by a Muslim dervish from Mostar who had been invited into the apparitions room:

> I felt in my heart such energy that I could have cried aloud. I thought that I too would go into ecstasy. I decided to pray the whole night . . . The world is looking for God. If it looks for Him, it will find Him. If it finds Him, it will cling lovingly to Him, and he who is in love with God cannot ever be separated from him.

So powerful did a Hungarian-born English priest find the reconciling spirit of Medjugorje that he was moved to see it in a global context:

> May the reconciliation in Medjugorje and in the diocese of Mostar become a channel for a wider reconciliation between Catholics, Orthodox Christians and Muslims of the region, so that the reconciled people of Hercegovina may become an inspiration to other regions of the world in need of reconciliation: between Jews and Arabs, between Christians and Muslims in Lebanon, between Catholics and Protestants in Northern Ireland, between Greek and Turkish Cypriots, between Hindus and Muslims, between Iraq and Iran, between rich and poor, between oppressors and oppressed everywhere.

But where *was* that "reconciliation in the diocese of Mostar" of which he spoke? Despite all proclamations to the contrary, it seemed no less elusive than peace in any of the world's major trouble spots.

The Commission established by Bishop Žanić to investigate events at Medjugorje had been dragging its feet and showing little interest. Each of the four members worked individually and had to prepare his own report. Of the four, only Ivan Dugandžić, the Franciscan novice-master, had visited Medjugorje at all regularly since the earliest days; and the man charged with investigating the cures and the phenomena of light had not so much as set foot in the village. The dead hand of the bishop lay heavily on the Commission. "There was a serious question of authority at stake," says Ivan Dugandžić:

> No one doubted that apparitions were possible. What struck most members of the Commission as suspect was that they should have occurred in a Franciscan parish. Voting was secret and the results were never officially published. But it was rumoured that its verdict was that the visionaries' claims were false.[5]

It was no secret that the four men were divided and unlikely to reach a conclusion. In January 1984 Cardinal Kuharić of Zagreb asked Žanić to set up a larger, more serious Commission. Meanwhile, the Yugoslav bishops instructed the visionaries and their advisers to refrain from making public statements of any kind until an official verdict had been reached. The new-look Commission was expanded to fourteen and included members of the medical profession and representatives from all the theological training centres of Croatia and Slovenia. None, however, was known to the public, and none had the remotest connection with the events they were investigating. Moreover, the mixture was no more balanced than before, as ten of the fourteen were known opponents of Medjugorje. Indeed, one of Žanić's fellow-bishops drily observed that disapproval of Medjugorje seemed to be a condition of selection.[6] It seemed improbable that any of the new members would welcome statements from enthusiasts for the apparitions. None of the doctors was invited to the Commission's first session in April, when Bishop Žanić, pronouncing himself chairman and president, declared his intention of "crushing the apparitions". "I am the Commission," he asserted, leaving little doubt as to its eventual verdict.[7]

But not even the bishop could turn back the tide. Though he tried to have the pilgrimages banned altogether, it was out of the question, since pilgrims are individuals who may go where they will, unless, as in the case of the Communist bloc countries, their own authorities restrain them, or there is a real moral reason why they may not – if, for example, the Medjugorje events were proved to be of Satanic origin. But the Archbishop of Split, Frane Franić, had cut that particular bit of ground from under Bishop Žanić's feet by his claim that the apparitions had done more for popular religion in Yugoslavia in three years "than all our pastoral letters in forty". A strange result for Satan to achieve!*

---

*It seemed to be common knowledge that the Split representative on the Commission would like to have seen Žanić as Archbishop of Split instead of the increasingly embarrassing Frane Franić.

In March, the new enlarged Commission issued a report which was published in *Glas Koncila*. It deplored "those priests and laymen who organise pilgrimages", and demanded silence on the subject until their own verdict should be made known. A thorough investigation into all the phenomena, including the cures, was promised. The report was an exercise in wishful thinking; no more than a holding operation. But the Vatican newspaper, *L'Osservatore Romano*, gave it front-page prominence, and from there it spread round the world, creating the false impression, highly satisfactory to Bishop Žanić, that Medjugorje had been placed out of bounds to faithful Catholics. And for a time the number of pilgrims fell dramatically.

In June, on a rare visit to Medjugorje, the new Commissioners attended Mass and witnessed the children in ecstasy. Nicolas Bulat, Professor of Dogma at the University of Split, applied the brutal medieval test of prodding an ecstatic. He twice inserted a large unsterilised needle into Vicka's left shoulder-blade – but provoked no reaction. When Vicka got up to leave, however, a blood-stain marked the spot where the needle had penetrated her blouse.[8] Though impressed by the "inner transformation among the local population", the Commissioners nevertheless stayed only two days, since "nothing of any interest" was happening in the village.

In making this assertion, the Commissioners were obviously being less than accurate. For ever since the beginning of the year, the Lady had been asking, through Jelena, that all the parishioners should assemble once a week in the church to receive a special message. The friars had suggested a Thursday, and on Thursday, 1st March 1984, the following message was transmitted through Marija:

> Dear children,
> I have chosen this parish in a special way and I wish to guide it. I watch over it with love, and I wish you all to be mine. Thank you for your response this evening. I hope that you will come in ever greater numbers to be with me and my Son. Every Thursday I will speak a message specially for you.

The second message on 8th March was even briefer:

> Dear children,
> You in this parish must begin changing inwardly. If you do so, all those who come here can be converted. Thank you for responding to my invitation.

As the messages followed the liturgical year, and on the first Thursday after Easter there was no message, Marija concluded that they had been intended solely for Lent. A few days later, however, she learned that the Lady's silence stemmed from her displeasure at the lukewarm response given her: "Only a very few have accepted the Thursday messages," she told Marija. "At first there were more, but now boredom has crept in. Quite a few are now asking about the message in a spirit of idle curiosity rather than one of faith and devotion to my Son and myself." She had, in fact, already complained to Jelena on 18th November that too many people in Medjugorje had begun looking for material profit and abandoning their concentration on spiritual good. "There is no prayer there any more." The messages did, however, start again on 10th May, after a gap of two weeks. Mostly they were a request for prayer – some of them said no more than "Pray, pray, pray" – and stressed the world's need for repentance:

> 6 September 1984
> Dear children,
> Without prayer there is no peace. Therefore I say to you, dear children, pray at the foot of the Cross for peace.

The following week she added:

> You are wondering what all these prayers are for. Turn around, dear children, and you will see how much ground sin has gained in the world. Therefore pray that Jesus may overcome.

"Dear children," she said, in Advent:

> You do not know how to love, nor how to listen with love to what I am saying to you. Be aware, my beloved ones, that I am your mother and that I have come to earth to teach you how to listen and pray – not because you must, but out of love for the cross you are carrying. Through the cross, God is glorified in every human being.

And the heaviest cross the children carried was undoubtedly the Bishop of Mostar. "Pray for the bishop every day," the Madonna had told them; "he carries a heavy burden." "You pray for the bishop as though he were a sinner," Žanić complained one day to Marija. "Oh no," she smiled, "I pray for you as my bishop."

Jelena, too, was receiving messages. On the Thursday before Easter, the Lady told her:

> Today I shall tell you a spiritual secret. If you want to rise above evil and temptation, create an active conscience within yourselves . . . Pray in the morning, read a page of the Gospels to root the Divine word in your hearts, and meditate on it all through the day, live by it, and by evening you will have become stronger.

And again: "If you want to be happy, lead a simple, humble life. Pray a great deal, and leave all your problems in God's hands."

A message of a more controversial kind to Jelena at the end of May exasperated Bishop Žanić yet again. The Lady, it seemed, had asked for her two thousandth birthday to be marked on 5th August instead of on the traditional feast day of 8th September – though Father Vlašić's chronicle for 1981 recorded that the Lady had solemnly acknowledged the children's birthday greetings on 8th September! When Vlašić approached the bishop with this mind-boggling request, Žanić ordered him not to broadcast such "anti-ecclesiastical" rubbish. But it was already too late; the news had spread. "Perhaps," spluttered the sorely-tried bishop, "we should therefore expect 'Our Lady' to change the Feast of the Immaculate Conception as well, from 8th December to 5th November?"[9]

In the same document, he referred to a letter sent by Father Vlašić to the Pope on 2nd June after Jelena had asked the Lady for more details in order to convince the bishop. ("He is against the whole thing".) "Tell the Holy Father," counselled the Lady. "If he agrees, celebrate the Feast as I have told you." And if he doesn't? "Pray and leave the rest to me. I'll sort everything out." The Holy Father did not apparently set great store by this message, since he did not vouchsafe a reply. The Feast continues to be celebrated on 8th September.

In July 1984, Bishop Žanić ordered Tomislav Vlašić to ban the visionaries from the church. The priest refused on the grounds that this would leave them dangerously exposed to the crowds, to say nothing of the police who would pounce on any religious gathering not held on church premises. Vlašić's obstinacy was, argued the bishop, "damaging to the negative verdict being prepared by the Commission". He persuaded the Franciscan Provincial Superior (not elected by the friars themselves but foisted on them by Rome as a punishment for their misdeeds) to remove Vlašić to a parish at Vitina about fifteen kilometres away. Slavko Barbarić replaced him as the visionaries' spiritual director.

As the Communist authorities came to realise that Medjugorje was indeed a purely religious phenomenon and not a slow-burning fuse to a nation-wide insurrection, their hostility began to cool. They were said to be enjoying the spectacle of the Catholics at each other's throats. Besides, they were beginning to see that Medjugorje could be a goose with a whole quiverful of golden eggs! Ljubljana TV in Slovenia broadcast a sympathetic thirty-minute documentary programme about Medjugorje, and Ljubljana radio organised a phone-in. In June 1984, however, as 50,000 pilgrims made their way to the village for the third anniversary celebrations, the restrictions were still very much in force. Helicopters patrolled the skies, militia vans lurked round every corner. Lucy Rooney, a Notre Dame nun who has co-written several books about Medjugorje with Robert Faricy, SJ, reported that the police were still being as obstructive as possible:

> We were stopped at the crossroads leading to the village; passports were examined, bags searched very thoroughly. Some buses were turned away. Passengers from other buses were made to walk the last few kilometres, even though they included sick pilgrims. Those who were camping in tents near the church were turned out.[10]

A group of twelve British pilgrims had been warned that they might be turned back at the airport; and that hotel and tourist agency employees could well be government spies. They had been told to beware, if they succeeded in getting to Medjugorje, of "people who look out of place in or around church and ask a lot of seemingly friendly questions".[11] As the previous winter had seen massive propaganda for the Winter Olympics in Sarajevo, one of the Irish pilgrims in the group could not resist making a moral point. "Doesn't it show that Satan controls the media which made such a fuss of the Games when the Queen of Heaven is apparently nightly just down the road?" Obviously the civic authorities had not yet awakened to the fact that the Medjugorje bonanza could help offset the considerable losses incurred by the Winter Olympics!

Tomislav Vlašić was there for the anniversary Mass. "Prayer means a searching for God," he told the crowd. "It is not just a case of reciting the Rosary. It means opening the Gospel and trying to become the Word that is written there. It would be enough for a whole lifetime to read the fifth, sixth and seventh chapters of St Matthew. Only by prayer and fasting will we be able to change the world."

"I found myself wishing that the whole world could be like Medjugorje," said Tonka, a teenager who admitted that she herself had not felt able to pray a great deal while there. "I cried for all the millions of people whose lives are just centred on themselves."

Though Medjugorje's amenities had not greatly improved, and most of the pilgrims merely lived rough or took pot luck with the villagers, Richard West, a journalist accompanying the group of pilgrims referred to above, noted undeniable signs of approaching change: "half-finished buildings, higgledy-piggledy stacks of stone and brick, and pipes for the drains that have been dug but not yet filled".[12]

Word was spreading far beyond the confines of Europe. By chance, John Hill, a Boston millionaire and lapsed Catholic, heard an audio-cassette about Medjugorje, and instantly dedicated his entire fortune to promoting the messages. Setting up a Center for Peace in Boston, he despatched a team to make an hour-long television film, began organising monthly charter flights for pilgrims and arranging for the free distribution of booklets, video and audio-cassettes, in a variety of languages to people all over the world.

All these developments served to increase Bishop Žanić's frustration. His problems seemed to be multiplying. In all fairness, it must be admitted that he had begun to deal more sensitively with the continuing Hercegovina problem: "Diocesan priests are still being refused admission to five churches on Cathedral ground," he wrote to a friend in September 1984. "I sent some Franciscans in to cool the highly inflamed atmosphere. What a terrible example for the Church to be giving the Muslims and Orthodox, not to mention the Communists."[13]

One of the ten anti-Medjugorje theologians on the Commission had gone over to the other side. The bishop, however, believed that even with a more precarious nine-four majority, he could still guarantee a negative final judgement. But when the Commission met again on 11th October, it was rapidly deadlocked, and could manage no more than a re-issue of its earlier communiqué with its promise to investigate the Medjugorje affair thoroughly and its dissatisfaction that pilgrimages were still being made. Priests and visionaries were asked to desist from making public statements to the press.

When this revised communiqué was sent for endorsement to the Yugoslav bishops, the latter inserted the adjective "official" in front of "pilgrimages", thus recognising that though there could be no major pilgrimages led by a bishop or cardinal to Medjugorje, private pilgrimages remained a matter of free choice. They further suggested that a wider Commission – possibly with an international membership – might have more chance of breaking the present impasse.

On 30th October 1984, a polemical document which lengthily set out Bishop Žanić's officially "unofficial" opposition to Medjugorje was sent to bishops round the world, and – with more immediate impact – to the world's press. Foreign journalists, choosing to disregard the finer points of the argument, uniformly gave the impression that the Holy See was solidly behind the bishop. "Yugoslav Bishops Ban Pilgrimages to Madonna of Secrets", announced an Italian paper. "Medjugorje: Bishops Ban Pilgrims", the Portuguese were told. "No to Pilgrims. Rome Speaks Out", proclaimed a headline in France. Rome had done no such thing, but it was difficult for the Holy See to issue a denial without compromising Bishop Žanić.

Many Christians were distressed. Was the Church really against Medjugorje? Had they been hoodwinked? Had they just been chasing dreams? In vain did Archbishop Franić protest in his diocesan newsletter (16th December 1984):

It would be absurd to call a halt to the pilgrimages while the episcopal Commission has still not decided whether these events are of God or of Satan. If the pilgrimages are stamped out, we should have no way of finding out the truth. We should be left wondering only whether the phenomenon had died a natural death or been extinguished by illicit force.

Deservedly or not, victory in the battle, if not the war, had unequivocally gone to Bishop Žanić.

13

Medical Evaluations

You must mix some uncertainty
With faith, if you would have faith be.
Robert Browning

"All these signs are to re-inforce your faith until I send you the final, visible sign," the Lady had told the children. Appearing to Ivan and a group of friends on the Crnica hillside in 1982, she had repeated the message: "Now I will give you a sign to strengthen your faith." All the boys saw two bright beams of light coming from the sky, one shining over the church, the other over the Križevac cross.

Since that time, many strange phenomena had been sighted: crosses spinning and vanishing from sight; the sun surrounded by multi-coloured rings dancing like a Catherine-wheel in the sky. Bishop Žanić was understandably sardonic. "Once," he remarked, "I sent a priest to make a recording in Medjugorje. He was bent over his microphone when a group of Italians nearby started shouting: 'Look at the sun.' He looked up, and of course he saw nothing, because there was nothing to see. But those pilgrims probably all returned home with their heads stuffed full of miracles."

But some had photographs which, if they did not actually prove their claims, at least took some explaining away. One photo was taken by a lady from Mostar who was one of a huge crowd on Križevac on 14th September 1983. When the film was developed, the crowd had become a blob, dominated by a white cross with a white-robed woman standing next to it. Another photograph was an innocent "snap" taken of the rural setting around the church. When his film was returned to him, the photographer was surprised to find that the rural scene had given way to the vague outline of a veiled woman. A third, taken of a blank wall in the apparitions room by a Belgian lady at six o'clock in the evening on 6th September 1983, clearly shows the face of a beautiful woman.

Although photographs answering to these descriptions have come into my own possession, their authenticity is almost impossible to verify. It is known that a great deal of clever faking goes on.

131

Early in the morning of 5th September 1984, Louis Desrippes, from Bordeaux, was standing outside the church at Medjugorje.[1] Looking up at Križevac, he was surprised to see the cross gradually disappear from view. Its base turned into a globe, surmounted by the indistinct silhouette of a woman. Five of the six people standing with Desrippes saw what he saw; the sixth saw nothing at all. With only a little film left in his cine-camera, Desrippes managed to film the final two minutes of an occurrence which had lasted about half an hour. Unexpectedly, the film provided confirmation: it showed the globe and a flashing, seemingly rotating silhouette. As globe and figure gradually disappeared from view, the arms of the cross slowly re-emerged into the picture. At 7 p.m. on 25th May 1985, two pilgrims in Bijakovići, one Belgian, the other Italian, filmed a very similar phenomenon from different angles.[2] As with Desrippes, the cross disappeared, to be replaced by a globe and a luminous figure.

Such extraordinary happenings have so far defied rational analysis – which is not, of course, to claim that there *is* no rational explanation for them. Jean-Louis Martin, an opponent of the apparitions, spent seven months in Medjugorje and many times saw strange phenomena. And he continues to search for a natural explanation for them.[3] We may not go all the way with the British Jesuit, Richard Foley, who wrote in the *Catholic Herald* that, "The reporting of these facts by a multitude of eye-witnesses representative of diverse nationalities, age-groups, backgrounds and cultures adds up to evidence which is fully credit-worthy for being so convergent and compelling." But it is nevertheless inconceivable that such evidence should be completely ruled out of court.

Even stranger claims have been made. In March 1985, Professor Bogusław Lipinski of Boston, using nuclear-research equipment – a BT 400 (Biotech-Canada) electroscope – recorded phenomena which he believed explicable only in terms of spiritual energy. There was, he said, an incredible amount of such energy in Medjugorje: on one occasion, in the chapel of apparitions, his machine registered 100,000 millirads p.h. energy. Considering that the usual figure registered at big Yankee football matches was a mere twenty, the concept of 100,000 was hard to grasp. A comparable degree of physical energy would have killed anyone exposed to it![4] When Professor Lipinski tried to return to Yugoslavia to repeat these tests the following year, he ran into trouble at the airport. Suspicious of his high-tech equipment, the authorities decided that he was a spy (if they were right, surely he was a rather ostentatious one!) and banned him from entering the country for two years.*

---

* Other nuclear physicists and engineers who investigated radio-activity in Medjugorje, did not achieve the same extraordinary results as Professor Lipinski. They considered the latter's concept of spiritual energy to be eccentric and unscientific.

For its own good reasons, the Yugoslav government was resisting all demands for a national scientific commission to examine such claims – along with the phenomena of light, the 300 or so reported healings, and the radio-activity which was said to increase in the apparitions room during the time of the visions. For the first time in all the history of apparitions, science had an opportunity to investigate extraordinary phenomena while they were actually happening. Medjugorje opened up for the scientist possibilities for research that neither Lourdes nor Fatima had been able to provide. It was too good – and exciting – an opportunity to miss.

Isolated tests had been done on the children from as early as 1982. The first doctor to have examined the visionaries while in a state of ecstasy was a Yugoslav psychiatrist and parapsychologist from Slovenia, Ludvik Stopar, who in 1982 and 1983 paid four visits to Medjugorje, each lasting between five and ten days. At this time the apparitions were of between three and ten minutes' duration. As Dr Stopar considered that hypnosis was the best method for deciding whether the children were being manipulated or not, he hypnotised Marija, in his view "the most intelligent and mature of [the six] and . . . therefore the most suitable for the test" – without her knowledge or consent. "If I had asked," he said. "I am sure she would have refused. In therapy one does not ask permission."[5] To the casual observer that comment is more than a little shocking!

Dr Stopar asked Marija to describe the visions; and then repeated the request under hypnosis, when her subconscious was giving the replies to his questions. (When she came round, Marija apologised for having "dropped off to sleep".) The two accounts were substantially the same – with the important difference that under hypnosis Marija had revealed the closely guarded secrets. Dr Stopar claimed that his experiment did not put Marija at risk; and, in a conversation with Laurentin,[6] dismissed the objection that he had violated her conscience. "You can trust my professionalism," he assured Laurentin. "The secrets remain as secret for me as they are for Marija. It is as binding as the seal of the confessional."

Various clinical tests – neuro-psychiatric, medico-psychological and somatological – convinced Dr Stopar that the children were quite normal. Unlike Laurentin, he was reluctant, however, to describe their state as "ecstasy", since they remained in contact with the outside world and, to some small extent at least, continued to react to it. (Though impervious to camera flashes and the infliction of pain, Marija admitted to having seen a "light mist" around the apparition on the occasion when the portly Dr Stopar had stood immediately in front of her line of vision.) He was impressed. "In Medjugorje," he said, "I had the impression of coming into contact with a supernatural reality" – but he was well aware that his own resources were limited and that a lot of scientific investigation remained to be done. In a report sent to the Bishop of Mostar in December 1984, he suggested that an ecclesiastical commission should examine the parapsychological phenomena in order to determine whether they were of divine origin, or the result of human manipulation.

Tests by Italian doctors in March 1983 had established that the visionaries' heartbeats were normal. The evidence of these and a number of clinical tests suggested that the apparitions did not affect physiological reality in any way. Dr Mario Botta, a heart-surgeon from Milan, returned in December to carry out an electrocardiogram on Ivan. His second conclusion confirmed his first: "that ecstasy does not suppress normal physiology but somehow transcends it".[7]

In February and March 1984, Dr Lucia Capello observed the five children during ecstasy, noting their calmness and cheerful normality. At one point, Jakov, the lightest of the five, was lifted off the ground; but he did not react and when put down again "his legs went from the vertical to the horizontal in the most natural and spontaneous fashion". This response excluded the possibility of catalepsy. All in all, the visionaries "appeared to be discreet, well-mannered, careful in their dress and in their speech and absolutely aware of their surroundings. Their behaviour seemed to conform perfectly with that of other young people of the same age."[8] She also noted, as have many doctors before and since, the various synchronisations: the way the visionaries fell to their knees at the same instant, their voices becoming inaudible, though their lips continued to articulate; the fact that their voices all became audible again on the third word of the Our Father, the apparition having recited the first two words; that when their ecstasy was over, eyes and heads were raised at exactly the same moment and in the same direction, and the word *ode* (she's gone!) was uttered.[9] As Laurentin remarked, the first of these synchronisations might be attributed to natural causes, but there seemed to be no explanation for the second and third.

The French professor, Cadilhac, who later conducted psychological and psychiatric tests on the children, attached great importance to the fact that the word *ode* was uttered (by one or more of the visionaries) *after* they had lowered their eyes. Had they spoken first, the word could have been interpreted as a pre-arranged signal. Moreover, *ode* was not always synchronised. Out of fifty apparitions studied by the French team, Jakov came in first with it fourteen times, Vicka eight, Marija four, and Ivanka only three.

In April, Dr Enzo Gabrici, a neuro-psychiatrist, agreed with the findings of the French team and added:

> Clinical observation has also excluded hallucinatory phenomena, as well as the habitual signs of epilepsy or of any other malfunction capable of

producing altered states of consciousness. There are no symptoms which would suggest that the subjects are living out something previously suggested under hypnosis. The visionaries can recall with absolute lucidity what has happened to them . . . [They] retain perfect consciousness of their own identity.[10]

Professor Maria Franchini, making more or less the same observations, concluded that: "The group is made up of a number of independent individuals. Each has his or her own attitude, but all are drawn towards an external object which holds their attention with an intensity which I have never before experienced, and which in my view makes their experience unique."[11]

An extremely important and comprehensive series of tests was conducted by a team of French doctors, in short but frequent visits to Medjugorje between March and December 1984. The French medical team's programme aimed at "a clinical and para-clinical study of the visionaries of Medjugorje, before, during and after the apparition, from the point of view of differences in the functioning of their principal receptive organs: brain, vision, hearing, voice and, in particular, the vegetative cardiac functions".[12]

Professor Henri Joyeux, the team's co-ordinator, was Professor of Cancerology in the Faculty of Medicine at Montpellier and a surgeon at Montpellier's Cancer Institute. Having read René Laurentin's book, *Is the Virgin Mary Appearing at Medjugorje?* he and a group of colleagues were "intrigued but not convinced", and resolved to see for themselves. His first impressions are worth noting:

Vicka, Ivan, Marija and Jakov are like any other youngsters of their age. We saw no signs of hallucination, pretence or invention. They were calm, serene and deeply serious and did not play at being celebrities. They remained normal in all the circumstances in which we observed them. They did not collude with each other, either before, during or after the essential event of their day, and they all returned home to their families.

These young Yugoslavs are easy to communicate with . . . they allow themselves to be photographed or filmed but they do not seek this out; rather, they appeared to be somewhat annoyed by all the fuss that surrounded them. They are country youngsters who do not appear to need either a psychologist or a psychiatrist. They dress in the normal fashion of other young people of their country. They give no impression of being bigoted, each seeming to have his or her own personality; we felt at ease with all of them: they are neither geniuses nor simpletons; they are not being manipulated but remain free and healthy in mind and body.[13]

He also offered thumb-nail sketches of the five children who were still receiving daily visits:

> Jakov Čolo, aged 13 . . . as impulsive, roguish and wild as any youngster of his age.
>
> Ivan Dragicević, aged 19 . . . a very reserved, almost solitary, young man; he likes sport – (some of the team played football with him); he answers questions precisely, appears to reflect a good deal and tends towards introspection. He refused very firmly to answer a precise question about his future: it is his private life and nobody else's business.
>
> Marija Pavlović, aged 19, is a calm young girl, open and smiling. She is discreet and keeps to the background but is at the same time positive and reassuring in dealing with questioners. One feels that she has enormous inner reserves . . .
>
> Ivanka Ivanković, aged 18, has regular features and the assured walk and deportment of a student closely in touch with her times; she is accessible, sympathetic and open, but does not lack strength of character.
>
> Vicka Ivanković, aged 20, is the most open and smiling of the group. Her angular features, piercing gaze, and strong voice, all combine to give her a particular character; she is extrovert, her approach is simple and direct, and she is incapable of hiding her feelings.

During the French team's first visit, in March, purely clinical studies of the visionaries were made. In June, they returned to continue these studies, and also in hopes of making electro-encephalographic recordings. Here they ran into an unforeseen obstacle. The children, with Jakov as their spokesman (he had been almost completely silent during the doctors' first visit), refused the recording, on the grounds that the Lady had said it was unnecessary. Laurentin and Professor Joyeux both argued that the test would be invaluable for countering doubters and unbelievers; but all they got was a promise from Jakov that he would ask the Lady again.

Later, rather to everyone's astonishment, Jakov reported, smiling, that the Lady had given the go-ahead for the experiment. All opposition seemed to have melted away. Electro-encephalographs were then made of Ivan and Marija (Marija had to stay motionless on her knees, with wires attached to her hair), and one recording of the heart rhythm and blood pressure of Ivanka.

In September, Professor Joyeux went to Vicka's house where, at the time of apparition, he was able to film not only Vicka herself but also a pseudo-ecstatic who had knelt beside her. The latter went into a very different kind of ecstasy: exaggerated, pretentious and incoherent. The contrast between these pathological symptoms and Vicka's calm concentration was striking. It was, commented Laurentin, a contrast "between the supernatural which fulfils nature and the pathological which distorts it; between spiritual moderation and a spiritual self-indulgence which takes pleasure in aping the appearance of spiritual gifts".[14]

When the team returned in October, this time it was Ivanka who objected (Jakov being at home with measles). "Today you want to do another test: tomorrow it will be another one. Where is it all going to end? We're not guinea-pigs." Gently, Laurentin persuaded her to consult the Lady. This time the reply came back: "You must decide for yourselves." Fortunately for the medical team, the visionaries decided to co-operate. On 6th October, further electro-encephalograph and ophthalmic studies were made. Similar tests were performed next day; and video-recordings were made before, during and after the ecstasy.

The final tests in December dealt with vision, hearing and larynx function; and again video-recordings were made. The clinical studies made during the entire series[15] persuaded Professor Joyeux's team that there were no signs of:

(1) individual or collective hallucination – such as is normally encountered in drug addicts, among users of hashish and other hallucinogens.

(2) individual or collective hysteria, usually characterised by debility, suggestibility, inconstancy, theatricality, emotional immaturity and childish egocentricity. None of these indications was observed in the visionaries.

(3) neurosis. "The visionaries have no symptoms of anxiety or obsessional neurosis, phobic or hysterical neurosis, hypochondriac/or psychosomatic neurosis, and there is no indication of any psychosis."

(4) catalepsy – in which there is complete suspension of voluntary muscular movement leading to complete immobilisation; assumed positions are retained and there is no capacity for spontaneous movement. All gesticulation ceases. "This phenomenon has not been observed in the visionaries who quite naturally drop to their knees together when, as they say, they see Our Lady. They remained quite naturally in the kneeling position while the medical team were carrying out their tests; rather than freezing, the muscles governing gesticulation remain relaxed. The visionaries move spontaneously and without the slightest difficulty right from the end of the ecstasy. During the ecstasy they are not in a state of catalepsy, but in one of prayer and peaceful contemplation."

(5) a pathological ecstasy, such as is frequently observed in pathological mystics, hysterics, the chronically delirious and those suffering from hallucinations. In this state, "ecstasy alternates with excesses of exaltation and lewd excitability although the subjects remain useless in the face of practical activity". None of these signs was present in the visionaries of Medjugorje. "The daily ecstasy does not excite them, does not constrain them, does not make them ill and does not give them a false sense of their own importance."

Professor Joyeux claims that his tests "are based on sound medical judgement and on common sense. In the last analysis it is not necessary to be a doctor in order to be aware that these young people are normal and healthy in mind, soul and body."

Electro-cardiograms showed the heart contraction to be normal and regular during the ecstasy. The rhythm of the heartbeat increased and remained high for the minute following the ecstasy. The electro-encephalographs made on Ivan and Marija were normal and identical, allowing the doctors to exclude the possibility that the subjects were asleep, dreaming, hallucinating or epileptic. During ecstasy they had remained "in the alpha rhythm . . . the rhythm of wakefulness and receptivity, the rhythm of the contemplative in calm prayer".

Meanwhile, Dr Jacques Philippot, an ophthalmologist, was studying the ocular and visual functions of the visionaries. No organic abnormalities were found, and the possibility of visual hallucination was excluded. Recordings made by an electro-oculogram showed frequent eye movements before and after ecstasy, while during it there was no movement of the eyeballs at all. Examination of the inner eye indicated a normal state, identical before and after the ecstasy. The pupils contracted normally in the presence of light, but it was noted that while Marija and Ivanka blinked in the bright light before and after the apparition, during it they did not blink even once.

In a study of Ivan's hearing function, Dr F. Rouquerol observed that before the ecstasy, sound was conducted in a normal manner as far as the upper part of the brain. The boy jumped, as was to be expected, when exposed to a seventy-decibel noise. During the ecstasy, however, although the sound was conducted along the auditory passages in the same way, Ivan did not react to a ninety-decibel noise, and afterwards said he had heard nothing at all. It would appear that, at this time, the sound had not reached the cortex of the brain.

Finally, in an attempt to find out why and how the visionaries' voices became inaudible from the moment ecstasy began, Dr Rouquerol investigated Ivanka's voice and larynx. He found that:

> During the recitation of the Rosary before the apparitions began, the needle indicating that the larynx muscles were working moved up and down the scale.
>
> When ecstasy began and the voice became inaudible, the needle stopped and the larynx no longer moved. The lips continued to move, as the visionary spoke to the apparition; but no sound was registered on the equipment.
>
> When the voice returned to normal on the third word of the Our Father, the needle moved again; and ceased when the voice disappeared again.
>
> As soon as the apparition had gone and the visionary began to speak normally, the movements of the larynx returned.

One essential question which the tests did not answer with any certainty concerned the subjectivity or objectivity of the apparition seen by the visionaries. A screening test had shown that the children's vision was not impaired – which meant that the normal visual pathways were not being used. Hearing tests had similarly proved that during the ecstasy the normal auditory channels continued to function but were not used. Those results might suggest that the vision was subjective in origin. On the other hand, "the convergence of gaze (confirmed by video-recordings); the simultaneous cessation of eyeball movements; and the simultaneous raising of eyes and heads as the apparition disappears, incline one to the objective explanation. The truth of the matter is that we have no way of deciding; what the visionaries see is beyond our limited powers of perception." As Professor Joyeux's report concluded:

> the phenomenon . . . is scientifically inexplicable . . . The visionaries of Medjugorje are not drop-outs or dreamers, nor are they tired or anxious; they are free and happy, at home in their country and in the modern world . . . The ecstasies are not pathological, nor is there any element of deceit. No scientific discipline seems able to describe these phenomena. We would be quite willing to define them as a state of active, intense prayer, partially disconnected from the outside world, a state of contemplation with a separate person whom they alone can see, hear and touch.[16]

On 20th October 1985, the diocesan paper, *Glas Koncila*, carried a report by the bishop's Commissioners who, in September, had attended what they called "an experience" and talked to the visionaries afterwards. In the Commissioners' view, the foreign doctors' testimonies were inadmissible since, however sophisticated their technology, they did not speak Serbo-Croatian and had to rely on interpreters!

Professor Louis Bélanger, an expert on paranormal phenomena at the Theological faculty of the University of Montreal, was equally sceptical.[17] While agreeing that the earliest visions were probably genuine, he pointed out that Ivanka, who had been in a state of grief over her mother's death – and therefore highly emotional and suggestible – had been the first to see the apparition. He also reported seeing Vicka flinch slightly when fingers were suddenly poked into her eyes; a proof that she was not "in a true trance". "Of course she wasn't," countered Fr Slavko. "She was not in a trance but in ecstasy: a state in which the person is only partially disconnected from reality."

Fascinated by what he agreed was an extraordinary phenomenon, he suggested in an interview with Gitta Sereny the possibility that geophysical forces were releasing some electro-magnetism which was affecting the brain and causing hallucinations.[18] The character of the hallucinations would depend on the subject's own cultural background; and in a Catholic village like Medjugorje, it would be natural enough for the vision to be of the Virgin Mary. Self-hypnosis might do the rest. How then, asked Miss Sereny, did he explain the fact that Marija had given two identical accounts of the same happening to Dr Stopar, one under hypnosis, the other not? How did the idea of self-hypnosis fit in with that? "Ah, Marija," sighed Professor Bélanger. "That extraordinary girl – she defeats any thesis I can propose."

On 7th, 8th, 9th September 1985, an important series of tests by Italian doctors confirmed the findings of the French team.[19] Psychological tests done by this group of doctors showed that the seers were of only average intelligence and were not possessed of a vivid imagination. Considering the intolerable pressures brought to bear on them, the mental balance of the two most prominent visionaries, Vicka and Marija, was agreed to be remarkable.

Professor Santini used an algometer – an electronic instrument for measuring resistance to burns – to test the children's sensitivity to pain. When a heated silver disc was applied to Marija and two of the other visionaries before ecstasy, they reacted within three or four tenths of a second – in other words, normally. During ecstasy, however, they did not react at all. The test was limited to seven seconds, for fear of inflicting serious burns if the period were extended. During that time, the visionaries appeared to be completely insensitive to pain.

Santini used an estesiometer during the ecstasy, extending, with varying amounts of pressure, a nylon thread on to the cornea of the eye. The visionaries did not flinch, nor so much as blink. It seemed too that they were impervious to strong light, since a 100-watt bulb shone full in their faces produced no ocular reaction.

Next it was the turn of the visual and auditory nerve-impulses. Using an ampliphone, Dr Paolo Maestri and engineer Savario Brighenti traced the passage of nerve-impulses from eye and ear as far as to the cortex of the brain where transmitted messages are interpreted. The result, they found, was like a telephone ringing in an empty house: "the visionaries' consciousness was elsewhere, and did not reply".

The visionaries, therefore, presumably neither saw nor heard what was going on around them while they were in ecstasy, even though the input of nervous signals to the brain was exactly the same as usual.

Professor Margnelli, a neuro-physiologist who specialised in the study of ecstasy, tested the visionaries with an American polygraph, a sophisticated type of lie-detector capable of revealing the hidden reactions of anyone intending to deceive. Earlier researches had proved that ecstasy causes heightened neuro-vegetative activity. With his polygraph – the

Diplomat One 1010 – Margnelli set out to explore the various physiological parameters of the vegetative nervous system: heartbeats; arterial pressure; electrical resistance of the skin; the flow of blood into the end-joint of the fingers; and the rhythm of breathing.

He studied Jakov on 7th–8th September, Ivan on 9th September, and his most important findings concerned the heartbeats and the flow of blood to the heart. Jakov's were abnormally fast: 150 per minute, while the flow of blood to the middle finger of the left hand was one third of the normal rate: "This reduced flow induces pallor of the skin, dryness, lowered temperature. We are speaking of an orthosympathetic hypertonia, with closing of the precapillary sphincters. The lack of feeling in Jakov and the other young people is therefore total."[20]

These tests showed variable results. During the French tests, Vicka's heartbeat had been abnormally fast, whereas that of Marija and Ivanka had actually slowed down during ecstasy. In Marija's case, the heartbeat never accelerated: it seemed that her concentration was complete. In the others, the acceleration was said to be linked to the conveying of secrets or messages. On one occasion, Jakov's breathing appears to have stopped altogether for about ten seconds – when he was being given a serious message about the future of the world.[21]

Interestingly enough, while the tests were being done, the ecstasies which until then had averaged two minutes each went down to forty-five seconds – although the very first apparition after the tests were finished lasted for six minutes. The Madonna appears to have asked, both about the French and the Italian tests, "Is all this really necessary?" Perhaps it was this that made Slavko finally decide, when the Italians had gone home, that enough was enough. There were to be no more instrumental tests during the ecstasies, unless they were deemed absolutely vital by the doctors concerned.

To Professor Margnelli, the visionaries of Medjugorje had opened up new horizons. Until this time, two extremes of ecstasy had been recognised. In the first of these, the subject showed a complete break with the world, exhibiting pathological symptoms, even sometimes catalepsy and rigidity. At the other extreme was the mystic, remaining partially earthbound while acting as an intermediary between the people present and the apparition. This was the role – one foot in both worlds – that the children had played in the first weeks.

But they had undeniably matured since then, evolving into a state of consciousness – not at all morbid – in which all their attention was concentrated on the apparition, to the exclusion of everything else. This was the new dimension provided by the visionaries of Medjugorje; and Professor Margnelli was forced on their account to introduce a third, completely new, category: ecstatics who are partially and significantly disconnected from the exterior world, yet who are completely normal, relaxed, well-integrated and happy:

> Ecstasy for these young people is invincible and spontaneous – and authentic. Normally an emotional stimulus provokes an immediate, though possibly brief, reaction from an individual. But in the present case, neither normally painful stimuli, nor a nylon thread in the eye, nor any of the other experiments provoked any reaction at all. In every case, the (metaphorical) telephone rang for someone who wasn't there. We must therefore be dealing with an authentic ecstasy.[22]

14

A Campaign of Disinformation

If the hallmark of Satan is chaos and confusion, one is driven to discern his presence in this conflict.

René Laurentin

All through 1984, the Abbé Laurentin had been a frequent visitor to Medjugorje and a painful thorn in the side of Bishop Žanić. When Žanić had warned the Frenchman that he would lose his reputation if he got mixed up with Medjugorje, Laurentin had understood this to be a simple plea for caution. Only after Žanić had launched several attacks on him in the Catholic press, accusing him of being a stooge of the Franciscans and of having made a fortune out of his book on Medjugorje, did Laurentin realise what he was up against. On 7th October 1984 he listed his grievances in a firm letter to Žanić:

> Since you are such a lover of the truth, Monsignor, let us clear away all suspicion of lying. To this end I beg you to stop telling your house-guests and casual visitors untruths which they then go away and reproduce in writing. For example:
>
> that the Abbé Laurentin has made a fortune out of his book on Medjugorje. The truth is that I spent a great deal of money in writing the book, money that has not as yet been recuperated. This will continue to be the case for some time to come.
>
> that Father Vlašić is a liar and a perjurer. The diary that you imagine exists does not in fact exist. If there *are* other diaries and notebooks, they make no mention of you.
>
> when I asked you on 26th December last not to make certain specific allegations public, it was out of regard for the Truth, not the fear of scandalising the faithful.
>
> finally, do not make the categoric assertion that the Medjugorje apparitions are hallucinations. Encephalograms and clinical observations by doctors have ruled out such a possibility on scientific grounds.[1]

The letter made some attempt to be conciliatory, Laurentin declaring that he accepted the bishop's authority and expressing admiration for the openness and courage Žanić had shown in the past. He did wonder, however, why such admirable qualities had not been put to the service of Truth! If at times Laurentin's tone was more in anger than in sorrow, it must be remembered that he had been sorely provoked.

It was wasted effort, anyway, since the bishop did not deign to reply. Laurentin sent him a second copy of the letter on 9th November; and this, too, went unanswered. When a third letter was delivered directly into the bishop's hands on Christmas Day, he threw it impatiently aside, saying he had no time to waste on reading such things.

By that time Žanić was being swamped by an avalanche of his own making. He had told the parish priest of Medjugorje, Tomislav Pervan, at the end of September 1984 to "cool and gradually extinguish" the Medjugorje events; but in the meantime he himself was taking no chances. In a twenty-three-page document, dated 30th October 1984 but not circulated till December, he sharpened his attack on Medjugorje. *The Present (Unofficial) Position of the Diocese of Mostar on the Medjugorje Events* was written in Italian and ostentatiously aimed at the world's press. "Unofficial" it indeed was – it had no legal authority to be anything else. But it was signed by the bishop and adorned with his episcopal seal; thus giving it the hallmarks of a definitive pronouncement.

"Collective hallucination", cleverly exploited by a group of unscrupulous Franciscans, was the bishop's considered verdict on Medjugorje. Of that, whatever the doctors might say, he was now "morally certain". Right from the start, he said, referring to himself as usual in the third person: "the bishop invited the Franciscans of Medjugorje . . . not to indulge in unbridled propaganda . . . but the desire to push themselves forward in order to defend their position on the notorious Hercegovina issue – plus their desire for not inconsiderable material gain – has swayed their every action."

He had warned the friars, he said, not to stand out against the Church, adding that if Our Lady *were* to leave a credible sign of her presence, he and others like him would come to Medjugorje and eat their words. (He had promised, in those circumstances, to walk there barefoot!) "But if one day it becomes obvious that the apparitions are fraudulent, what explanation will the advocates of Medjugorje give to the people?"

Meanwhile, the bishop argued, Catholics throughout the world were in a state of euphoria, thanks to "all kinds of news reports, articles in newspapers and magazines, bulletins, pamphlets, books written by well-known but irresponsible theologians, television films, video-cassettes, shallow journalists and excitable charismatics." It was to throw cold water over such euphoria that the bishop had rushed into print. Otherwise, when all the hysteria burst like a soap-bubble, the damage to the Church would be incalculable and the faith of believers everywhere might be damaged beyond repair. The visionaries, he claimed, were no more than unwitting pawns in a game they did not understand, manipulated so effectively that already they were making their moves "like mindless robots". In the early days, he later told journalist Gitta Sereny,[2] "they spoke like peasants . . . then their language changed. They were taught what to say to journalists and how to conduct themselves with doctors. It is all a lie."

All Žanić's old objections were given an airing: the non-appearance of the promised sign; the "ludicrous" banality of the weekly messages; the contradictions in the children's accounts of the first day; the disobedience of the two friars; Vicka's secret diaries and Ivan's attempts at "intimidation". In addition, he derided the cures that had been claimed, suggesting that few of these had been authenticated, and that some of the "cured" had since died.

But his greatest spleen was reserved for Tomislav Vlašić, and (to a lesser extent) for René Laurentin whom he publicly charged with deviousness and with having made large sums of money out of his book. On the subject of Vlašić he was unrestrained, reviving the old charge of perjury and calling him "confidence trickster" and "charismatic sorcerer":

> It is often said that the "messages" of Medjugorje are evangelical. Of course they are, especially the ones which have been given most publicity. How could they not be evangelical, when they were composed by Fra Tomislav Vlašić who has studied theology and knows what to say? Appeals for prayer, penance and conversion can be extremely effective, but they do not constitute proof that the apparitions are authentic.

Laurentin wrote to the bishop to protest. He dealt first with the charge of "collective hallucination". The bishop, he said, had wilfully ignored the electro-encephalograms carried out by French and Italian doctors, which provided scientific evidence that the visionaries were neither asleep, dreaming, nor hallucinating. In reply, Žanić said that, on the contrary, it was psychiatrists who had first suggested the idea of hallucination to him, but that he was quite prepared to withdraw the charge. For indeed:

> The word hallucination is too flattering for what goes on in that apparition room. There are witnesses to testify that there are no ecstasies, no hallucinations, but simply parrot-like performances of a comic show. Therefore I declare the word "hallucination" too generous a description for such wicked play-acting. It will all blow up in your face sooner or later, and then your precious encephalograms and cardiograms and all your scientific apparatus will sink without trace.[3]

Laurentin, who still insists that the bishop was influenced by the ideas of Marc Oraison, a progressive French priest who dismisses all apparitions as hallucinatory, and all miracle cures as psychosomatic, published his point-by-point refutation in a small book.[4] He quoted the Italian Professor Emilio Servadio as saying that "collective hallucination" was a contradiction in terms:

> Genuine hallucination (as distinct from optical illusions or mass hysteria), is always peculiar to one individual. It is not possible for a group of people to have repeated identical hallucinatory experiences which they insist are real, without showing signs of psychic abnormality. One cannot but be surprised that a bishop should pronounce a psychiatric diagnosis based on criteria which are psychiatrically unsound. (*Il Tempo*, 12 December 1984)[5]

Unfortunately, observed Laurentin, the bishop had turned his back on all evidence that did not fit his prejudices while accepting blindly any and every statement that did.

The trivial differences in the children's accounts of the first day were just one example. Ivanka had claimed they'd gone up the hill to look for sheep; the others said variously that it was to pick flowers, to listen to pop music or to smoke. So when Ivanka began telling the Commissioners about looking for sheep, the bishop reminded her sharply that she was under oath. "Then she panicked and admitted that she'd really gone up the hill to smoke and listen to pop." How, the bishop had witheringly inquired, could he be expected to believe in the apparitions, when the visionaries told such lies. For answer, Laurentin quoted a Jesuit from Split who had denounced the bishop's methods as being worthy of the KGB: first intimidating the children, then tricking them into contradicting themselves. "His brainwashing techniques recall those used on Cardinal Mindszenty of Hungary," claimed the Jesuit. In any case, said Laurentin, the children had always claimed they went twice up the hill on the twenty-fourth and only on the second occasion to look for (Milka Pavlović's) sheep.

And what did it matter that, as the bishop complained, the promised sign had not materialised! After all, the early Christians had lived in hourly expectation of the end of the world almost 2,000 years ago, and it had still not happened. As for the forty-seven copycat visionaries who were claiming to see the Virgin Mary, they were only to be expected. At Lourdes, after Bernadette's apparitions, there had been fifty such reports, all of them easily proven false.

There had been no "unbridled propaganda", insisted Laurentin. Editors publishing positive articles about Medjugorje had done so on their own initiative. In Yugoslavia, where there was no press freedom, the two Franciscan journalists who had written about the place had been given stiff prison sentences. Bishop Žanić himself cared little for press freedom, Laurentin accused; he had done his own share of muzzling free information, so that it was now almost impossible to find any article about Medjugorje that was not defamatory.

As to the bishop's accusations against Laurentin himself, they were laughable: any author could have told him that there was very little money to be made from publishing books. He had received an advance of 2,000 francs and had spent forty times that sum on expenses: travel, secretarial help, photographs etc. The ten per cent royalties payable on sales were divided three ways among Father Rupčić (author of the original text), the translator and himself.

In a codicil written in Croatian, Žanić had sneeringly suggested that Laurentin had been seduced by the attractions of the girl visionaries. "It appears," retorted the Frenchman, "that I preferred to take the word of Ivanka, who is 'beautiful' and Vicka who is 'charming', rather than that of the bishop who most certainly is neither."

But worst of all was the uninhibited attack on Tomislav Vlašić – a priest loved and revered in Medjugorje. One British pilgrim (Delia Smith in the *Catholic Herald*) had written of him:

> On reflection I think it was the experience of this priest celebrating Mass that did more than anything else to convince me of the genuineness of the apparitions. It would be wrong to say he had charisma – he is too humble for that – but everything about him has the ring of truth, communicating gentleness and serenity.

Sent to the parish to take charge after Fra Jozo's arrest, Tomislav Vlašić had for two years been the visionaries' spiritual director, guiding them and helping to interpret what they saw and heard. But, said Laurentin, he was no puppet-master: the children remained in charge of their own lives. Žanić had accused the Franciscan of authorising the two expelled friars to hear confessions in Medjugorje; but this was not the case. He had specifically asked them not to do so. And though indeed he had welcomed the friars to the village, in order to avoid any misunderstandings about their role, he had asked them not to broadcast their presence by wearing the Franciscan habit.

Why had Bishop Žanić spoken out so prematurely? Why not at least wait until after the Commission had done its work? Was he so sure of his Commission that he could afford to pre-empt its findings? Had they already prejudged the matter? For the comparable investigation in Lourdes in 1858, Mgr Laurence, the Bishop of Tarbes, had included Bernadette's parish priest in his Commission, and had, within certain

necessary limitations, left its members free to reach their own conclusions. Such was far from being the case in Mostar, where nobody from
Medjugorje itself, no close witness of the events there, was invited to
participate. It would appear that Bishop Žanić wanted a rubber-stamp
Commission to endorse his own views.

Yet it was still not clear why he had rushed in feet first, before the
Commissioners had made even a nominal review of the evidence available. "A judge who made his own opinions public before passing sentence
would be automatically disqualified," wrote a canon lawyer, "and this
communiqué likewise rules itself out of court. In thus publishing his
views, the bishop has invalidated any future work done by the Commission – including its eventual judgement."

But despite the criticisms, Bishop Žanić's position paper almost came
near to torpedoing Medjugorje, as the international press danced to his
tune. Tomislav Vlašić was pilloried and reviled, his reputation irremedi-
ably tarnished. In Italy, in America, the document was given maximum
publicity; but nowhere was the onslaught deadlier or longer-lasting
than in France. "Žanić wrote to all the French bishops himself,"
said a Franciscan in Medjugorje angrily. "It was a real campaign of
disinformation."

His efforts bore immediate fruit. In France, public opinion veered
sharply against Medjugorje; books on the subject disappeared over-
night from bookshop windows and shelves. Pilgrimage places were cancelled; charter flights stood empty. Many who had been as pilgrims to
Medjugorje felt let-down and disillusioned. *La Croix* (6th December)
was to fire the first broadside:

> The Bishop of Mostar, after careful study in which he was assisted by a
> properly constituted Commission, is morally certain that the Medjugorje
> events represent "a collective hallucination".
>
> The young seers have been manipulated by a group of Franciscan friars
> led by Fra Tomislav Vlašić, whom he describes as an "arch-deceiver and
> charismatic magician . . . who stands convicted of perjury to the bishops
> and the Commission . . ."
>
> The pseudo-mystical exaltation . . . which has been floating over
> Medjugorje is about to burst like a soap-bubble.

Four days later, in its issue of 9th–10th December, *La Croix* summed up
the position, albeit mistakenly:

> Collective hallucinations. This is how the Yugoslav Bishops describe the
> apparitions of the Virgin Mary at Medjugorje . . . These apparitions were
> faked by a fraudulent friar who has been expelled from his Order [*sic*].

148

The Yugoslav bishops had, in fact, hastened to re-assert that their ban applied only to "official" pilgrimages; they had never spoken of "hallucinations" nor about Father Vlašić – who had certainly not been expelled from his Order. Communist journals in Zagreb and Belgrade were claiming that Cardinal Ratzinger, head of the Vatican Congregation for the Doctrine of the Faith, had banned the pilgrimages. But Ratzinger had maintained a prudent silence on the subject of Medjugorje, and *Glas Koncila* had to publish a denial.

Other foreign periodicals jumped on the bandwagon, the *Croix du Midi* spicing its remarks with elaborate sarcasm:

> Well, it had always taken some swallowing. There she was, the not usually very talkative Virgin Mary, chatting away every evening to four or five Yugoslav kids. And those secrets! Strewth! – I know something you don't know, and I'm not telling you! It was so ridiculous that the local bishop, after an inquiry, is now talking of "collective hallucination" and "fraud". But Laurentin's all right: his book has already sold out!

"Lord, forgive your Church for its impostures, above all for the apparitions at Medjugorje," prayed a French priest at Mass.

In one adroit move, Bishop Žanić had all but swept his opponents from the board, dealing Medjugorje a far more effective blow than the Marxists had ever managed. Yet his triumph was not unalloyed, for the strident, polemical tone of his document had alienated not a few who might otherwise have supported him. They resented the gratuitous insults hurled at the defenceless Vlašić – and at the internationally renowned Laurentin. They deplored the lack of balance, the wilful disregard of the graces and strengths that so many had found in Medjugorje. If the tree was so palpably rotten, how come it produced such excellent fruit? It was clear to all but the most purblind that the document revealed nothing so much as Žanić's mounting obsession with the Hercegovina issue. In his view, everything that happened in Medjugorje could be reduced to the simple syllogism: the Virgin of Medjugorje has spoken against the bishop, who represents the authority of the Church; therefore it is impossible that such a subversive and wrong-headed oracle could actually be the Virgin Mary.

It was left to the eminent Swiss theologian, Hans Urs von Balthasar, to voice the not inconsiderable disquiet. On 12th December 1984, in an open letter to Bishop Žanić, he wrote:

> My Lord, what a sorry document you have sent throughout the world! I have been deeply pained to see the episcopal office degraded in this manner. Instead of biding your time, as you were recommended to do by higher authority, you fulminate and hurl thunderbolts like Jupiter. While

you denigrate renowned people who are innocent, deserving of your respect and protection, you bring out accusations that have been refuted a hundred times over.[6]

To Laurentin, von Balthasar expressed his horror at the slanders thrown at Vlašić: "Father Tomislav," he wrote, "seems to me a model of humility, of deep wisdom, of discretion, a man whose obedience is nothing less than heroic. He is a true Christian man of God."

Archbishop Franić also sprang to the rescue. He had little to lose, since he had already come under heavy fire – both from Rome and within Yugoslavia – for his championship of the apparitions. Through the children, Our Lady had foretold that he would have to suffer much; and it seemed to him that her words were coming true. In an interview for *Glas Koncila*, he expressed his personal satisfaction that, in spite of everything, pilgrims kept coming to Medjugorje, since he for one was totally convinced that Our Lady was appearing there. He spoke of the boost to ecumenism, of the "real faith, real Church, real Pentecost" he had found. "It is a profound voice which transcends the littleness of human politics," he said:

> Our Lady said the same things at Lourdes and Fatima, but people in the West have short memories. They arm to the teeth, in order to achieve supremacy over Eastern Europe, and they call that preserving the peace. But the peace they preserve is not the peace of Christ. Christ's peace is a peace of heart and conscience, a total peace made up of truth, justice and love. It is a peace of soul which involves satisfying all legitimate human needs, whether personal or social, just as Christ's redemption was for the whole man, to set him free from all his burdens – spiritual, corporal, material and social – and from all forms of oppression and slavery.

But Medjugorje did not appeal to simple people alone, said Franić, recalling the huge numbers of teachers, doctors, politicians who had visited him on their way home:

> Am I to say to these intellectuals, theologians, specialists, that their prayer, their confession, their conversion, are the work of the Devil? That seems to me absurd. And it is no less absurd, in my opinion, to put a stop to the pilgrimages.

Of course there were faults to be found, he admitted; there were indeed discrepancies in the visionaries' stories. But these were not reason enough to condemn them as frauds. The visionaries were only intermediaries, the messages they received had to be filtered through their own subjective interpretation. He believed them to be essentially truthful, and denied that they could be hallucinating: after the three years that had gone by, they would by now have been in a state of nervous collapse. If indeed they *had* been hallucinating over such a long period, then the clear evidence of their sound mental health must be a miracle in itself.

Franić's increasing impatience with both sides in the clerical dispute was obvious:

> I believe that justice demands that the Holy See be obeyed, that agreement be reached and that some of the disputed parishes be handed over to the bishop. I believe that the two Franciscans who have been expelled from the Order should submit and begin seeking ways of rehabilitating themselves . . . This outcome would certainly be pleasing to Our Lady. But human weakness is at stake here.

In France, *La Croix*, which had so eagerly broadcast Bishop Žanić's anathemas, reported (15th December 1984) merely that the Archbishop of Split was apparently in favour of Medjugorje. After that, no article favourable to Medjugorje appeared in France until June 1985 when *Paris Match* reported on the tests carried out on the visionaries by Professor Henri Joyeux and his team.

Žanić scornfully attributed the archbishop's eccentric views to a recent enthusiasm for the charismatic movement. He was sufficiently alarmed, however, to ask Cardinal Casaroli of the Secretariat of State to stop Franić interfering. Whereupon Franić referred the matter even higher, to Casaroli's chief, Cardinal Ratzinger, putting the case for the apparitions, noting the "large number of authenticated cures", defending the Franciscans, and pleading in his turn for something to be done to stop Bishop Žanić.

> An international Commission should be set up, to stop the Bishop of Mostar forbidding all pilgrimages to Medjugorje – which would cause great scandal not only in Yugoslavia but throughout the world . . . Medjugorje belongs not only to the Church in Yugoslavia but to the universal Church.

Both men were warned by the Vatican to stop making inflammatory public statements which raised temperatures all round and caused opinions to become polarised. It was said that when a group of reformed drug addicts had arrived in Mostar *en route* for Medjugorje, the Vicar-General of the diocese had told the priest in charge: "From the moment you so much as set foot in that Medjugorje coach, you are excommunicated." Though the Vicar-General firmly denied he had said anything so improbable the rumours persisted.

The diocesan Commission met again in Mostar on 7th–8th March 1985. On the night of the seventh they were present during an apparition in Medjugorje, though they remained completely detached and sceptical about the whole occurrence. "What message has Tomislav Vlašić told you to put in the Virgin Mary's mouth today?" they sneeringly asked the visionaries.

The children were hurt by these cynical remarks. When two Italian doctors arrived next day to carry out tests, Marija, Ivanka, Ivan and Jakov were too upset to see them. Dr Frigerio and his colleague went to see Vicka at home, and fitted her with a laryngophone, a device to enable those who have lost their voice to be heard. The experiment was not a success. Vicka's apparition lasted only twenty-two seconds, and though the instrument registered a positive result, it was undecipherable. According to Vicka, the Madonna had greeted her, then, with a glance at the laryngophone, had said: "There's no need for that thing," and disappeared.

Nor did the doctors have much better luck on the following day when Ivan allowed them to apply a stapedio – to explore the mechanisms of the inner ear. As the apparition began, and Ivan fell to his knees, the stapedio dropped off.

In May, Professor Giorgio Sanguinati, a teacher of psychiatry in Milan's Faculty of Criminal Anthropology, published a report on clinical observations he had made in Medjugorje in April. "Neither before, during nor after the apparition," he said, "did I find any trace – in gesture, behaviour or word – of psycho-pathology, whether delirium, hallucination or hysteria."[7]

But, unfortunately for the advocates of Medjugorje, events were playing into Bishop Žanić's hands. He was temporarily delivered from the scourge of Laurentin's presence when the latter was arrested at Dubrovnik airport carrying "subversive" (i.e. about Medjugorje) literature and banned from Yugoslavia for twelve months.[8] Even more importantly, his charge that the visionaries were liars had received a fresh impetus.

On 7th March 1985, three members of the episcopal Commission asked Ivan directly if what he had written on the paper in the sealed envelope really concerned the Sign. "No," said Ivan. They then opened the envelope and found the paper headed: "Declaration of visionary concerning the sign to be given by the Blessed Virgin at Medjugorje. "What sign will the Virgin leave?" went the question. And Ivan had clearly replied: "The Blessed Virgin has said that she will leave a Sign . . . There is to be a great shrine dedicated to her in Medjugorje in honour of her apparitions there." "When will this Sign come about?" Answer: "In the sixth month." Signed, Ivan Dragicević.

There was no escaping the disgrace. Fra Slavko Barbarić (another *bête noire* of Bishop Žanić, who wanted him removed from Medjugorje) went to investigate.[9] Ivan was at home, working on his family's farm. After three months in the seminary, said Ivan, he had told the Madonna he could stand no more; and she had told him to pack his bags and leave. "I know why you're here," he said when Fra Slavko found him, standing in front of Vicka's gate. "The Commissioners have opened the envelope and found something there. But it isn't the Sign, and I didn't reveal the date."

"How do you know that's why I've come?" demanded Slavko.

"Because the Lady told me you were coming," Ivan replied. "She was angry with me for what I did." And the boy wept with shame.

"Only prayer will undo Ivan's silly mistake," the Lady reportedly told Vicka. "He should have written nothing, and told everyone so. Then there could have been no doubt."

Slavko tried again on 16th March, when all five visionaries came at nine o'clock to begin a day of prayer. Marija and Vicka had both been ill that winter. Marija, suffering from overwork and excessive fasting, had pains all down the left side of her body; and Slavko had now persuaded her to cut down on the fasting. Vicka had undergone emergency surgery for peritonitis in December; and in the course of that operation, the surgeons had discovered an intestinal tumour. She was also suffering from continual violent headaches.

This day was no exception. As soon as she arrived at the clergy house, she was prostrated by a violent headache and had to lie down. It was not till the afternoon that Slavko could put his questions to all of them together:[10]

"Did Ivan write about the Sign?"

"Did he reveal the date?"

"Does Ivan really see the apparitions?"

Ivan and Marija both answered "No" to the first two questions, but Vicka, Ivanka and Jakov were unsure. All five, however, answered the third question with a "Yes". (Appearing to Mirjana on her birthday on 18th March, the Madonna said, "It wasn't Ivan's fault. I've scolded him enough now. Let him alone.")

A report on the Commission's latest session, published in *Glas Koncila* on 24th March, made no reference to the Ivan affair, though it covered a wide range of subjects. There were practical matters, such as the attitude of Archbishop Franić; the general criticism of the Commission's membership; the theological problems involved; and the continuing problem of the two expelled Franciscans. But they could not ignore the apocalyptic dimension of Medjugorje: the alleged power of Satan over the world; the threat of imminent catastrophe; the secret signs. The Commission had also discussed the growth of charismatic practices, prayers and hymns among the foreign prayer-groups pouring into Medjugorje. No conclusion had been reached on any of these matters.

When Fr Robert Faricy asked the bishop what would happen if the Commission failed to reach agreement, "[he] replied that the judgement of events at Medjugorje would not come from the Commission but from him, and that he had already made up his mind that the Blessed Virgin was not appearing in Medjugorje".[11]

The bishop wasted no time. On 25th March, the Feast of the Annunciation of the Blessed Virgin, Žanić wrote to Tomislav Pervan, demanding to know why he had taken no steps to "cool and eventually extinguish" events in his parish, as he had been instructed six months ago. The time for compromise was now past, and the following eight demands were to be implemented immediately.

> The visionaries were to make no further public appearances.
>
> There were to be no more apparitions in the church. ("Let them stay at home and see their visions.")
>
> The new statue of Our Lady, fashioned according to the children's description of her, was to be taken down from its place in front of the altar and replaced by the original statue.
>
> There was to be no more mention of the apparitions in homilies, no more passing on of "messages".
>
> Pious practices and devotions related to the apparitions were to stop.
>
> No souvenirs or publications aimed at spreading the cult of Our Lady of Medjugorje were to be put on sale. Mass might still be celebrated and confessions be heard, however.
>
> Fras Jozo Zovko, Tomislav Vlašić and Ljudevit Rupčić were henceforth banned from celebrating Mass or preaching in the parish of Medjugorje.
>
> The visionaries were to hand over to the diocesan authorities everything they had ever written down about the apparitions.

It was a devastating blow for the Franciscans, torn between obedience to the bishop and the pastoral realities of their extraordinary parish. Were they to bow to this legitimate but indisputably fallible authority, or keep faith with what they believed was divine revelation?

Their decision was never really in doubt, the only question being how they might abide by the letter of Žanić's demands while still preserving the spirit of Medjugorje intact. In the end, they agreed to stop the children leading the prayers in the church (the seven Our Fathers, Hail Marys and Glorias that preceded the nightly apparitions). If they came to the church, it would be as private individuals with no special privileges. The ban on the three priests was similarly accepted, though reluctantly: a parish with the special needs of Medjugorje required many more priests than were available; and the loss of three valuable extra hands would be painful. The new statue was obediently relegated to the small apparitions room; the number of saleable artefacts was reduced; and the messages would henceforth be written down rather than spoken. As for the sermons, if the bishop had done his homework properly, he would have realised that they contained very few references to the apparitions, being mainly about Christ, about the Gospel message of reconciliation and conversion.

Where could the children go for the evening apparition, now that they were banned from the church? (There was an undeniable irony in the thought that it was the Marxist authorities who had originally driven them into the church, and the bishop who was now driving them out!) The astute Slavko Barbarić (with the approval of Archbishop Franić) solved that one. Despite the bishop's continuing relentless pressure on the Franciscan Provincial to remove him from Medjugorje, the multi-lingual Slavko was far too valuable an asset to be disposed of lightly; and for the time being there was a stay of execution. At Slavko's suggestion, the children were transferred to his own study-bedroom in the clergy house. In this way, the bishop was technically obeyed, while the children were afforded protection both from the unmanageable crowds and the police.

In April, at the Yugoslav Bishops' conference, of which he was currently chairman, Archbishop Franić and his adversary battled it out for half an hour on the subject of Medjugorje. The archbishop was particularly incensed by Bishop Žanić's unsubtle attempts to lay hands on Vicka's "secret diaries":

> The Bishop of Mostar has ordered the Franciscans to extinguish the pilgrimages and suchlike at Medjugorje; and the visionaries to hand over all written material, even when this involves the secrets. No bishop is entitled to make such a demand. He has no right to force matters of conscience to be revealed.[12]

In any case, as Vicka told René Laurentin, she had already handed over everything she could: "I have nothing to hide. But I have always told you there are some things I am not at liberty to divulge." By this she meant the secrets, and the "Life" which the Madonna had recently finished relating to her. Feeling a little better, Vicka had gone down to the apparitions room with the others from 7th–9th April, (the beginning of Holy Week) but on the tenth the headaches and the comas that now accompanied them had returned. The apparition which she had at home that same day lasted for twenty-five minutes, and apparently covered the last episodes in the life of the Madonna. ("She talked a lot about her childhood," said Vicka, "and a lot about Jesus. But she didn't say much about Joseph. Perhaps that's because there isn't a great deal to say about him."[13]) On the following day, during an eleven-minute apparition, the Lady authorised her to hand the account to an as yet unspecified Franciscan with a view to eventual publication. There was no question of handing it over to Bishop Žanić.

Vicka's personal dilemma echoed that of the Franciscans. How could they obey a bishop who was ordering them to betray the spiritual renewal which they saw all around them? On 6th April, they wrote to Rome for guidance. True to form, they did not get a reply. Two months later, it was announced in Rome that Archbishop Alberto Bovone, Secretary for the Congregation for the Doctrine of Faith (whose head was Cardinal Ratzinger) had asked the Italian bishops "publicly to discourage the organisation of pilgrimages and all other forms of propaganda for Medjugorje". The archbishop referred approvingly to Bishop Žanić's efforts, saying that such propaganda caused "confusion among the faithful" and hindered the investigations being conducted by the Church.

Was this the end of Medjugorje? Would this disclaimer be the *coup de grâce* for what Archbishop Franić had called "the dynamic of pilgrimages"? It appeared not. Five days later, on 25th June, over 50,000 people streamed in to Medjugorje for the fourth anniversary of the apparitions, during which Mass was concelebrated by sixty priests of various nationalities (forty of them Italian). The British journalist, Mary Kenny, probably summed up the general feeling of those present:

> Whether the apparitions at Medjugorje are pronounced genuine or not almost became irrelevant for me; pragmatically, I felt, whatever it is that is present here, it works. There is a holiness, a simplicity and an energy that is felt and transmitted. We learn and feel things in mysterious ways, and I am content to leave it at that.[14]

15

Miracles or Illusions?

> He comes to us as one unknown, without a name, as of old, by the lakeside, He came to those men who knew Him not. He speaks to us with the same word: Follow thou me! and sets us to the tasks which He has to fulfil for our time. He commands. And to those who obey Him, whether they be wise or simple, He will reveal Himself in the toils, the conflicts, the sufferings which they shall pass through in His fellowship, and, as an ineffable mystery, they shall learn in their own experience, who He is.
>
> Albert Schweitzer, *The Quest of the Historical Jesus*

Politicians, even at the federal level of Belgrade, were waking up to the advantages of such massive international interest centred on Yugoslavia. "There are a lot of people here, perfectly good Socialists," a journalist friend told Gitta Sereny,[1] "who would welcome any decrease in isolation, any opening of doors, any opportunity for all people to reaffirm their moral independence." By that summer of 1985, daily tour buses were coming to Medjugorje from other parts of Yugoslavia – not by any means from all, since the amount of flexibility depended on the degree of ideological fervour in the local authority. Drivers of these transports were both apprehensive and curious about what they might find. "I half-believed I'd see something special, maybe even the Blessed Virgin," confided Vito, a driver from the state tourist agency, Kompas:

> but I also half-believed it was all a hoax. Well, I saw the sun spinning, but there didn't seem anything religious about it. I told myself it was probably due to humidity caused by the air evaporating over the mountains. So, as I say, I went prepared for anything – or nothing – and what I found there was peace. It was very impressive. I suppose most people come looking for one particular thing, and go away with something quite different. But most of them seem to find this peace, this feeling of being completely relaxed.

Medjugorje had changed little in the course of four years and nearly 2,000 visions. Unlike Lourdes, with its 204 hotels, the village was still what it had always been, a cluster of houses indistinguishable from any other village. "The sweet peasant ladies who offer you such hospitality," wrote

Mary Kenny, "have a picture of Tito in the front hall, and Our Lady, Jesus at Gethsemane and the Holy Family in the back bedroom."[2] To serve its 10,000 pilgrims a day, the village still had only "a hole in the ground, into which an unending stream of urine and excrement is deposited". The offer of a rich American pilgrim to have toilet facilities constructed at his own expense was still being rejected by the politicos. "If they were ever to agree, that really would be a major miracle," laughed Slavko Barbarić.

By this time between two and three million pilgrims had visited Medjugorje. For many the primitiveness and lack of strident commercialism – the first stalls were only now putting in a tentative appearance, and there was not as yet even any holy water on sale – was blessing rather than blight. It was, wrote Delia Smith, "a far cry from the contrived showiness of unauthentic holiness".[3] Obeying that powerful urge of the human spirit to transcend itself, people were coming to Medjugorje seeking to escape, however briefly, from the pain or boredom of their own lives. The protestations of the Bishop of Mostar were an irrelevance. It was, as Shelley had put it:

> The desire of the moth for the star,
> Of the night for the morrow,
> The devotion to something afar
> From the sphere of our sorrow.

By far the largest number came by bus: sometimes up to a hundred buses a day would crawl through Medjugorje's inadequate streets. Some, like the Italians, could cover the entire journey in their pilgrimage buses, with a short ferry trip in the middle. The Portuguese came by bus too, flying first from Lisbon to Milan or Trieste. Other foreigners would fly to Split or Dubrovnik and get a bus; or arrive by rail at Mostar, Čapljina or Čitluk and take a taxi. By this time there had been pilgrims from as far afield as Japan, Korea, Israel, Vietnam, the Philippines, Egypt, the Ivory Coast, Zaire, the Caribbean islands, Haiti, Brazil, Nicaragua, Argentina, Uruguay, Peru, the Dominican Republic and Mexico. Pilgrims from Communist Hungary came for the most part as individuals, except for one coach-load that had somehow slipped through the net in 1984. Hungarians would join an officially-sponsored shopping-weekend to Yugoslavia, do their shopping at record speed and fit in a lightning visit to Medjugorje.

And there were also those who came in the time-honoured way of all pilgrims since pilgrimages first started in the Middle Ages. At least 3,000 had walked over 100 kilometres to get there, fasting on bread and water all the way. Some had taken ten days to walk from Zagreb, or two weeks from Austria, even four weeks from Mainz in West Germany. It had taken one young man from Belgium forty-nine days to cover the distance to Medjugorje.

Some few, like the artistic and multi-lingual Austrian, Milona von Habsburg, came to stay permanently. "Medjugorje acted on me like an electric shock," she says:

> I'd lost my faith, or at least everything that until then I had called faith. I was plunging down into emptiness, with the taste of humiliation in my mouth. But somehow there, something new and alive warmed my heart. I made up my mind to go back to Medjugorje and look for God there. You have to give up your own pre-conceived ideas in order to discover what God really is.

Beyond question, many came looking for miracle cures. "We are such poor creatures," sighed Bishop Žanić. "We need to go looking for miracles where there are none." Cures continued to be reported; and the bishop continued to denounce them as illusions. The Franciscans at Medjugorje noted all the cases in a book, and asked for further medical documentation to be sent in. But the member of the bishop's Commission who was detailed to investigate the cures did not even ask to see the written record.

It is hard, if not impossible, to provide satisfactory scientific proof of a miracle. In Lourdes, it has usually taken anything from six to thirteen years for a cure to be authenticated; and over a period of 130 years only sixty-four cases were accepted as genuine cures. It may well prove to be the same with Medjugorje. But a balance must somehow be struck – between the necessary patient and hard-headed search for empirical proof, and the actual joy that is brought into the life of a person who believes himself or herself cured. Human beings, despite the scientific advances of the twentieth century, are still more than statistics.

Of the fifty-six original cases reported in Laurentin's book, nine were said by Dr Mangiapan of the Lourdes Medical Bureau to be worthy of further study. "A good score," he wrote to Laurentin. Nevertheless, in the April 1984 issue of the *Bulletin of the Lourdes International Medical Association*, Dr Mangiapan deplored the lack of acceptable hard evidence. The cures claimed had not been confirmed by an independent medical examination:

> Rarely is the duration of the cure mentioned . . . [nor] are the treatment, the diagnosis or the grounds for any prognosis indicated. In conclusion, if we are to follow the norms of this Bureau, the entire dossier is of no practical value and as such would give no grounds for an argument in favour of the apparitions.[4]

Bishop Žanić was delighted to endorse this final sentence of Dr Mangiapan's otherwise carefully encouraging report. With a fine disregard for the general context, he claimed that the doctor's considered verdict was "completely negative".

In his *Posizione* of November 1984, Žanić milked this "completely negative" line for all it was worth, referring to a handful of "cures" which had turned out badly: a child who had died after being promised a cure; a young woman who had died after being advised by the visionaries not to have a mastectomy; a Franciscan who had died of cancer, although his mother had been promised that he would recover. The visionaries protested that they had never promised anyone anything: they had merely said that prayer and fasting were capable of accomplishing miracles.

More aggressively, Bishop Žanić referred to the case of Marco Blažević, who had died during heart surgery in June 1984, after being assured by the visionary, Ivan, that the operation would be successful. Melanie, the man's daughter, protested that she had merely asked Ivan to pray for her father.[5] But her written disclaimer only urged the bishop to a fresh outburst of cynicism:

> The daughter of the late Blažević, no doubt instructed by Tomislav Vlašić, confirms that she was at Medjugorje and asked a question about her father. She now expects us to believe that though the visionaries instructed her to pray for her father throughout the operation, they nevertheless made no mention of its possible outcome.[6]

Žanić, complained Laurentin,[7] was determined to focus on the failures, while ignoring the successes. Why did he continue to state that no medical evidence was available, when he had medical evidence in abundance? Dr Ludvik Stopar, the Slovenian psychiatrist and parapsychologist, had submitted three full dossiers to the bishop. These related to:

> Maria Brumec who had had a fractured spine. All treatment had failed and she had been told she would be an invalid for the rest of her life. On pilgrimage to Medjugorje, on 8th August 1983, she was instantly and inexplicably cured.
> Damir Corić (see p. 161), a hydrocephalic youth, for whom the possibility of a cure seemed nil, had been cured instantly in the summer of 1981, after Vicka had prayed for him.
> Iva Tole, a multiple-sclerosis sufferer, who had been carried into the church at Medjugorje on 13th September 1981, and later that same day had climbed the hill of Križevac for the annual Mass celebrated on the Sunday nearest to the Feast of the Exaltation of the Cross.

Yet Dr Stopar had received no acknowledgment of his dossiers from the bishop; and the latter spoke as though they did not exist. Why, asked Laurentin, did the medical members of the episcopal Commission not investigate these and similar cases for themselves, if indeed they were not satisfied with the evidence available? There was no sign that they had done or were about to do so.

Other doctors, notably Dr L. Frigerio and his colleagues at the Specialist Clinical Institute of Milan, were, however, showing a keener interest. They had compiled a dossier of 143 items on the cure of a forty-three-year-old Italian secretary and mother of three sons, Diana Basile. Multiple sclerosis had been diagnosed in 1972. Signora Basile suffered from total urinary incontinence – which caused perineal dermatitis; was blind in one eye, and could walk only with difficulty. In January 1984 all this was compounded by a severe clinical depression, as her physical condition continued to deteriorate. In May a colleague in the office where Signora Basile had worked suggested that she should join a group going from Milan to Medjugorje.

On the evening of 23rd May, she was in the church and a friend, Signora Novella, helped her to climb the steps up to the apparitions room:

> At that point I no longer wanted to enter the room . . . [but] the door was opened and I went in. I knelt just behind the door. When the children came in and knelt down . . . I heard a loud noise. After that I remember nothing, except an indescribable joy and certain forgotten episodes of my life passing before my eyes as though on film. When it was all over, I followed the children, who went straight to the main altar in the church. I was walking just like everybody else, and I knelt down just as they did. It didn't actually occur to me that anything extraordinary had happened, until Signora Novella came up to me in tears.

The cure had been instantaneous. On the pilgrimage bus returning her to the hotel in Ljubuški, the other pilgrims embraced her and wept with amazement. That evening, Signora Basile found that she was no longer incontinent, and the dermatitis had completely disappeared. Her right eye, useless for twelve years, had regained perfect vision – even better than that of the left eye which was only ninety per cent good. Next day she walked the ten kilometres from the hotel at Ljubuški to the church at Medjugorje – barefoot. As if that were not enough, in the afternoon she climbed the rocky path up the hill of apparitions.

When Bishop Žanić heard about Diana Basile, he professed amazement at the absence of any certificate authenticating the cure. Dr Frigerio accordingly sent him a dossier which already contained over 100 items. (Later there would be many more.) The bishop objected that he had not seen the woman in person. So Signora Basile returned to Yugoslavia and went to Mostar to see him; only to find that he had gone away. The Vicar-General received her, and gave her the routine bland assurance that the Church must exercise great caution before pronouncing on a cure.

Žanić sent the dossier to the Lourdes Medical Bureau, and thereafter was able to refer to certain negative comments made by Dr Mangiapan:

> that multiple sclerosis is notoriously difficult to diagnose, the only real proof being afforded by a post-mortem autopsy;
>
> that it would take at least three or four years before judgement could be arrived at;
>
> that the bishop should exercise great caution in either approving or denying the alleged miracle.[8]

The Milan doctors, however, not all of them believers, considered that the signs – and the tests so far carried out – pointed to Signora Basile having multiple sclerosis; and that there was no conceivable explanation for what had happened. Her case is still under investigation.

In Bishop Žanić's judgement, Dr Mangiapan had rejected all the supposed cures of Medjugorje; and he accused René Laurentin of ignoring Mangiapan's report of April 1984. But Laurentin, whose book was published in February of that year, had been sent an advance rough draft of the report by Mangiapan himself, and had incorporated both its positive and negative elements in his own book.[9] He had asked Mangiapan to comment on the list of fifty-four cures originally drawn up by Father Rupčić. Whereupon the doctor had suggested his eliminating all those cases which were not easily verifiable by medical science: as, for example, the curing of persistent alcoholism. He made the fair comment that without exhaustive documentation about relevant medical tests, the cures had no credibility. But, Dr Mangiapan admitted, thirty-three of the cases were at least interesting and might merit further research. All this Laurentin had duly reported. The bishop, however, had ignored Mangiapan's main directive: that a serious investigation should be undertaken.

In any case, in a later (still 1984) edition of *Is the Virgin Mary Appearing at Medjugorje?* Laurentin had reproduced Dr Mangiapan's report in full. He adds that one of the doctors on the episcopal Commission, and one only, came to Medjugorje in the summer of 1984. He came on his own initiative, somewhat embarrassed that he had not been asked to go there in an official capacity.

Fra Jozo Zovko, exiled now to Tihaljina, expressed his conviction that the greatest miracle was the interior one. He told of two Italian women who had arrived in their wheel-chairs:

> The elder of the two women was healed. The younger, Manuela, remained in her wheel-chair. The one who was healed returned home, delighted at being able to walk again; Manuela stayed behind to give thanks and praise to God. They had both come with the desire to be healed, and they were

both healed. But healing is not only physical, it is something that takes place in the heart. Manuela was healed in her heart. Full of joy, she praised God for having come to her, for shedding light on the cross she carried, for showing her its value and meaning. She understood that from her wheel-chair she could bring people spiritual solace, telling them about the love of God, about goodness, about the wisdom that patience can bring. Manuela took a far greater joy home in her heart than the woman who went home able to walk. The Church was grateful for both blessings. Deeply grateful.[10]

Even for sceptical theologians, if there is a miracle of Medjugorje, it can be found in the outpouring of faith that the Virgin has inspired – from the heart of a Marxist society. All the rest, says Fra Ivo Marković, a Professor of Theology at the Franciscan seminary in Sarajevo, dismissing the visions and the prophecies along with the signs, is "kitsch". For Laurentin, however, "all the rest" is a test of faith: modern Catholic scholars, he believes, are too sophisticated to accept evidence of the miraculous. "In the prevalent deterministic atmosphere", he told an American reporter,[11] "God seems forbidden to perform any miracles at all."

16

A Time of Grace

And in the silent, sometimes hardly moving times
when something is coming near,
I want to be with those who know secret things
or else alone.

Rainer Maria Rilke

Just over a month before the fourth anniversary in June 1985, Ivanka received the tenth secret, and with it her regular apparitions came to an end. At six o'clock on 6th May, she, Marija, Ivan and Jakov had all as usual reached Medjugorje. (Vicka's health had deteriorated yet again and more often than not she was seeing the apparition in front of a home-made altar in her own bedroom.) In the clergy house, Marija's, Ivan's and Jakov's apparition lasted two minutes; and when they stood up, they were astonished to see Ivanka still on her knees. It was the first time they had ever seen one of their number in ecstasy, and they were quite alarmed by the spectacle. Ivanka remained kneeling and abstracted for a further six minutes, as the others watched and waited. When she finally got to her feet, it was to say in a flat voice: "*Gospa* has finished giving me the messages about the future of the world. She has told me the tenth secret, and my apparitions are over. But, as from next year, I shall see her once a year on the anniversary day. Tomorrow she will come at the same time – not here, but at home, to say goodbye."

"May we all come?" asked Slavko.

"No, she wants to see me alone."

Next day, Tuesday, Ivanka's apparition lasted for an hour. As she described it later to Slavko:

> I had never seen her so beautiful – she wore the loveliest dress I have ever seen. Her dress, her veil, her crown cast reflections of gold and silver. Two angels were with her, in similar dress. It was so beautiful I can't begin to describe it. You'd have to have seen it to be able to understand.

Ivanka asked the Lady if she might see her mother:

> *Gospa* smiled agreement. And suddenly my mother was there, also smiling. *Gospa* told me to stand up. I did so, Mama took me in her arms, kissed me

and vanished. Then *Gospa* said: My dear child, this is our last meeting. But don't be sad: I'll come back each year except this one on the anniversary . . . Don't go imagining you've offended me in some way, it's nothing like that. You have accepted my Son's plans with all your heart, and have carried them out faithfully. Few people on this earth have known the grace which you and your friends have been given. So, be happy: I am your mother who loves you. Thank you, Ivanka, for responding to my Son's call, thank you for persevering, thank you for staying with him . . . Tell all your friends that my Son and I are always near them when they call us. Do not reveal any of the secrets, until I give you permission.

I then asked *Gospa* if I could embrace her. She nodded, and I did so. She blessed me, smiled and said "Go now, in the peace of God."

"How do you feel?" asked a sympathetic friend. "Lonely," replied Ivanka. "Even lonelier than after my mother died."

It was rumoured that Ivanka, like Mirjana, had received from the Lady a paper or piece of material with the secrets written on it. Not so, as Ivanka told René Laurentin: the Lady had merely taught her a code in which to transcribe the secrets safely. Mirjana, however, claimed to have been given a "paper" inscribed with all ten secrets. As she told a group of Italian pilgrims on 25th June 1985:

> It is of an indescribable material. It seems like paper but it isn't; it seems like material, but it isn't. It's visible, you can touch it but not see the writing on it. My cousin, an engineer in Switzerland, has examined the stuff but can't identify it. When the right moment comes, I am to give it to a specially chosen priest, who will then be given the grace to read only the first secret from it.

Since her regular apparitions ceased, at Christmas 1982, Mirjana had made only rare visits to Medjugorje. For two years she had been immersed in the secular atmosphere of the city of Sarajevo, relentlessly shadowed by the secret police. On her coming-of-age eighteenth birthday, 18th March 1983, she was detained in police custody all day until nine-thirty in the evening. The Madonna, she said, "was waiting" when she eventually got home. But for the rest of that year and part of the next, she had no apparition to console her, the Madonna reappearing only towards the end of 1984. In September 1984, Mirjana said, the Madonna shed tears for all the unbelief in the world, but said that prayer and fasting had already toned down the awfulness of the seventh secret. At Christmas the Madonna told her that the time for revealing the first secret was fast approaching, and promised to speak to her (though not to appear) again in February. In February 1985 the Lady spoke to Mirjana for twenty minutes, and promised a proper three-dimensional visit for the girl's twentieth birthday on 18th March. On that day: "After wishing me a happy birthday, she began to speak again about unbelievers. They are all my children, she said. I suffer for their sake, they do not know what lies in store for them if they refuse to make the inner change. Pray for them, Mirjana . . . Tell everyone to pray."

Mirjana had prepared a thousand questions to ask, but the vision quickly silenced her: "When you need to know the answers, I shall tell you," she said.

At the end of August 1985, Jakov revealed that Mirjana had made her choice of priest. The task of revealing the first secret to the world had fallen on another young Franciscan, who was shortly afterwards transferred to Medjugorje, thirty-nine-year-old Fra Pero Ljubičić. "It looks," said Fra Pero calmly, "as though the first secret will be very disturbing." In September, Mirjana heard the Lady's voice promising to appear to her on 25th October and asking for Fra Pero to be present. Mirjana reported that the Lady again wept for sinners and showed her, as though on a filmed sequence, the coming revelation of the first secret, the chaos and desolation that would ensue. Mirjana wept too. Why so soon? she asked.

"Because there is so much sin in the world."

"But can God have so hard a heart?"

"God's heart is not hard. Look around you and see how people behave. How can you say it is God who is hard-hearted?"

"The time that remains is a time of grace," the apparition told Mirjana. "Use it well and change your lives." The visionary stressed the mounting urgency of the Madonna's plea. The time of grace would be followed by:

> the time of purification which will end with the third warning, that is to say, with the visible sign to the world. When this sign appears, no one will any longer doubt that God truly exists. But it will be too late then for conversions: the encounter with divine reality will be catastrophic for those who have not already turned towards God. But for those who have done so, it will be a time of great joy.

Mirjana was given more warning visions in November and December. Yet she continued to insist that there was no need for fear and despondency. "If we love God, it is obvious that no evil can befall us." In a fleeting visit to Medjugorje, Tomislav Vlašić attempted to interpret such apparently unjustifiable optimism. The coming revelations, he explained, were not to be understood apocalyptically; on the contrary, they were an invitation to love, to accept the will of God in all humility, joyfulness and hope. Speaking also to René Laurentin, Mirjana reiterated this view: the secrets were not all sad, and God would not abandon any who wanted Him. "Why have the apparitions gone on so long," Laurentin asked her, voicing a question that was turning many one-time sympathisers into sceptics, "and why the delay in announcing the secrets?"

"It is because so few have changed their lives," said Mirjana. "There are more unbelievers than ever."

"So the delay is a merciful one?" pressed the Frenchman.

"Yes."[1]

Vicka, having come to the end of the Virgin's life-story, had begun (on 17th April 1985) receiving revelations about the future of the world. She was more than ever troubled by violent headaches and sudden black-outs, though still smiling and saying she was perfectly all right. In spite of frequent medical check-ups at the Rebro Clinic in Zagreb, doctors were mystified as to the specific nature of her illness. They had offered pills, and suggested that she should rest more and fast less.

"Why don't you ask the Madonna to cure you?" asked friends. But this she would never do. "The Madonna and I know the reason, and it doesn't concern the rest of you," she once told an anxious priest, adding: "I've already told you how she taught me to offer up my sufferings for the conversion of sinners, and to leave the rest to her." Vicka had learned to see her sufferings as redemptive, to be accepted cheerfully and endured for the sake of others. "I am glad," she said, "to be able to endure what He sends me, with love. I can only be grateful for it." She had made an unconditional gift of her life to God – and indeed she seemed to have more dread of the apparitions coming to an end than of the death that always lurked in wait for her.

In view of Vicka's declining health, it was no longer possible for her to receive the groups of visiting pilgrims. Hitherto, they had arrived in a steady stream all day, draining her, leaving her little time for work in the fields or even for snatching a bite to eat. Unlike the other visionaries, she had seemed not to feel the need for peace and quiet – although she admitted to a Franciscan friend that she felt "torn apart": "People come, they settle in the house, they wait . . . I come home, I talk with them for a bit."[2]

It didn't end there. In the evening after Mass, the visionaries would stay behind, to pray over and with the sick pilgrims, especially those in wheel-chairs: "After the prayers, each of them wants to talk a bit, tell their troubles. What can you do? What can those poor people do? You have to listen to everyone . . . It's exhausting, but that doesn't really matter."[3]

From the summer of 1985, though Vicka still made every effort to be available to those who wanted her, the role of pilgrims' confidante was increasingly taken over by Marija. Quieter and more subdued than Vicka, in many ways she was the most compellingly attractive of them all. The life of this shy and gentle girl had been turned upside down by the apparitions. "What did they change for you?" Laurentin once asked her. "Absolutely everything," she replied. Interviewed by the producer of a BBC film unit, she was more explicit:

Before the visions, whenever I gave any thought to the future, I assumed I'd finish school, pass my qualifying exams, get a job, get married, have a family. At school I studied to be a hairdresser, and I enjoyed that; though what I'd really wanted to do was floristry. I adore flowers and love handling them. But that wouldn't have been possible. I'd have had to go to Sarajevo, and it was much too far.

Anyway, suddenly everything changed. I now have only one ambition: to live as God wants me to live. I want to pay back as much as I can, to give back something of all He's given me.

Unlike Vicka who loved the Rosary but who confessed to being "not very good at contemplation", Marija preferred silent meditation to more mechanical forms of prayer. She responded to silence, loving to get up early and see the sun rise over Križevac. "The sun rises in my own heart too. I think God gives special gifts to those who pray."

Deep though her inner spirituality undoubtedly was, Marija's feet remained firmly planted on the ground. In many ways her life was still that of a Hercegovinan peasant girl. "When I've done the housework, I put the sheep out to graze. And when there's work to be done in the vineyards and tobacco fields, I do that too." *Gospa* had recently reminded the visionaries that prayer must always have its practical side; it was not just a matter of private fulfilment:

> She told us to go out and visit people who are lonely or abandoned. We went to see some of those people, though we didn't think they'd want to let us in. But at one house the woman who opened the door exclaimed, "*Gospa* has sent you to me," and she hugged us with great emotion. We had a guitar with us, and we sang to her and she joined in. Then we all said a prayer together. Next day we went again. We girls cleaned her room and the boys chopped firewood for her. Since then we've been to see her about three times a week. She looks forward to our visits, because we're all she has. She tells us all her problems and all about her sheep. I often find myself thinking about those poor sheep: when she dies, they'll have no one to look after them.

It was common practice for the pilgrims to offload their problems on to Marija. As so many of those who came in convoy to her house were Italians she began to learn their language, and soon became a surprisingly fluent and accurate Italian speaker. With her almost uncanny ability to put people at their ease, she was in constant demand. It was a revelation to her. "I'd had no idea there were so many sick people in the world," she told the BBC:

> so much sickness of so many kinds, so many problems great and small. People confide in me, they're not aware of any barriers between us. A lot of

them are able to face up to their disability and come to terms with it. But others are frightened, especially of dying. They want to talk about it, getting it off their chests helps.

Inevitably there was a high price to be paid in terms of exhaustion. The pilgrims, especially the volatile Italians, put an incalculable strain on all the visionaries. The Italian pilgrims were, as anyone could see, inclined to "over-dramatise, or even to behave as if they were in an opera, throw themselves on their knees before the children, kissing their hands, paying deep homage".[4] The strain was greatest of all on Marija. The pilgrims might leave her with a lighter step, but her own burden became heavier, the more they loaded their fears and worries on to her:

> They go away relaxed, but I am left feeling oppressed. Sometimes I can't shake off the profound depression they leave me with. When I shake it off even a little, I try to offer it to God – all those problems, all those people – because I know that once I manage to do that, the load is shared. When I really succeed in offering him everything without reserve, then I feel a tremendous calm deep down in my heart.

Marija's whole life bears witness to her conviction that there is a loving God. Her calm and her clear-eyed serenity have become almost legendary. Even for those who have remained untouched by Medjugorje, she remains in the mind as a very special memory. But the calm has been achieved at a price that few have recognised; and her only solace is prayer:

> I know that talking to the pilgrims is prayer too. But sometimes I have to get away from them and find a little solitude in which to pray. I can't live without praying. I have to find time for it. Sometimes I go right outside the village. But if that's not possible, I just go into my room with the Bible.

The recollection of that evening on the hillside, when a weeping Madonna made an impassioned appeal for peace and reconciliation, remains the guiding force of her life. Of everything that has happened to her since, nothing has made such a profound and indelible impression.

And when in October 1985, in a striking volte-face, Belgrade TV showed a two-hour documentary film on Medjugorje over the whole country (except for Bosnia-Hercegovina!), Marija appeared on the screen.

"At your age," speculated the interviewer roguishly, "I expect there's someone you're very fond of?"

"Yes," replied Marija, "someone I love very much."

"And his name?" pursued the unsuspecting media-man, delighted at the success of his crass question.

"His name is Jesus Christ."

Marija had already decided that, when the apparitions finished, she would enter a convent. When Laurentin* asked her later that year what 1985 had meant to her, she replied quite simply, "I have grown closer to Him."

Ivan, too, had been interviewed for the Belgrade film. In spite of all his problems – *l'affaire Ivan* had rumbled on all through 1985 – Ivan had changed out of all recognition. Always a loner, a nervous and timid boy, he had emerged out of that solitary chrysalis as an assured, even sociable, young man. Ivan, like Marija, had been "changed utterly". "I am filled with an inner content," he said. Leaving the seminary may have helped the change along: he had never liked study nor found it easy, and looking after his family's small-holding, he no longer troubled himself to do any. When asked if he still wanted to become a priest, he replied calmly that the decision could be best left to the Madonna. His life revolved round the apparitions. "I cannot tell you the happiness I feel when I wake up. I always expect something new . . . And in the evening, after I have seen her, I feel complete inside. Calm, peaceful."[5] From October 1985, Ivan and Marija (and Vicka when she was well enough) began their own prayer group, meeting three times a week on the top of Križevac at night. Quite frequently, the Madonna would appear to them there.

Jakov, now aged fourteen, had finished his primary education in Medjugorje and was attending middle school in Mostar. He was, wrote Gitta Sereny:

> about as boyish a boy as one might wish, enjoys reading out loud and does it well. But the prayers, although he frequently tries to cover his eyes, bore him. He fidgets, looks around and is likely to smile, or even wink, at visitors he considers receptive. It is precisely because of this that the change – from relative boredom to total concentration, from childlike impatience to pure joy – is most apparent in Jakov, once the vision . . . begins.[6]

Whether or not it was true that prayer bored him, Jakov had decided to become a Franciscan friar. He had wanted to join the seminary straight away, but had been persuaded at least to finish one year of middle school first.

Then something happened which upset his plans and made him think again. Out of the blue, Bishop Žanić summoned to Mostar Fathers

---

* Laurentin returned to Medjugorje in December 1985 after being banished for a year by the civic authorities.

Pervan and Ljubičić, Sister Jania (to represent the sisters' community at Medjugorje), Marija, Ivan and Jakov. As though it were stop-press news, he announced to them that in 1976 "a certain Franciscan", formerly of Medjugorje (and it didn't require much imagination to divine who he meant), had fathered a child on an ex-Franciscan nun, now living in America. The information, he said, had come to him as a written denunciation from Cardinal X in Rome.

The rumour was about a year old, and all the Yugoslav bishops had already been told about it by Bishop Žanić. For days now, ever since the written confirmation had arrived from Cardinal X, the bishop had been spreading the news to all who visited him, parading it as the ultimate proof that the apparitions were nothing but a hoax. The Italian doctors who had come to investigate the children in September had all been presented with this vital evidence, the missing link, as it were, in the pattern of treachery. "Either I or Medjugorje must die," the bishop replied melodramatically to those who queried his near-paranoid vehemence.

As it was obviously intended to do, the rumour spread through Italy and France, gathering distortions and absurdities on the way. "It appears that one of the visionaries has had a child by a Franciscan priest," a journalist in Nice confronted a startled Laurentin.

The unfortunate man at the centre of this scandal was not summoned to Mostar until 12th December. Laurentin does not actually mention him by name, so I will also refrain from doing so. Nevertheless, his identity was left in little doubt, since Bishop Žanić then accused the friar directly, inviting him to confess "that the Virgin is not appearing and that the whole Medjugorje business was your idea in the first place". The accused man, on whose head Bishop Žanić had so often heaped so many choice insults, protested. "The Virgin *is* appearing, how can I possibly say she is not?" he demurred. "As for what you accuse me of, why am I the last person to be told of the charge?" For the rest, he lapsed into silence.

According to Laurentin, the ex-nun in question had indeed given birth to a child in 1977; the putative father – a Croatian Franciscan but a different one – had left the Order and gone to live in America where he had subsequently married. The ex-nun had gone to keep house for an nonagenarian widower in exchange for a home. The man whom Bishop Žanić was now charging with the offence had been the nun's Father Superior and had continued to keep contact with her at Christmas and Easter, with an occasional affectionate letter besides. These tokens of affection had been enough to start the rumours and suspicions. The old widower, by then aged ninety-five and blind, had sent Bishop Žanić a letter allegedly written by the former nun to the accused man. When the woman heard what he had done, she too wrote to the bishop, protesting that the letter was a forgery:

Excellency, that letter was not written by me, it is not in my hand-writing. I have never revealed to anyone the name of my child's father. As for the old man whom I have dutifully served for the last nine years, when I understood how falsely he had served me, I left his employment and his house forthwith. His extreme old age may excuse the lies he told about me, but what puzzles me is how anyone can have believed them.

Everybody in the room with Bishop Žanić was profoundly upset and embarrassed. But poor Jakov was absolutely devastated. The accused man had been his hero. What was he to believe? The boy wept in the bishop's office, and remained visibly shocked for days afterwards. And as a result of the scandal he dropped all idea of becoming a priest, and decided to become a locksmith instead.

On 29th–30th November 1985, the bishop confronted the newly convened Commission with the accusation. The members, naturally enough, failed to see what it had to do with the apparitions, though it was obvious that for Bishop Žanić the connection was self-evident. The Commission was dismissed, to give time for further reflection in the light of this momentous discovery, and a further session (the eighth) was fixed for May 1986. The bishop confidently forecast a negative final verdict.

At the end of April 1986, however, he returned visibly chastened from a visit to Cardinal Ratzinger in Rome. When the Commission of Inquiry assembled on 2nd May, the bishop began by offering the members lunch – which, since it was Friday and a fast day, Father Dugandžić did not eat. After the meal, Žanić asked for a secret vote, with each member giving reasons for the way he had voted. Then he dismissed them.

Voting *was* secret, and Father Dugandžić is adamant that not even the members were told how it went. "Bishop Žanić collected the voting papers and took them away. The results were never officially published." Nevertheless, the bishop himself freely spoke of the results, and one of his diocesan priests, Fr Petar Vuletić, felt confident enough to tell a BBC interviewer in September that:

> after expert and persistent work, these fifteen doctors of theology reached their conclusions. Eleven of them categorically asserted that there was nothing supernatural about Medjugorje. Only two said that there *was* something supernatural and that the Madonna *was* appearing. Of the other two, one said that at first he believed there had been something, but had changed his mind. The other handed in a blank sheet of paper.

Yet *four* members of that Commission were known to support Medjugorje. What had happened to the other two? Father Dugandžić disputes the diocesan priest's account and claims that he himself had heard two different versions: some said there were five positive votes, others only four:

> My own diagnosis is this: two psychiatrist members of the Commission were against a vote being taken at all, since they wanted to go on considering the phenomenon indefinitely. They abstained from voting, saying that they were psychiatrists not theologians, and were not competent to make a theological judgement. Four of the theologians were certainly favourably disposed, and I cannot imagine any of them casting a negative vote. One member whom I would presume to be negative believed that the Commission should continue its work to the end before taking a vote. He probably abstained. So I would make it eight votes against, four in favour and three abstentions. And I should add that of those eight who were against, some did not take the Commission seriously at all, and some were so prejudiced that they devoted more time at our sessions to the Hercegovina issue than to the apparitions.

But then, in the bishop's mind, the two were inextricably intertwined, the former providing the whole *raison d'être* for the latter.

The die was cast. The Commission may not have completed its work, but it had voted. The ballot papers were sent to Rome. Three weeks later, in May, Cardinal Ratzinger dissolved Bishop Žanić's Commission, and ordered the Yugoslav Bishops' Conference to set up a new one. He gave no reasons for this action, unprecedented in the history of the Vatican, which has always left such investigations to the local bishop. In October, Cardinal Kuharić of Zagreb and Archbishop Franić of Split sent a joint letter to all the bishops, asking for nominees from each diocese.

It seemed that Bishop Žanić had finally overreached himself.

17

Five Years On

Mary Immaculate, [who]
This one work has to do –
Let all God's glory through.
Gerard Manley Hopkins

Slavko Barbarić had his bags already packed, knowing only too well that the bishop was determined to remove him from the scene. He asked for an explanation. It was unfair, he said, to send him away as though he had done something criminal. Bishop Žanić, however, saw no reason to explain himself. On 15th September 1985, the Franciscan Provincial, yielding to episcopal pressure, sent Slavko off to Blagaj, twenty-five kilometres away. "What could you expect?" shrugged a fellow-friar resignedly. "Rome took away our real leaders and put a yes man in charge of the province."

But Slavko had been left a loophole. Being still so near to Medjugorje, he was able to slip over there for part of each day. With his five languages, it was he who looked after the needs of the foreign pilgrims, switching from one language to another with obvious ease. This talent rendered Slavko indispensable, especially since his successor, Ivan Dugandžić, spoke only two, Italian and German.

The bishop, of course, was not pleased at being thwarted in this flagrant manner, and in January 1986 Slavko joined Tomislav Vlašić in being banned from saying Mass or preaching in Medjugorje. This did not affect his daily visits, and by the following August, the furious bishop was threatening both him and Vlašić with the full blast of canon law, if they continued to disobey his orders.

Vicka meanwhile was being almost completely prostrated by her headaches, which reduced her to a state of total lethargy; and although they usually stopped just before the Lady was due, she had had three apparitions in this weakened state. Early in January, when a group of psychiatrists came to examine the visionaries, they expressed some reservations about her character. They had visited her one afternoon, when she was in what her family described as a "coma", but which *they* preferred to designate as a hysterical stupor. One of the three observed that she had a tendency to exaggerate for effect, always wanted to be the centre of attention, and was inclined to court popularity.

To the bishop's immense satisfaction, the men conveyed their (guarded and not unreservedly unanimous) doubts to the Commission of Inquiry, which found them preferable to the more positive findings of the Italian psychiatrists and psychologists. On behalf of the latter, Dr Gagliardi had reported:

> During the interrogation, Vicka looks first at one, then at the other, but rarely at the camera. She neither looks at it nor avoids it – but she has no desire to be appreciated, only a desire to give an adequate reply. Her responses do not reveal an unreal, imaginary situation, but a real, positive world, lived with simplicity and joy. During the time we spent at her house, we did not observe any neurological or pathological symptoms related to her cerebral pathology. She was completely simple, coherent and vivacious.

Vicka was admitted to the Zagreb Clinic in February 1986. Her zombie-like lethargies could easily be laid at the door of her ferocious headaches and general exhaustion. On this visit, psychiatric reports spoke of "an excellent rapport with the subject . . . a warmly emotional person with no neurotic or psychotic symptoms". The clinic's psychologists noted a "highly developed altruism, a lack of aggression, a high degree of social adaptability".

But all the psychiatrists recognised the dangers to mental health represented by continual exposure to the pressures of Medjugorje, and suggested that the visionaries might do better to leave the place. Common-sense advice, but, given the circumstances, out of the question.

On 6th January the Madonna told Vicka that she would not appear to her for fifty days; and asked her to carry out three tasks. (Vicka would not tell anybody what these tasks were.) Being deprived of the sight of the Madonna was a great hardship for this girl who was not at all afraid of death, yet who lived in dread of the day when the apparitions would end. Oddly enough, however, her health dramatically improved during this time, the pallor left her cheeks and the headaches disappeared.

The fifty days came to an end on 25th February. Vicka was well enough to walk to the clergy house and the reunion between her and the Madonna was a joyful one. According to Ivan and Marija who were also present, the conversation during the three-minute apparition was all centred on Vicka. "You stole our Madonna from us today," Marija laughed. "She had no time for us." In April, Vicka was given the ninth secret, and wept in dismay. "You're a slow-coach, Vicka," said Laurentin, knowing that the others had all long since received this secret. "No, it's the Madonna who's taking her time," she replied. Next day she was given the final message on the future of the Church and the world, which had begun a year earlier;

and the Madonna announced a further separation: this time she would not appear for forty days. It was a devastating blow for Vicka. Matters were made worse by complications resulting from the appendicitis operation in December, during which an intestinal tumour had been found; and by a fresh infection at the site of an old tonsils operation. More surgery seemed called for.

Vicka returned to the Zagreb Clinic again in June, at the end of the forty days, and on 4th June she saw the Madonna again, in the clinic. On 7th June, the surgeons investigating her throat discovered a swab that had been left behind and was responsible for the infection. She returned home just in time for the fifth anniversary, her throat raw and painful. She had lost a lot of weight, but none of her habitual cheerfulness. Laurentin visited her twice; the first time, she was up and sitting on the edge of the bed; on the second occasion, pain forced her to stay lying down. "But the smile was still there. I asked about her suffering. She said: 'When the rust attacks us, we have to do our best not to be eaten away. If we continue to love, we can keep smiling.'"[1]

Just before the anniversary, a Belgian painter of some renown, Léopold Baijot, presented a portrait of the Queen of Peace to the parish. He had come as a pilgrim to Medjugorje in June the previous year, when the American nun, Briege McKenna, told him, "You are not here by chance. Jesus has sent you to glorify his mother. You will do the portrait of the Madonna of the apparitions."[2] Undismayed by this pronouncement, he had accepted the task as a sacred trust, and made several journeys to Medjugorje to question the visionaries and pin them down as far as possible on the physical details of the apparition. He got them to mime her characteristic gesture of praying and inviting to prayer. Baijot had started work on the painting early in 1986, and produced a vaguely spiritual symphony in blue; a simple, uncluttered picture of a woman whose striking blue eyes look straight at the beholder. He did not claim that the finished portrait was or could possibly be a faithful representation of the vision, and when the visionaries were shown a photograph of it, they were critical: the Madonna's robe was too blue, her hands not in the right position, and she was unsmiling. But no picture, they admitted, could ever do justice to the original. "To us she is a living, warm, friendly person. No portrait could convey the reality of that." But it would do well enough; at least it was an improvement on the stylised, romantic and garish Mainardi picture now reproduced on hundreds of thousands of picture postcards on the stalls.

A curious story is told about Baijot's picture:

> The artist so felt himself to be guided in his work that he had planned to paint a dove into the portrait, rather than his own signature, in recognition

of the work of the Holy Spirit. It was only after unsatisfactory attempts to do so that he noticed that there was already a dove – at the bottom right-hand corner of the painting. From photos taken of the canvas daily during its completion, it was discovered that the dove had appeared on the second day, though the artist had not consciously intended to paint it.[3]

From the weekend before the anniversary, traffic was almost at a standstill as the crowds poured in to Medjugorje. On the Sunday (the anniversary was on Tuesday) 120 priests, as usual most of them Italian, concelebrated Mass in the church. Old Medjugorje hands could not fail to notice how the place was changing; and not altogether for the better. It was, alas, succumbing to a creeping commercialism. Ice cream and Coca-Cola at the foot of Križevac; and round the church, giant hamburgers vied with plastic, luminous Virgins and cockle-shell crucifixes for the pilgrims' attention. The friars had wanted to buy the land for the parish, but the authorities had refused, and were busy handing out permits to gipsy, ethnic Muslim and Communist stall-holders for the sale of tasteless religious "kitsch". There was still a dearth of lodgings – and most pilgrims were lodged in hotels many miles away – but on either side of the road from the church to Bijakovići houses were springing up, a well-appointed guest-house was already completed, and it was rumoured there was to be a wine-bar at the foot of the hill of apparitions. On the credit side, there were now eight taps for drinking-water and – wonder of wonders – a half-finished block of WCs. A bulldozer had been at work, the three holes in the ground had been filled in, and building had started in April.

The good behaviour of the pilgrims was by now taken as axiomatic by the civil authorities who had mellowed considerably. No longer was it a politically subversive act to climb Križevac or Podbrdo; and no attempt was being made to stop the thousands of pilgrims from doing so. Bishop Žanić was less amenable. Despite the fact that Rome had taken the matter out of his hands, he had no intention of allowing the children back into the church. Accordingly, the people followed them to the hill.

On the evening of the twenty-fourth, the prayer group centred on Ivan and Marija openly invited all the 50,000 pilgrims to join them on the top of Križevac at eleven-thirty. (Ivan himself was not there, as at the beginning of the month he had gone to Ljubljana to do his military service in the Yugoslav Army.) Everyone knew that the Madonna was likely to appear that night; even the police, who flew low and loud over the dark hill in their helicopter at the crucial time, as if to show who was still boss. Only Marija and Jakov were there, since Vicka, of course, was too ill to put in an appearance at the clergy house, let alone make the arduous climb to the top of Križevac. Marija announced the following message from the Virgin, who had duly appeared at 11.30 p.m.: "You are on a Mount

Tabor. Here you receive blessing, strength and love. Carry these gifts home with you when you go. To each of you a special blessing. May you grow in joy and prayer and in the spirit of reconciliation."

Next day – the anniversary – the six visionaries were scattered. Marija and Jakov were in the clergy house; Vicka in her own bedroom; Ivan in the barracks (where he had an "inner locution"). Mirjana was simply a pilgrim among other pilgrims; she had been promised no apparition, and received none. But for Ivanka it was a very special day, the first time in fourteen months that the Madonna had promised to come. Laurentin, who had been invited to join members of her family and Tomislav Vlašić in the little room in Ivanka's family's house, noted that the girl was calm, showing not the least sign of apprehension. She prayed for a long time. At six-forty, half-way through an Our Father, she knelt down, facing the right-hand wall on which hung a reproduction of the Holy Shroud of Turin:

> Her face was radiant with happiness. Her lips moved but soundlessly . . . from time to time she listened, then nodded her head vigorously as though in agreement . . . At 6.43, her voice returned as she prayed with the Madonna . . . "who art in Heaven" she prayed, as the Madonna had obviously started the prayer . . . After saying the second half of the Our Father and Gloria her voice disappeared again, and there was more conversation. Three minutes later, her voice returned, intoning the first half of one Pater and Gloria . . . It was the first apparition in which I had noted this two-sided prayer . . . Her voice went again . . . and a seemingly animated conversation ensued . . . At 6.54 [Ivanka] raised her head slightly. "*Ode*," she murmured.[4]

And so Ivanka returned to the humdrum, vision-less world for another twelve months, leaving it up to Tomislav Vlašić to recount the latest episode in her life as a visionary.

"The Virgin told her several things for herself alone. There was some talk of secrets, but no messages were given, simply an invitation to pray and to persuade others to pray. She passed on a blessing to all those present."

18

An Unhealed Wound

Outside this way of love, there is death by fire and ashes, death from
the multiple hatreds which divide humanity, whether of class, nation
or race. Against all such totalitarian concepts we must proclaim one
unique reality – the image of God in man . . . Each of us is called to
give himself for his friends, to follow lovingly in the footsteps of Christ.

Mother Maria Skobtsova

Marija had been making coffee and handing round bowls of grapes to the
entire BBC film crew. When the time came for us to go, she came with us
to the door. "God bless you," she said in English to Roger Stott, our
agnostic researcher and stills photographer, putting her hand on his
shoulder and looking straight into his eyes. He had never heard her speak
English before and was startled. "It was a strange moment," he said
afterwards. "I felt that somehow I *had* been blessed, yet I wasn't at all sure
that I wanted to be."

It was September 1986, and BBC *Everyman* producer, Angela Tilby,
had brought a team to the village – to make the film, *Madonna of
Medjugorje*. With her was co-producer John Bird of Westernhanger
Productions, whose idea the film had been.

Marija was the first of the visionaries to be filmed, and had impressed us
all by her simplicity and calm dignity. Her life, she said, was a before-and-
after: since the great turning-point of June 1981, she had been completely
focused on God: "Before, I knew God somehow at a distance. But since
that day, He has come closer to me. Through this experience, I have truly
experienced God and want to commit my life entirely to Him."

She recalled the special experience-within-an-experience when on the
third day she had seen the Madonna weeping:

That shocked me, and drove me to commit myself utterly to the search for
peace . . . Somehow I felt she was confiding one of her problems to me and
that she wanted to be my friend . . .

The Madonna encourages us all the time to live the way God wants us to
live. She tends each one of us like a flower, making sure that each of us
grows in the way we should. For instance, she's always telling Jakov he's

done something wrong, because he's still very young and full of mischief. The Madonna knows what he's like and is helping him to grow.[1]

If the Madonna had not helped them through the early months, said Marija, they could hardly have survived. And that help created a bond between them, a unity which allowed them to help each other and to appreciate the difficulties faced by those who loved them:

> At the time when life was most difficult, our parents were wonderful. It was really something special, because until then we simply hadn't realised how much our parents loved us. Nothing else mattered, not their work, not anything; we were the only important thing for them, and they gave us their undivided attention. I came on my parents one morning on their knees, praying for things to be just the way God wanted them to be. And that was an even greater incentive for me to change my life and to live more deeply the things that the Madonna was saying . . . We're all praying more and trying to live the Madonna's messages.

Looking at Marija's face, it was not hard to believe that her only ambition was to live her life according to "what God wants". She intends, when the apparitions stop, to enter a Franciscan convent; and in preparation for that life, she is often to be found helping the Medjugorje sisters or doing odd jobs about the church.

Jakov, fizzing with restless energy and as elusive as an eel, was less co-operative. Cameras, microphones, and indeed journalists, disturb and irritate him, though he protests that, "I do try to be patient, because I know people come here to learn something." He seemed like a carbon copy of teenage boys anywhere in Europe, a football enthusiast, keen on pop stars, Bruce Springsteen – and Madonna! Jakov wouldn't even try to describe the visions: "It's impossible to describe. You'd have to experience it. When I have a vision, I feel a special kind of joy. But I can't describe that either, well, not in words."

The naturally loquacious Vicka, on the other hand, talked to us at great length, though she agreed with Jakov that the experience itself remains incommunicable. Talking to people is like the breath of life to her:

> I like everyone, equally, without distinction . . . Some people want to take my hand and kiss it. They say, "let me touch you, then touch my own face", "put your hand on me where it hurts", and so on. Well, I don't really mind, although I could do without it, and it's a bit pointless. But people have so many problems and crosses, their load is so heavy that they say, "if I just touch you, it makes it easier". And if it makes them feel better, then why not? It's not going to hurt me, the fact that they touch me . . . I like to tell them what they can do to ease their burdens, even just a little bit . . . I beg them to be as patient as they possibly can.

Since 24th August, Vicka had not been receiving visions:

> I've had two breaks before, and now there's a third, because that's the way the Madonna wants it. The first time, she said there were three things she wanted me to do; and before the second break she told me one of them. Now she's asked me for the other two things. So that's where we are now. She's not appearing to me again until 20th October.

Further than that she wouldn't go: "Nothing can be explained yet, until the Madonna gives permission." When asked if she'd ever doubted the authenticity of the visions, her eyebrows shot up into her hair. "Me? No, I've never once doubted. No, never." She smiled as she sought to soften the terrifying content of some of the secrets, the threat of impending catastrophe that seemed to be integral to the Medjugorje story: "Look, the Madonna just says that her messages should be told, that we should all pray more, and that people should change their lives. That's what she cares about, she doesn't want to scare anyone. She wants us all to be saved, you, me, everyone. She doesn't want anyone to be lost."

Next door, between Vicka's house and Marija's, Marinko Ivanković and his wife, Dragica (she who had so berated the unfortunate Fra Zrinko and Jozo Zovko in the earliest days), were waiting for us. Both of them had believed right from the start, even though there had been nothing special about the children so dramatically singled out: "There was no difference between them and the others. God just picked them up."

"There were quite a few in the village who didn't believe at first," Marinko told me:

> although perhaps the majority did. But some of those who believed at first soon got bored. Like the Israelites who started demanding a golden calf. But there's been one good result: people have stopped all that cursing and swearing. And they used to spend their time quarrelling, but they don't any more. They've realised just how negative their lives used to be.

Medjugorje by this time was unashamedly wooing the pilgrims. Souvenir shops, food stalls, coffee, soft drinks and snack bars fringed the church – and the toilet block was at last fully operational. The Franciscans had opened a new parish office and shop, with rooms on the upper floor for three of the sisters to live in. Building work was going on all along the route from Bijakovići to the church and beyond, and more and more pilgrims were able to stay in the village itself rather than several kilometres outside. Already the government had established a compulsory rate for accommodation, sixty per cent of which was payable to the local state tourist board. The amount of tax charged on accommodation in the Čitluk-Medjugorje area was two to three times higher than that charged anywhere else. All guests had to be registered, and regular police checks meant that hosts who did not register their visitors were liable to a hefty fine. The villagers resented the restrictions and the high prices, and tried to find ways of circumventing the law. Some of them were registering their private houses through hotels outside the heavily taxed Čitluk area, so as to pay a lower tax. Private tourist agencies from outside were cashing in on the villagers' dilemma and causing even greater confusion by setting up their own agencies offering more favourable conditions.

Waving a hand in the direction of the burgeoning new buildings, Fra Ivan Dugandžić acknowledged that there was a high price to pay for Medjugorje becoming an international pilgrimage centre. The villagers now faced considerable temptation; and he could only pray they'd be spiritually strong enough to withstand this challenge:

> When the first foreign pilgrims began coming here, our people did not have so much to do. They were few and far between, and our villagers could show them, by their own example, how to pray. Today, unfortunately, the situation is reversed and it is the foreign visitors who set an example for the local people. Many of our people find it impossible to come to church every day because they are too busy providing accommodation for the visitors, preparing their rooms, cooking their meals. And that's on top of their work in the fields which is now in full swing.

"Medjugorje is going through a crisis," said Jozo Zovko, when we went out to his church of St Elijah at Tihaljina: "There are many people doing their best to exploit it. All those guest-houses have brought envy and greed in their wake. The Devil failed to subvert the children, but it seems to me that with some others he had considerable success."

In the short term, he sighed, commercialism would "enslave the spirit of Medjugorje". That was a prospect which a hotel-proprietor in nearby Čapljina found far from dismaying. "Five years ago," he gloated, rubbing his hands as he watched one coach-load depart and another arrive, "this hotel was more than big enough. But today it's far too small. We're going to build a new one with two hundred and fifty beds. We get Italians, French, Spanish, Austrians, Irish, British coming here. We've done good money."

Jasminka Ostojić, a cousin of Marija's whom we found serving soft drinks in a bar near the church, shared Fra Jozo's gloom. The village had changed out of all recognition, she told us sadly – houses built, telephones installed, running water indoors, the restaurants and snack bars, all so different from what it had been. (The Sarajevo TV documentary had shown stills of Medjugorje taken in 1954, when there was no tap-water, no electricity, and people were still digging their land with spades.) She did not agree with Marinko about the good effect of the apparitions on village life. True enough, more people were praying – at home as well as in church, but

> as for being better, I don't think so . . . People used to be so much calmer. Now it's all hustle and bustle, everyone's in a hurry, everyone's running, chasing something. They've lost their peace, they used to have time to spend with each other, but not any more. Especially now with all this tourism, it takes up nearly all their time. Foreigners have to be taken in, and now you've no time to waste in visiting or just chatting, in just being together, the way we used to. Nowadays we only see each other in the evenings in or around the church.

Even the bond with the Franciscans was not what it was:

> The people go one way, the priests another. They've no time any more for the village people. The trouble is there are so few of them to cope. They can't spare anyone for the religious needs of the village, to go round the houses talking to people and discussing their problems, putting themselves in the picture. Each of the priests has a few people that he visits, plus his family and friends – they don't have any time left over for the rest of us.

If Jasminka were able to change anything in Medjugorje, what would she choose? Everything, she answered with vehemence:

> I'd try and calm people down, for one thing. And I'd look for priests like we used to have, real priests who lived for their faith and for God. As for Medjugorje, its souvenir shops and all those buildings, I'd tear the whole lot down, so that Medjugorje would be the way it was before. Oh, if I had the power, I'd change everything back again. Except for the Madonna. I'd want to keep her.

"I'd love to have been one of the visionaries like my cousin Marija," she added. "Of course, I've daydreamed about that, but I know that it won't happen." She had always longed to "feel a little of God's power", but "only for myself, not in public". Maybe since the apparitions, she had prayed more than before, "but I've not experienced anything special. I'm just a bit more peaceful. Yes, I'm really quite peaceful . . . I used to be more carefree and cheerful, but now I've found a little corner inside myself where I can be by myself. I have my own path to follow."

Unlike Marinko, Jasminka *did* believe that the visionaries had always been different and special, "always somehow set apart". They had a difficult time now – the pilgrims made excessive demands on them, the priests didn't protect them enough, "but Mary has given them the strength to endure it all. They're always smiling, you can't see that they're having a hard time. In any case, they wouldn't want people to know how exhausted they feel."

For Mass most evenings, the crowds were so dense that we were unable to get inside the church. Outside, on the steps, in the forecourt, under the trees, thousands knelt, stood or sat, heads bowed, some with arms outstretched. Gnarled old peasant women, bent with age, kneeling for hours on the rough, broken stones; young and old, the chic and the shabby, the drab and the outrageous. No amount of discouragement by Bishop Žanić and the opponents of Medjugorje had succeeded in keeping the numbers of pilgrims from growing.

It was obviously crucial for us to visit the bishop and hear his version of events. One morning, therefore, the whole team set off for the beautiful Turkish town of Mostar, and, more specifically, for the episcopal palace opposite the modern Catholic cathedral. Sitting in his book-lined study, Bishop Žanić looked resigned rather than delighted to meet us. He made no attempt to play down his hostility to Medjugorje, and kept insisting that our visit was a waste of time, since the whole tissue of lies would soon be exposed for what it was.

Though, as he told us, he had himself led several pilgrimages to Lourdes and other shrines of the Blessed Virgin and was therefore "predisposed to accept the possibility of miracles", he had no time for the pilgrimage centre on his own doorstep. "Of course, the sermons and liturgy are all very fine," he said irritably, "but I'm quite convinced the only way those children have seen Our Lady is on a statue or a holy picture." They were just like all the others, hundreds every year, who claimed to have seen the Virgin Mary but who were merely letting their imaginations run riot. Questions about the apparitions obviously annoyed the bishop: "You *will* keep on referring to 'apparitions'. *My* point is that we in the Commission don't believe there have been any," he interposed testily. "I have always been extremely suspicious of religious women who claim to have seen this, that or the other thing. These fantasies of theirs, usually no more than hallucinations, can do the Church a lot of harm."

Bishop Žanić was well aware that pilgrims to Medjugorje had cast him in the role of villain. "Anyone who doesn't believe in the place is dismissed as an atheist," he complained. "People are looking for miracles, and if they can't find them they invent them. They're trying to prop up their faith with things they know nothing at all about, intangible things. But a great deal of caution is needed: you can't use apparitions as a basis for faith. They may prove false – and then where are you?"

People seemed unable to understand that his refusal to accept Medjugorje was based on valid objections: "I have a responsibility to God, to the Holy See and to my own conscience, to examine this matter thoroughly and discover the truth about it. If in so doing I were to speak against the dictates of my own conscience, I should deserve the terrors of Hell. And if I must suffer for the truth, then so be it."

Telling us yet again that we were on a fool's errand, and ought to find better things to do with our time, Bishop Žanić bade us a polite if chilly good morning. "He prefers ideology to truth," commented Slavko Barbarić acidly, and, in the light of the bishop's remarks, somewhat unfairly; "he doesn't ask himself whether these things are true, he's only concerned about winning."

"But of *course* the Bishop is trying to find the truth," flared Fr Petar Vuletić, a secular priest who was unshakeably in the episcopal camp. As we sat eating grapes and drinking coffee under a tree outside Father Vuletić's church at Domanovići, near Čapljina, he eagerly defended his patron to Angela Tilby:

> It seems to me that he's already found the truth, and is deeply hurt because it is unacceptable to those who insist on pushing on with this Medjugorje nonsense at all costs. This present situation makes us all unhappy, especially the bishop. Don't people realise how happy he would be if Our Lady really *were* appearing? I believe he's actually sworn to walk barefoot from Mostar to Medjugorje if Our Lady gives him a real sign of her presence there.

It seemed that, unlike the foreign scientists, who were at least prepared to express themselves baffled by events at Medjugorje, Father Vuletić would not allow that there was anything to be baffled by. He'd visited the place twice, he said, and though indeed the pilgrims were very devout, and the liturgy and sermons well presented, that was all there was to it: "I don't believe the Madonna is present there any more than she's here in Domanovići . . . In Lourdes and Fatima, she confirmed her presence. In Medjugorje, it's all talk."

Had the Madonna confirmed her presence in Lourdes and Fatima? Certainly in Lourdes a spring of fresh water had appeared at the site of the apparitions, but it is unclear what constituted confirmation in the case of Fatima. Both places had, however, been granted official Vatican recognition, which may have been what Father Vuletić meant. Or again, he may merely have been reiterating his loyalty to Bishop Žanić.

As regards the Franciscans, Father Vuletić was obviously very angry indeed. He was in no doubts as to what *they* were up to. Brushing aside Angela's tentative suggestion that some good things had come out of Medjugorje, he exploded:

> Good things? And what about all the problems it's caused our bishop? . . . In my view, most of the Franciscans in our diocese have used Medjugorje to

bolster their own opposition to the bishop, their refusal to implement Pope Leo XIII's decree on the distribution of the parishes of Hercegovina. They want the ordinary laity to say, "Look, even the Blessed Virgin is on the Franciscans' side" . . . The problem is that the Medjugorje Franciscans are making their bishop's life extremely difficult; and, in my opinion, any priest who disobeys his bishop is disobeying the Church.

Subdued by this partisan outburst, we returned to Medjugorje in the early evening. It was about six-fifteen and the crowds had begun to gather outside the clergy house, waiting for Marija and Jakov to appear. Roger Stott and I were trapped in the crush. A sudden flash of light and a tremor of excitement in the crowd made me turn and look in the direction of the sun. Almost to my horror, I witnessed what so many have called the "dance of the sun": the sun moving back and forth as though on a yo-yo string, its central incandescent white disc surrounded by spinning circles of yellow, green and red light, for all the world like a Catherine-wheel firework. "My God," said an American to his wife, "it's a Mediterranean sun that I've been staring into. Yet I'm not even dazzled when I look away." Startled by the thought that I too had been staring into that sun for about ten minutes, I hastily looked away. I didn't even have spots in front of the eyes.

"Are you seeing this too?" I asked Roger.

"I think so," he replied tentatively.

"Have you ever seen anything like it before?"

"Well, no, but I'm sure there's an explanation."

"But have you ever . . . ?"

"No, but then I've never looked."

All around us, people were on their knees praying. To my regret, I felt no such impulse. Why, I don't know, but I had no sense of the numinous, only of the passing strange. Like Roger, I felt that somewhere there must be a rational explanation.

Wisely, the Franciscans of Medjugorje ignore or play down reports of such phenomena. They are a side issue, of undeniable interest but irrelevant to the main theme, as indeed are the visionaries themselves. "The latter," said Tomislav Pervan,

are to Medjugorje like the ignition system to a motor. When the ignition has fired the motor, it switches off. That's how it is with the Medjugorje visionaries. They had the task of igniting the world, igniting people, being witnesses, then withdrawing. Their role is like that of the prophets: to ignite, to move people out of their apathy, so that the world can fulfil the mission they have set in motion. They are necessary only as witnesses.

So what did he think was the purpose of the apparitions?

> I would say the apparitions point to the need for man to be converted, to choose life. The Virgin Mary stands in the service of life . . . Our age has reached the limit of its powers, it has a death-wish, the cult of death faces us at every turn. We are characterised by pleasure-seeking, self-indulgence, forgetfulness of God (even to the point of declaring that He is dead), and countless weapons that threaten death to the world. Look at Chernobyl which has infected one third of Europe with radio-activity. Doesn't all this point to the world's need for salvation, for a message of salvation which offers a way out, a blue-print for a better future, for life instead of death? And that message is the message of God, the message of the Scriptures, the message of Jesus Christ. Through the Virgin Mary, that message has been brought here to Medjugorje, to be beamed to the world, not just to this parish or to our Church, but to the whole world. Medjugorje presents a planetary call for conversion.

Further north, in Sarajevo, regional capital of the republic of Bosnia-Hercegovina, we stood and looked at a plaque commemorating an event that more than seventy years earlier had unleashed a trail of death and destruction on the world. The murder of the Austrian Archduke Franz Ferdinand by a Serb patriot in 1914 had sparked off the First World War. In 1986, Bosnia-Hercegovina was sending out shock-waves of a different kind. Could they, this time, put the process in reverse, and save the world from auto-destruction?

Filip Simić, the Minister for Religious Affairs, was disposed to take not a global view, but "our own, localised, regional and republican view of the phenomenon", though he would go so far as to claim it was also the federal view as seen from Belgrade. Choosing his words with a politician's caution, he combined pride in his regime's tolerance of religious absurdities with an unabashed delight that these same absurdities had brought an avalanche of tourists into Yugoslavia:

> Medjugorje is a phenomenon . . . connected with people's religious beliefs. They have an absolute right to believe that something supernatural is happening there, if they choose to. The state is neither competent nor called upon to make a judgement on whether there is, or is not, any foundation for their belief . . . Whether or not the Madonna has appeared in no way pre-occupies the state. We are faced, though, with another fact – that a great many people are coming here on a surge of religious fervour . . . They must be made welcome . . . We are an open country. We are also a significant and powerful and beautiful country for tourists.

That Medjugorje could provide a much needed shot-in-the-arm for the ailing Yugoslav economy was now belatedly accepted:

People come to Yugoslavia to ski; to relax on our beautiful Adriatic coast; to do business; to play football; and they are all made welcome. So why shouldn't we welcome those who come because they believe there is something in Yugoslavia which has to do with their beliefs, and to which they want to pay their respects?

But, Mr Simić added darkly, such visitors must refrain from abusing Yugoslavia's hospitality and exploiting Medjugorje for their own ends. Apart from this possibility, we asked, was the situation in any way threatening to a socialist society? Not at all, said the Minister. Mere numbers were not proof of intensified religious feeling in the country at large. The fact that we had asked such a question, he said indignantly, betrayed our lamentable misunderstanding of the role of religion in a socialist society such as Yugoslavia. "I do not take the question amiss," he told us charitably. In fact, it was not the first time he had been asked it:

But I must tell you that our Yugoslav socialist society has never tried to wipe out religion. Our society recognises the religious feelings of its citizens. We see no reason why a religious-minded citizen should not be fully engaged in the struggle for socialist self-management structures. We see no reason why he should not be whole-heartedly committed to the equal progress of nations and nationalities within this country, to the development of brotherhood, unity and mutual affection . . . Our ultimate goal is that our country should enjoy peace and security, as the homeland of all the nations and nationalities who live in it, regardless of national, religious or other allegiances. In the pursuit of these unifying goals, there is room for everyone – Catholic, Orthodox, Muslim, Communist, indifferent or whatever. No one is excluded from our national struggle.

Admittedly, he said, Medjugorje had presented the regime with difficulties at first:

Some church people revealed an ulterior purpose when they wrote about the events. They stressed in print that the Madonna had come to Yugoslavia because of its Communist regime. This was a purely political stance . . . It is hard for any Yugoslav citizen, who has personally suffered from the divisiveness caused by religious and ethnic divisions, not to hear political alarm bells clanging when people begin gathering in large numbers, and claim that Our Lady is appearing in order to bring freedom to this or that nationality.

But that was all in the past, and, well, frankly, Medjugorje was now a welcome boost to the economy.

Mr Simić's tendency to classify pilgrims as tourists was not limited to government officials. It was echoed by one of the villagers in Medjugorje who took a jaundiced view of the visiting multitudes: "Yes, there are those who come to pray and to undergo a change of heart. But many come only because they are curious about the strange things that are said to happen here. And then there are the scoffers, who come looking for proof that the visions are not real."

Tomislav Pervan disagreed most profoundly: "Pilgrims come here first and foremost to seek God. They don't come to have a good time, they come to look for the living God. And that is what most pilgrims find in Medjugorje."

On several occasions, I myself was fortunate enough to be present in the study-bedroom where the visionaries received their apparitions. Nowadays, this is a rare privilege usually accorded only to visiting priests or distinguished lay people. The first evening that Fra Slavko invited me, I got there early and was put into the corner from which I could get the best possible view of Marija and Jakov as they went into ecstasy. When the thirty or so priests had filed in, the room was filled to capacity and unbearably hot and stuffy. The arrival of the two children was the signal for the Rosary to begin – each decade being said in a different language, according to the nationality of the priests present. Finally, Marija and Jakov, who were kneeling in the doorway, took over the prayers, speaking of course in Croatian. Suddenly, they were on their feet and coming quickly into the room, to kneel facing the wall against which I was sitting. I could clearly see their rapt expressions and the very slight movement of their lips. It didn't last long. No more than about half a minute. Then it was over, and the children had gone.

On Monday, 8th September, the BBC's camera man, John Goodyer, filmed the event while sound recordings were made by Dave Brinicombe. (Dave, who had been brought up in India, and had gone barefoot in Medjugorje, even while climbing Križevac, was persuaded to wear sandals on this one occasion.) That night the usual contingent of priests was excluded from the little study-bedroom. Once the camera equipment had been installed, there was little room for anybody but the members of the team and the resident Franciscans. Jakov arrived wearing a bright orange singlet covered by a check shirt. He had left his rosary beads at home, and had to keep borrowing Marija's. ("Jakov is my cross," she would sigh later in mock protest.) The two visionaries led the Rosary prayers in turn, but after a while Jakov got tired of kneeling upright and went and squatted on his haunches in a corner. In contrast to this restlessness, the total silence and absorbed concentration in which, at six-forty-five, both visionaries knelt before what to the rest of us looked like a blank wall, were electrifying. So was the silence of the huge crowd outside the window. The only sound anywhere around was the whirr of the television camera capturing the whole scene – the ecstasy, the valedictory *ode*, the upward glance, and the abrupt return to normality. When it was over, the two children ran from the room and down the outside steps, heads lowered against the by now ecstatically waving crowds beneath. Having run the gauntlet of those milling thousands, Jakov, his old self once again, rushed off to join his friends under the trees outside the church.

Someone else who left that room with a firm step was Agnes Heupel, a nurse from Munich who was on a return visit to Medjugorje to give thanks for a cure. Only three months earlier, in May, she had climbed to that room on crutches, having been paralysed for ten years. She had witnessed an apparition, thrown aside the crutches and walked unaided down the stairs. When she left Medjugorje, her wheel-chair joined the crutches. "Keep them as a souvenir," she told the friars.

Yet almost more than this complete physical cure, which baffled the Munich doctors, Agnes Heupel valued the ensuing inner calm: "The physical well-being is marvellous. I take no medicines, I walk, jump, everything. But the condition for that is the spiritual conversion. You have to love more, forgive more. I no longer have any problems – I find the quality of all my relationships has completely changed."

During our visit, we had seen Marija, Vicka, Jakov, and resigned ourselves to missing Ivan who was away in the army. There remained Mirjana and Ivanka, both of whom shunned publicity and disliked talking to journalists. But Svetozar Kraljević had managed to talk them into seeing us.

The house where Ivanka lived when in Bijakovići was apparently not known to the pilgrims. Large numbers of them had walked across the fields from Medjugorje *en route* for Marija's house, and were passing Ivanka's gate without a second glance as we arrived, completely unaware of the two girls sitting in the garden waiting for us. Two very pretty twenty-one-year-olds sitting in the sunlight beneath a canopy of grapes: Mirjana, artificially blonde, quite heavily made-up, wearing a turquoise sweat shirt, patterned cotton skirt and yellow sneakers; Ivanka, dark and classically beautiful, in a vivid magenta cotton jacket and skirt, a bright pink T-shirt, flowers in her hair, and wearing black pumps.

Taking myself out of the way of the cameras and sound equipment, I went inside the house with Tonka, one of our two interpreters – into the room where on the June anniversary Ivanka had seen the Madonna. A shabby, unremarkable little room with a reproduction of the Holy Shroud on one wall; a makeshift shrine; a hideous picture of the Pope worked in chenille, and one of Ivanka's sister in a ballet costume; a vase full of cheap plastic roses and a handful of fluffy toy chickens.

Outside, the girls were starting to tell their well-worn story. "On 24th June, Mirjana and I went for a walk. And when we were coming back, I happened to look up the hill. And I saw the figure of the Madonna. 'Mirjana,' I said, 'look, it's the Madonna.' 'Aw, come on,' she said, 'why would the Madonna appear to the likes of us?'"

And so on, more or less as they must have told it countless times before. They were adamant that the Madonna had chosen them because they were like everyone else and not because they were specially good. "She needed us just the way we were," smiled Mirjana. "We're all six different from each other, but none of us is particularly good at anything. She said herself that we were ordinary and average, and that she needed us that way."

The filming over, I came out into the sunshine and was able to talk to the two girls. "My faith has deepened, but I've not changed," said Ivanka, taking up Mirjana's theme. "The Madonna doesn't want me to change. What's different is that Mary is with me all the time, and through her I know that God lives in me. I didn't know that before." Mirjana, too, said that Mary was always with her. As an agronomy student at Sarajevo University, Mirjana lives in a completely secular environment in which many of her fellow-students have no knowledge of God, and no sense of a meaning to life. "Of all the young people I know in Sarajevo, only two or three are believers," she said. She never spoke about the apparitions even to these few, but she tried to pass on the Madonna's messages as though she had thought of them herself:

I want to pass on these messages to all the young people I meet. I say, even if you can't believe in God, at least try and spend five minutes a day in silence, just thinking. They *must* think about God, even though they deny that He exists. They think it's embarrassing to be a believer, but *I* think that belief is something beautiful. If all people truly believed, there'd be no more war.

Like Jasminka, Mirjana was nostalgic for the old Medjugorje, now presumably disappeared for ever. The village had been at its best in the first year of the apparitions. Everyone went to Mass every day, and there was a wonderful spirit of neighbourliness. "But now, they think the Madonna's going to be in the village for ever, and they've got blasé about it." She herself is far from blasé: the experience of knowing the Madonna has meant "drawing closer to God, praying to Him as though He were my own father". Ivanka had decided to get married,* but Mirjana wanted to finish her studies before reaching a decision. "Then God will tell me what He wants for me."

On 14th September, the anniversary of the erection of the cross, there was to be an open-air Mass on Križevac. Angela Tilby wanted to film this

---

* She married just over a year later, in December 1986.

event which would attract crowds from all over Yugoslavia, and had commissioned two local carpenters to build a platform for John Goodyer and his camera on top of Križevac. The plan nearly came to grief, as the police, suspicious of any building activity on the hill, went to investigate. They took the two carpenters in for questioning and ordered them to return and dismantle their work. Three of us had to go to the police station at Čitluk to sort things out with the local authorities and get the necessary permits before the men were released and allowed to continue their work.

For several evenings before the event, lights (presumably fires) could be seen twinkling on the top of Križevac; and each evening the police climbed the hill to extinguish them. On the eve of the Mass, a beautiful moonlit night, lights were again glowing – and a police car was parked at the bottom of the hill as we passed. That night, however, there were people as well as lights up there, for many were spending the night on the mountain to prepare for the celebration next day. John Goodyer and Dave Brinicombe had carried their equipment up in the afternoon; and John Bird was guarding it, with his assistant, Peter Bigg. (The second cameraman, John Sennet, was to film from the Hill of Apparitions, opposite and slightly lower than Križevac.)

Next morning, most of the crew left the hotel before dawn in order to film the earliest pilgrims at sunrise. The rest of us left our hotel in Čapljina at six-thirty, by which time a steady stream of people was making its way through the town, slung about with bottles of drinking water and plastic bags filled with sandwiches. At the foot of Križevac, there was an air of expectancy, fruit vendors were already displaying their wares, and a coffee bar had been set up. The crowd began snaking slowly up the hill, singing hymns, reciting the Rosary, pausing in groups to pray at the fourteen Stations of the Cross, each marked with a crucifix. Sandalled youths with crew cuts, wearing singlets and patched jeans; women, young and old, shod in every variety of footwear – espadrilles, boots, even carpet slippers; women weighed down in ceremonial national costume with its pinafores, billowing skirts and thick wool stockings. Men and women hobbled up on sticks, a few (one of them one-legged) on crutches. Girls brightly plumed as aviary birds, and tough old *babcias* built like tanks, carrying flowers, plants, bunches of herbs, and clutching umbrellas to ward off the atrocious heat. Ancient crones with wizened skins and bent backs skipped barefoot across the rocks; while the sweating foreign pilgrims puffed and panted and swore as they tore their clothes on the brambles. Most were hampered by bags, some by large boxes and even suitcases.

By nine the heat was already intolerable, but still intensifying. The loud prayers dropped to a whisper or disappeared altogether as people concentrated on merely breathing. As clothes stuck to the body like a damp skin, sweat stung the eyes, gathered in globules at the end of the nose and dropped saltily into mouths gasping for air. By 10 a.m. with an hour still to go before Mass, there was little open space left on top of the mountain. People were searching in vain for shade, cold drinks, and somewhere comfortable to sit. The distant Dinaric Alps encircled us, blurred and unfocused in the shimmering hundred-degree heat. By the time Mass began at eleven, half the pilgrims were permanently stuck down the side of the mountain, and many of us could see nothing at all but a heaving sea of humanity. I had to take it on trust that Mass was being said. When we finally staggered and tumbled down the hill in the afternoon heat, we felt almost literally at our last gasp. The fruit carts could barely keep pace with the demand for water-melons, figs, pomegranates; and the soft-drinks stall had long since been cleared out. People were knocking on doors, asking for water – and frequently being offered grapes, figs or sandwiches as well. It looked for all the world like a crowd swarming out of an open-air pop concert.

Our visit to Medjugorje was nearly at an end. Throughout it, one question had consistently nagged us. It seemed to us that there was an unhealed wound at the village's heart. Marija had seen that weeping Madonna crying for peace; and if ever there was an area that needed peace it was this one; for throughout most of its history, it had been soaked in blood. We had read a great deal about the war years, the Ustaša atrocities, the terrible fratricidal slaughter perpetrated by both Croats and Četniks. Roger and I had seen, in the Orthodox Monastery at Žitomislić, a plaque that froze our blood. It commemorated the day, forty years earlier, 21st June 1941, when seven of the monks, from the Father Superior down to the youngest novice, were buried alive by the Ustaše in the pit at Šurmanći. Three days after that plaque had gone up, the apparitions started a few miles away in Medjugorje. That weeping woman, could there be a connection? Was this why Medjugorje had been chosen? Had those six children absorbed the hopes, desires, fears – and guilts – of a suffering people?

It was not easy to discover the truth of what had happened in the war years. A wall of silence was erected against our inquiries. The subject, it was clear, was taboo. No one was willing to talk about that dreadful pit in Šurmanći. As the Communists won't admit to the crimes of the Partisans, seemed to run the objection, why should we talk about the excesses of the Ustaše? On one occasion we obtained a quite horrifying admission by default. Was it really true, we had asked, that in a single day in 1941, more than 700 Serbian Orthodox women and children had been buried alive in Šurmanći by the Ustaše? No, came the reply, which stunned us, "I have it on good evidence that it was only half that number."

What happened in this place? Angela Tilby asked Ivan Dugandžić.

What was it that left such a terrible scar on the people? Here at last was someone who did not shy away from the subject:

> Well [he said], it was in the maelstrom of the Second World War, when passions on all sides were so highly inflamed. An act of retribution took place here within this parish – I'm not sure how to describe it – and people of another religion and nationality were thrown into that pit in Šurmanći. That left an ineradicable mark on this place, and the issue is still a sensitive one.

As with every crime, he agreed, there was a deep need for expiation:

> and it is in that context that I personally have always viewed these apparitions summoning us so urgently to peace. We can use these events very positively – they are calling us to replace senseless hatred by reconciliation and mutual understanding.

Is it possible that on some buried sub-conscious level the Medjugorje visionaries are the repositories of a tribal memory which is as yet unredeemed? Have they absorbed into their own psyches community sufferings, guilts and hopes of which, on a conscious level they are not even aware? However unlikely it may seem, it is a hypothesis that cannot altogether be ruled out of court. Slavko Barbarić, himself a trained psychologist, admits that the possibility exists and that it may be important:

> This place is a place that remembers. The people carry the memory in their consciousness, the memory of great sufferings, many terrible wars, famine, persecution, but also continuing hope. At a given moment, it is possible for a medium to emerge who personifies that hope, who then projects it and sees it in visual form. And this hope generally takes the form of a mother-figure who comes to console, to ease the pain, to promise a new beginning.

Yet, while conceding that the hypothesis may be quite valid, Slavko argues that in this particular case, it falls down:

> Admittedly, all the elements are there: the Madonna wept on the third day, Marija tells us; she pleads for reconciliation and conversion . . . But for a hypothesis to become a thesis, we must look at the visionaries themselves. Jakov, for one – what does he know or care about past – or present – history? The absence of peace from the world isn't causing him any sleepless nights. What he cares about is football, pop music and enjoying himself with his pals. When it's time for the apparition, he sees Our Lady; and afterwards he reverts to being the same old Jakov. He is as he is. Vicka next – now *there's*

someone who really does suffer. But the group as a whole is *not* a group that suffers. It is not even particularly cohesive. It has no sense of a joint mission: the only thing that unites its members is the visions. Visions apart, each of them behaves, dresses, prays in his or her own way. Each has a separate group of friends.

So I do not believe the hypothesis applies in this instance . . . If this is a place and a community that have known terrible suffering – and no one can deny that it is such a place – then we should expect the same sort of happening in other places of that kind. Why not Dachau, for example? Medjugorje is not the only place where extremes of suffering and hope meet.

"I feel both sad and sorry for this people among whom I have my own roots," added Svetozar Kraljević:

We admit our own need for reconciliation. But the wounds of our community are not so deep that they cannot be healed. One day this year, an Orthodox priest came to Medjugorje, was actually on the altar with us during Mass. We exchanged crucifixes, there on the altar, and our people were very happy. We *all* want reconciliation, and I think we *are* in process of healing. Young people today don't think like their elders. They do not believe in perpetuating old quarrels and hatreds.

Svet rejects the idea that past history has anything to do with the Madonna's choice of Medjugorje:

I know we've had our problems here in this very village. I'm sure the Madonna would like to heal those old wartime wounds, but not more so than the other wounds of the world; the drugs, the terrorism, the random violence, the break-up of family life. She speaks here to every human being on earth. There's a tremendous cost involved – for Medjugorje and for the visionaries – in being chosen as a sacrifice for the world. Just think of Judas, and how he ended. If Jesus had never called him, he might have lived and died a happier man.

No such shadow seemed to hang over Marija and Jakov when I saw them for the last time. Tony McAvoy, our assistant producer, had taken a team to film Marija at home, and I had gone with them. We found her standing under the overhanging vines praying aloud with a group of pilgrims. We made our way past them to the garden at the back of the house which looked out onto the hill where the Madonna had first appeared. Marija came to us there when the pilgrims had gone; and suddenly Jakov appeared from nowhere, clad in bright turquoise singlet and shorts. As John Sennet, the camera-man, filmed Marija, Jakov played the fool, pulling clown's faces at her, wiggling his ears in an effort to make her laugh. Marija's face twitched, but she kept it straight. Afterwards, she chased Jakov round the garden, and when she caught him, gave him a great hug. My last sight of them was standing there, arms entwined. For all Marija's twenty-one years, they were a couple of kids, as normal as anyone could wish. Mirjana was standing on the corner of the road leading to Medjugorje, on her own. "Show-off," snorted a young Croatian girl who was with us. "She hasn't changed at all," she went on, revealing an unconscious envy. "If the Madonna had appeared to *me*, it would have changed me completely." I couldn't help recalling Mirjana's words to us a day or so earlier: "She needs us exactly as we are. She doesn't want us to change."

At the end of the day, we all felt it was the sheer ordinariness and naturalness of the visionaries that was the best argument in favour of the apparitions' authenticity. And we could go much of the way – if not all – with our interpreter, Jozo Kraljević, a businessman from Mostar who summed up his own considered reactions for us:

I had my doubts at first, but now I believe that the apparitions are absolutely authentic. I'm not a credulous man, and I was a long time working out the reasons. Firstly the children: it would be preposterous to say they've been telling lies for over five years, making fools of the whole world. They are too simple, too guileless, too unsophisticated for that. And anyway, why would they? For money? No, they resent being offered money. Fame? No, they shun publicity. A better life? Oh, theirs would be a miserable life indeed if they were living a lie. People have been besieging them, pestering them in their own homes for five years, leaving them no peace. If their stories were false, they'd have been unmasked long since. So the only conclusion I am left with is that the children are not lying.

But what is it that they are seeing? Or rather, who is it? Well, I found the answer in the New Testament: a good tree cannot produce bad fruit. By their fruits you shall know them. I am sure that it is Our Lady who has planted this good tree in the rocky soil of Medjugorje. And the tree has already outgrown its local boundaries and overshadowed the whole world, producing many a good fruit.

As one of our young technicians said, "I don't know what the hell's going on here; but *something* certainly is." It was not the most thorough-going vote of confidence, but it probably summed up what most of the team felt.

19

Medjugorje Revisited

He is such a fast God, always before us and leaving as we arrive.
R. S. Thomas, *Pilgrimages*

A few days before the sixth anniversary in June 1987, I returned on a private visit to Medjugorje. Even before I got there, it was obvious that in six months much had changed; commercialism had been doing its ugly – if predictable – worst. A huge hoarding along the road from Ljubuški proclaimed the existence of a duty free shop in Čitluk, and advertised private (i.e. government controlled and taxed) accommodation throughout the Brotnjo region. The sight of Križevac looming into view was momentarily reassuring – until the eye was caught by the scores of new buildings along the approaches to the village. The decrepit old bridge over the little river Lukoc had still not been repaired, but was nevertheless being criss-crossed by taxis (150 were now in service) to say nothing of the crushing weight of the tourist coaches. There was a Kompas travel agency; a government Turist Biro; a mushroom factory. And from bridge to church a uniform sea of orange plastic canopies signalled the shape of things to come – as, beneath them, gipsy stall-holders displayed their highly-coloured wares. Rosaries, holy pictures, crucifixes, plastic Sacred Hearts and Madonna medals jostled for space with blouses, handbags, cotton sun-hats, sandals and woven rugs.

The piazza outside the church, I could see, had been flagged, and boasted a striking new statue of Christ, in bronze. And there was a new car park on the site of the old church. Not that it had made much difference – the traffic was hopelessly snarled-up, still reduced to its customary two speeds of dead-slow and full-stop. On either side of the road, building materials lay in a lake of churned-up mud. For two months it had not rained, and the crops had languished; but last night the rains had come with a vengeance.

Bronzed youngsters in shorts cycled cheerfully past the immobilised cars. Stuck in what seemed like a cat's cradle of traffic, I had time to observe the pedestrians, who, on first glance, all seemed to be from the USA. The Italians for the first time were outnumbered. A hundred groups of pilgrims from all over the United States had arrived at Dubrovnik or Split (only later in the year was the airport at Mostar opened to the heavy jets) *en route* for Medjugorje. They had come from New York, from Arizona, from Texas, from California, and over half of them appeared to be from Louisiana. They wore crimplene suits; bermuda shorts; baseball caps, cowboy hats; big, floppy cotton hats proclaiming "Medjugorje" or "Smile: Jesus Loves You"; hats that looked like up-turned meat-covers or waste-paper baskets. Women in floral-patterned bermudas were walking about singing "God reigns", or reciting the Rosary as they went. American hymns had clearly taken over from Italian, and the chorus to the Battle Hymn of the Republic (John Brown's Body) was much in evidence. Alleluias rent the air.

Village life was completely geared now to the needs of the pilgrims. There were few sheep to be seen, and even less tobacco in the fields. "We've no time to look after it." An article in the official press had accused the villagers of making fortunes out of pilgrims, and perhaps, in some cases, there was truth in the accusation. But the cost in human terms was high. They no longer had time to go to church, all their energies were devoted to cleaning and tidying, to finding and cooking meat, to preparing dinner for the pilgrims returning in the evening after Mass, or even later after a night ascent of Križevac. Pilgrims were rushing up the mountain at the merest hint of an apparition, and wild rumours abounded. "Some guy told me a woman broke her leg up there, and it healed immediately!" I heard an American pilgrim say. "What a load of bull-shit," snorted my companion, a Croatian girl who'd been brought up in Australia. The woman looked offended.

I asked for an update on events and people. Since January, a joint Commission formed by the Yugoslav bishops had superseded Bishop Žanić's old one. Ivan was now back permanently in Medjugorje, having finished his military service two weeks earlier. He, Marija and Jakov were still seeing the Madonna regularly; Mirjana had received a vision in January. Vicka's illness was now said to be not physical but spiritual: she was "suffering for the sins of the world". Ivanka, married in December to Raiko Elez and expecting a baby for November 1987,* was living in Medjugorje and working (apparently to the disapproval of the other visionaries) in one of the new snack bars in the village. Tomislav Vlašić was somewhere in Italy, his exact whereabouts known only to a few. The case of the two recalcitrant friars was now being judged by a Roman tribunal. And since 8th January, the weekly Thursday messages had been replaced by a monthly message – on the twenty-fifth of each month.

---

* Ivanka's baby was born in November 1987, a girl named Christina. She and her husband now live in Sarajevo with their daughter.

The guidebook to the Brotnjo area which I had bought the previous September had dismissed Medjugorje in a brief paragraph, a masterpiece of understatement: "In this place a modern Catholic church . . . has been built. Lately a number of church followers from Yugoslavia and other countries have visited this village and this church so that today it is known as a pilgrimage in Yugoslavia." Its updated successor had a full-length colour picture of the church on its back cover; thirteen pages of text; pictures of the visionaries, of the pilgrims, of the Križevac cross; and a splendid centre-fold showing the church and surrounding fields.

The two-day anniversary was now a licensed national event; and by Tuesday the twenty-third the villagers were bracing themselves for a further invasion. It scarcely seemed possible that Medjugorje could hold any more people than were already there; but clearly it was to be given no option. The militia took charge of the traffic, establishing a one-way system that considerably alleviated the chaos. "Here come the Gestapo," some of the visitors grumbled; but, all in all, the militia were a welcome presence. Less so to the hundreds of campers, perhaps, who found themselves unceremoniously evicted from their fields and despatched to a registered camp-site many miles away. Telephone lines were either clogged or unusable. And still the crowds poured in. Rumour had it that Yugoslav radio had announced the arrival of 15,000 AIDS victims among the pilgrims! The mind boggled. Was it possible that there were so many in all Europe?

On Wednesday the twenty-fourth – the Feast of St John, and the day when Ivanka and Mirjana had first seen the apparition – the whole village was astir by dawn. Iva Vasilj, having fed her chickens, was having great difficulty in crossing the road with a forkful of hay for her cow. Living at the foot of Križevac, she had to wait for a break in the continuous stream of pilgrims. The Americans, Irish, Egyptians, Koreans, Japanese, Austrians, Hungarians, Italians and French were being reinforced today by the Yugoslavs. Men and women, many of whom had walked for over two days to get there, straggled sturdily in with great carpet-bags full of provisions, ignoring for the moment the ice-creams, the cokes, and the souvenir shop open and ready. The women, for the most part, were bundled up in heavy black dresses, black cardigans and thick black stockings against what promised to be a broiling intolerable heat.

All day they went on up the hill, so many of them that from down below the hill seemed coated with ant-like figures. And on the other side of the valley, a mass of pilgrims on Podbrdo, jutting out like a spur from the larger mass of Crnica. To reach it, barefoot pilgrims were processing across the stony fields, carrying banners and crucifixes, praying aloud and singing hymns. Up on the hill, amid the rough boulders, crosses large and small were draped with ribbons, banners, scarves, flags, rosaries, bracelets, necklaces, and all things drapeable.

By five that afternoon there was no getting near the church; and Ivan, Marija and Jakov could barely make a way through the densely-packed mass to get to the clergy house. The congregation for Mass that evening stretched out beyond the forecourt, on to the road, and as far as the car park. Some people sat in the snack bars throughout, listening to the service – and long sermon – being relayed by the loud-speakers.

Later, the whole seething mass began once again to ascend Križevac; where the Madonna had promised to appear to the visionaries at eleven-thirty. By nine, almost all the available space on top had gone; and those of us who had secured a – desperately uncomfortable – perch between rocks and scrub, dared not move for fear of losing it. In any case, movement, even the stretching of cramped and aching limbs, was virtually impossible. As darkness fell and the air turned chilly, the pilgrims kept their spirits up by singing hymns – the Battle Hymn of the Republic again; and, more gently, "Let there be peace on earth, and let it begin with me". The words, "Praise God, Praise God", were sung over and over like a mantra, to the tune of "Amazing Grace".

Almost on the dot of eleven-thirty, a lone police helicopter began circling overhead, making an obvious point. As the visionaries went into ecstasy, its droning was the only sound that rent the otherwise total silence. (The silence of a 50,000-crowd is extraordinarily impressive.) TV camera lights split the darkness and the silence with vivid and brilliant flashes, lighting up the great cross. It was an eerie experience. Of supernatural experience we heard nothing, saw nothing, though Marija announced, to great applause, that the Madonna had indeed appeared, and wished everyone present to go home and change their lives.

Weary, aching, cold and full of sleep, we began the long descent. If there was a miracle that night, it was that nobody got hurt. And given that surging tide of humanity on the mountain-top, pushing and shoving towards the narrow bottleneck of the only exit, that was miracle enough. "Italians, please stop shoving," shouted an aggrieved American voice. In the dark, with few torches to light the way, large numbers of us missed the path, following like sheep behind the blind wanderers in front of us. We tore our clothes scrambling down the pathless scrub, crawling over the jagged and uneven rocks. Children cried with fright, terrified to jump from one rock to another. Mothers, some of them pregnant, waited helplessly for rescue.

Up there in the darkness of Križevac, I had found myself briefly able to pray. But the visit as a whole had done little for me; I felt isolated, alien and in a minority of one. Departing pilgrims in the next few days told me about the new-found peace in their hearts, of the way life was to be different from now on. All I had found seemed to be heat-rash and depression. Those pilgrims seemed so certain that they had found what they were looking for. Yet, to me, such certainty was intolerable; I was suspicious of "answers" that seemed to be rooted in formal prayers and orthodox Catholic practice. For me, God was a mystery, eternally hidden in a great "cloud of unknowing". I thought of the poet, R. S. Thomas, for whom the deity was:

> that great absence
> In our lives, the empty silence
> within, the place where we go
> seeking, not in hope to
> arrive or find.

Like the poet, I could only conclude that the search leads us all along different paths, some of them lit, others dark. My final question was the same as his:

> Was the pilgrimage
> I made to come to my own
> self, to learn that in times
> like these and for one like me
> God will never be plain and
> out there, but dark rather and
> inexplicable, as though he were in here?

For his own reasons, Bishop Žanić might have sympathised. A few weeks later, the bishop said Mass and preached in the church of St James, for the patronal feast of 25th July. Facing a packed congregation, he went for the jugular. The visions were false, he declared, and those who preached otherwise deserved "the lowest place in Hell". Strong words, which the people were not disposed to accept, not even from a bishop.* They murmured angrily, and Tomislav Pervan, the parish priest, rose to his feet and protested. But the bishop was adamant. Eleven out of his fifteen Commissioners had concluded there were no apparitions, he continued, and the new Commission was certain to reach the same conclusion. Like a bad fairy at a fairy-tale christening, Bishop Žanić lamented that, in spite of everything, the people kept coming, and that reports of sightings of the Madonna were increasing and multiplying. She had been seen, he said

* In September 1987 the Bishop of Mostar banned the visionaries from the clergy house since when their daily apparitions have taken place in the choir loft of the church. Marija and Ivan continue to receive daily apparitions there: Jakov, however, gets home from school too late to attend the evening Rosary and has apparitions at other times. Vicka is still too ill to attend.

witheringly, "in church, on the altar, in the sacristy, on the church roof, in the belfry, along the road, in cars, in buses, in schools, in Mostar, in Sarajevo, in Zagreb . . ." But for one thing the bishop was grateful: he must thank the Blessed Virgin, he said, for her eloquent silence in the face of all the requests for a permanent Sign.

That's part of the trouble with Medjugorje. The bishop has all the best lines; logic and reason would appear to be on his side. And yet . . . somehow, in spite of everything, I find myself hoping he's wrong.

20

The Doors of Perception

Das Ewig-Weibliche zieht uns hinan.
The Eternal Feminine draws us upwards.
Johann Wolfgang von Goethe

"You've sold out to the right-wing Mafia," a friend of mine shouted unreasonably when I first told him I had been to Medjugorje. "How can you even begin to think there's anything in that rubbish?" His furious reaction was not untypical, and I understood it well. Medjugorje represents a traditionalist Catholicism very different from my own. It is other-worldly, exclusive and moralistic; not a Catholicism steeped in the world's suffering and responsive to it. What would the average unemployed labourer, the starving peasant in India, an El Salvadorean caught up in a bloody civil war, make of Medjugorje? Yet the message of Medjugorje is aimed at the whole world. It represents, as Tomislav Pervan had said, "a planetary call for conversion". The dilemma has haunted me ever since, and I have come no nearer a solution.

It is claimed that at least ten million people have now (December 1987) been to Medjugorje. Ten million pilgrims, nursing what Matthew Arnold called "the unconquerable hope", expressing the yearning for self-transcendence. The phenomenon, whether or not it is officially recognised, is a growth industry; and it is difficult to see how it could be put into reverse even if the Yugoslav Bishops' Commission of Inquiry were to give a negative verdict. It seems likely that the new Commission will proceed slowly and with extreme caution. It will certainly make no judgement while the apparitions are still taking place. And if it does eventually find in favour of Medjugorje, that will mean far less than is generally supposed. It will not mean a Vatican blessing on the pilgrimages, merely a statement that since, after due deliberation, the reported events appear to be authentic and to pose no threat to either faith or morals, there is no reason why officially organised pilgrimages should not go there. Belief in the phenomenon will, of course, be optional; apparitions come very low down in the Church's hierarchy of revealed truths.

Even Lourdes was accorded no more than that cautious acceptance.

The Church has never resolved the question of what really happened there in 1858; but after a four-year inquiry it accepted that the place where Bernadette Soubirous had claimed to see the Virgin Mary could be turned into a shrine. Until the present, when Medjugorje threatens to outstrip it, Lourdes has been the undisputed pilgrimage centre of the Western world, receiving between four and five million visitors every year.

To the non-Roman Catholic, and even to many inside the Church, the whole question of apparitions seems strange and alien, even while it exercises an obvious fascination. Questions come flooding in, foremost among which seem to be: why is it always the Virgin Mary who appears; why always – apparently – to Roman Catholics? And why to inarticulate peasant children? Why, if the world is in such an awful state, does she not appear to world leaders, the shapers of the policies that threaten us with destruction? Why not to the Supreme Soviet or to the American Congress? *En passant*, it may be remarked that the disciples who claimed to have seen Jesus after the Resurrection were suspected of dreaming, hallucinating, wishful thinking and the same questions were asked. And from as early as the second century AD critics were asking why, if Jesus really had appeared as a Risen Christ, had it not been to his Jewish enemies, to Pilate, Herod, or – especially – to the Roman Senate.

Why not Jesus then, rather than Mary? It is important for us, in this context, to take a brief look at the latter's role in history. She is almost ignored throughout the New Testament, emerging only as the *de facto* mother of Jesus, a woman caught up in a real-life tragedy. Only Luke gives her a special role: that of the first disciple, the first to hear the Good News, the one whose "Yes" made possible the coming of the Redeemer. In Luke also, Mary speaks the Magnificat, that passionate and prophetic identification of the Redeemer with justice on earth: "He has put down the mighty from their thrones and exalted those of low degree; he has filled the hungry with good things, and the rich he has sent empty away."

But though, according to Luke (Acts 1:14) Mary was present in the early church of Pentecost, we hear no more of her after that, as the followers of Jesus began to work out the true meaning of his life and ministry. Nevertheless, thanks to Luke's identification of her as the one to whom and through whom the Redeemer came – fore-shadowed in the Old Testament as Daughter of Zion – it is now generally accepted that Mary was the "woman clothed with the sun" of the Book of Revelation, written by John at the end of the first century, when the persecution of Christians by the Emperor Domitian was at its height. Its theme of a terrible struggle between Good and Evil must have seemed no more than a reflection of reality, while its promise of divine intervention (through the woman) doubtless injected a note of much-needed hope.

Yet the early Church writers and teachers are virtually silent about

Mary. When they do mention her, it is only to provide an image of the Church or to prove to their Gnostic opponents that Jesus was a true man, born of woman. It must be remembered that Christianity was a religion of the East, and that a large part of the Near East had long worshipped the Goddess, the Ewig-Weibliche, the Eternal Feminine, bestower (and renewer) of life. The Mother Goddess, endowed with an understanding which no male god such as Jehovah could provide, was worshipped under many names: Ashtaroth, Astarte, Tanit, Isis, Cybele, Diana. The goddess-cult, and the fertility rites that went with it, had been fiercely attacked by the Old Testament writers; and it was not surprising that the early Christian writers were wary of giving any prominence to Mary. By AD 200 virtually all the feminine imagery for God had disappeared from orthodox Christian tradition. Any exaggerated claims about a Virgin Mother would have been both disastrously misunderstood and damaging to the doctrine of Christ's Incarnation.

Nevertheless, at the popular level, another current persisted. Romantic stories and legends about Mary's life abounded. The source of most of these, the apocryphal Book of James, was never accepted into the New Testament canon, but nonetheless continued to inspire belief. The certainty of Mary's assumption – her being taken up in glory into heaven – was common by the second century. Henceforth she was seen as ageless and immortal, able therefore to appear at any time or in any place to earth-bound visionaries.

When, in AD 313, Christianity became the official religion of the Roman Empire, three centuries of persecution came to an end. The ideal model for the Christian – that of the martyr – gave way to that of the ascetic, especially the virgin. In AD 325, the Council of Nicaea asserted Christ's birth from the *Virgin* Mary. The ground was laid for future Mary-worship, but as yet she was still only venerated, not worshipped.

In the late third and early fourth centuries, when barbarian hordes were tearing the fabric of the Roman Empire apart, there were many who blamed their fate on the wholesale desertion of the old gods. A spirit of fatalism and apathetic despair settled over the Empire, which in 395 split into an Eastern and a Western half. An infusion of hope was needed; it would come from the East.

It was in the East that Mary was first invoked in prayer. By the third century, the name Theotokos – God-bearer – the Greek equivalent of a term used in Egypt to denote Isis, had already been applied to the mother of Jesus. The use of the name spread. While Christians were ready to welcome a gentler celestial power than their all-male Trinity could supply, non-Christians found in Theotokos an echo of the old pagan deities. She could be seen as a protectress in an age of great insecurity and danger. When the Council of Ephesus (431) officially bestowed the title of

Theotokos on Mary, the fervour of her devotees was unleashed. In Ephesus, the centre of worship of Diana, a church was built to Mary on the site of Diana's temple. In Rome and other large cities of the Empire, churches sprang up on sites long-dedicated to Cybele, Minerva, Isis or Juno. Mary took over the attributes of all these goddess-figures, with the additional power of spiritual re-awakening, constantly renewed. As Geoffrey Ashe reminds us:

> Like Cybele, she guarded Rome. Like Athene she protected various other cities. Like Isis, she watched over sea-farers, becoming and remaining Star of the Sea. Like Juno she cared for pregnant women. Christian art reflected her new attributes. She wore a crown like Cybele's. Enthroned with her Child, she resembled Isis with Horus. The title and office of Queen of Heaven passed to her naturally from Isis, Anath and Astarte.[1]

For the first – but not for the last – time, the Christian Church had made a seemingly irrational but infinitely wise accommodation with more primitive beliefs, in the interests of its own survival. Christianity received a shot in the arm. From now on, until the twelfth century, the emphasis would be less on Mary, the mother of Jesus, than on the ever-Virgin and sinless Mother of God and Queen of Heaven. Contrary to the popular misconception, she was never allowed to be a goddess, the worship accorded her was the inferior hyperdulia, not the latria reserved for Christ. As Newman would later say, "The glories of Mary are for the sake of her son"; but there was no doubt that the emphasis was on her. By the seventh century, the Eastern feasts of her annunciation, visitation, nativity and purification were taken over; and her assumption into heaven was taken for granted throughout the Church. By the early Middle Ages she had in addition acquired a whole crop of minor feasts, and May had been designated as her special month. Soon she would have litanies of her own, recited publicly in church.

In the eleventh and twelfth centuries, returning Crusaders introduced a new art and a new poetry, along with a new romanticisation of woman. Mary was seen as the ideal of womanhood and knights fought battles in her honour. Thanks also to advocates like St Bernard of Clairvaux and St Francis of Assisi, she became known as the embodiment of compassion, the friend of the poor and humble. Christ might represent stern Justice, but Mary stood for Mercy, pleading with her Son on behalf of poor, suffering humanity. The sumptuous and resplendent new cathedrals dedicated to her in twelfth-century Europe acknowledged her as Queen of Heaven, but she was also seen as a human mother of great tenderness and warmth. Christian art depicted her as a Madonna, a beautiful contemporary woman, lovingly cradling her new-born child. The great religious art of the world has always been deeply involved with the female principle. It is noteworthy that the aggressively all-male religions (Judaism, Islam, Protestantism) produce little or no religious imagery, indeed in most cases actively forbid it.

It was towards the end of the twelfth century that the practice of saying the Rosary became widespread. The use of prayer beads as an aid to contemplation was known to all the major religions, and it is thought that Crusaders had picked up the habit from their Muslim enemies and introduced it into the West. The beads were for a long time called a "paternoster" (Our Father), but with the growing popularity of the Ave Maria (the repetition of which prayer on the beads was encouraged in the thirteenth century by the mendicant Dominican and Franciscan friars), a new name came into being. The term *rosarium*, or rose-garden, was in use by the fourteenth century, the rose being an ancient symbol of beauty, wisdom, love and mystery. But the word usually referred to the prayers rather than to the beads themselves, and it was not until the end of the fifteenth century that the Rosary as we know it was fully evolved. Within half a century, the familiar prayer pattern of one Our Father, ten Hail Marys and a Gloria, intoned as a kind of monotonous mantra while flicking over the beads, was established. It became a recognised way of freeing the mind for contemplation of the gospel scenes in which Mary figured (the five Joyful, five Sorrowful, and five Glorious Mysteries). The second half of the Hail Mary, "pray for us sinners, now and at the hour of our death", was not added until the sixteenth century, though the prayer itself dates from five centuries earlier.

The sixteenth-century reformers, of course, detested the Rosary, along with all other forms of Mariolatry, which they saw as obscuring the pure teaching of the Gospel and therefore to be destroyed. Protestantism, essentially masculine, rejected Mary as Theotokos; its creeds contained virtually no teaching about Mary as Mother of God. Luther continued to admit her as an intercessor, but Calvin would allow her no role at all. Erasmus of Rotterdam was more far-seeing. While protesting against those who gave Mary precedence over Christ, he warned against the suppression of genuine devotion to her. The elimination of Mary, he cautioned, would in the end produce a Church without Christ.

For simple, uneducated believers, the results of this suppression were traumatic. Mary was deeply rooted in their racial memory and could not be excised on the say-so of a handful of male reformers. "Imagine," wrote Kenneth Clark, in *Civilisation*:

> the feelings of a simple-hearted man or woman – a Spanish peasant, an Italian artisan, on hearing that the northern heretics were insulting the Virgin, desecrating her sanctuaries, pulling down or decapitating her

images. He must have felt something deeper than shock or indignation: he must have felt that some part of his whole emotional life was threatened; and he would have been right . . . He simply knew that the heretics wanted to deprive him of that sweet, compassionate, approachable being who would intercede for him as his mother might have interceded for him with a hard master.[2]

The Rosary, accordingly, became a weapon in the armoury of Rome's Counter-Reformation crusade. At the end of the sixteenth century, Pope Pius V formally endorsed its use, attributing the famous victory (1571) over the Turks at Lepanto (which marked the beginning of the end of their power over the Mediterranean lands) to the spiritual power of all the Rosaries that had been said. A new feast of Our Lady of the Rosary was proclaimed. Since that time, the Rosary has been a symbol of militancy, associated with the Catholic struggle against its enemies. "Devotion to the Rosary," wrote Marina Warner, "rises when the Church feels weak and insecure: the prayer, therefore, often indicates an embattled mood among Catholics."[3]

The reformers did their work well, and by the eighteenth century devotion to Mary, even among Roman Catholics, was a thing of the past. The ideas of the Enlightenment held sway.* During the French Revolution, a prostitute was enthroned as Goddess of Reason on the high altar of Notre Dame Cathedral in Paris. The nineteenth century had Darwin, the Communist Manifesto and the Industrial Revolution; and this deadly triple onslaught on the old beliefs at last provoked a reaction. In the West a new kind of extremist Catholic millenarianism arose, asserting a belief in miracles, and prophesying doom and destruction if the world didn't mend its ways. The Virgin Mary was, as it were, dusted off and given a new role as an autonomous messenger from heaven, intervening on behalf of a humanity threatened by the economic and political crises of industrialised mass society.

Three apparitions encouraged this resurgence of extremist belief. Lourdes (1858, four years after the Pope had proclaimed the doctrine of Mary's Immaculate Conception) was the best known, but before that – in 1838 – the Virgin had appeared to Catherine Labouré in Paris (resulting in the striking of the Miraculous Medal), and to two poor, illiterate children at La Salette in 1846. In 1871 she appeared to three peasant children at Pontmain, and in 1879 to a group of visionaries at Knock in Ireland. All of these visionaries were peasants, and all but Catherine Labouré were children. The visions did more than reveal a renewed belief

* Intellectual movement of eighteenth-century Europe which called traditional beliefs and prejudices into question and emphasised the primacy of reason and strict scientific method.

in the power of the supernatural to influence events, in the face of a rationalism that denied any such power; they also pointed to a longing for collective salvation whose focus was the Virgin Mary. Pilgrims began visiting the new shrines, as a new Marian Age began. A growing number of religious congregations were dedicated to her. Mary was now claimed as the defender of the uprooted and despised lower and lower-middle classes of Catholic Europe; she pointed to both Big Business and International Socialism as the major causes of the world's malaise.

In all these visitations, though the actual messages were often difficult to sort out, one request was constant: the Virgin asked the visionaries to say the Rosary. She seemed to have a special fondness for this prayer. Appearing to three young children at Fatima, in Portugal, in 1917, she again asked for it to be said at least once a day – for peace. Once again the Rosary was invoked in the cause of Catholic militancy: it was the year of the Russian Revolution, and the messages to the three Portuguese children were overlaid with warnings about the dangers of Communism. In Fatima, as later at Medjugorje, the visionaries were harassed and persecuted. The First World War, which Portugal had not entered until 1916, was going badly for her, and she had lost most of her expeditionary force in France in January 1917. There were strikes and industrial unrest, and the last thing the anti-clerical authorities wanted to see was a religious revival. The local administrator seized the children, put them in prison and threatened them with boiling oil. But they would not retract one iota of their story.[4]

As at Medjugorje, the Fatima children received apocalyptic secrets and appeals for repentance. (And the sun was seen to dance!) "Anyone predicting confusion and catastrophe round the corner would have had a fair expectation of being proved right," commented Peter Hebblethwaite.[5] But the Virgin did more than provide a commentary on the present. "The war will end," she said, "but if people do not stop offending the Lord, an even worse war will break out in the next pontificate."

Only three apparitions have ever been authenticated – Lourdes, Knock and Fatima (after a seven-year investigation), but hundreds have been reported. And, though few will have suspected it, our own century has been awash with them. In Belgium, Beauraing and Banneux were the sites of apparitions in 1932 and 1933 and both acquired shrines without gaining an official go-ahead. Of 210 visions reported between 1928 and 1971, ten per cent were adjudged false, while the remainder were still under investigation.[6] Appearing in Lithuania in 1962, the Virgin announced that she would next be seen in Egypt. And between April 1968 and May 1971, she made a series of spectacular, silent appearances over and around a Coptic Orthodox Church in a busy Cairo suburb which lies close to the route taken by the Holy Family during the flight into Egypt. Traffic congestion threatened to bring Cairo to a halt, as crowds of over a quarter of a million, of all faiths and none, came to witness the phenomenon for themselves. For the first time in history, Christians of all denominations, Jews and Muslims were publicly praying together. There were many healings, some of them from terminal illnesses. Even the Egyptian government was forced to the conclusion that, after thorough investigation, the possibility of fraud had been ruled out, and the apparitions were undeniable.[7]

The Cairo apparitions went unnoticed in the West. But they provide some indication that it is not only Roman Catholics to whom the Virgin appears. It is good to know that she appears to those of other faiths too, and the fact must surely be significant. It signalled also that Mary's visits were not confined to Europe. In 1985–6 among a positive explosion of apparitions (most of which were clearly phoney or at best ambiguous) eleven were considered authentic enough to merit further study. Apart from Medjugorje, one of the most outstanding is at Kibeho in Southern Rwanda, where in November 1981, Mary appeared to six girls at a Catholic boarding school and to one young man. She came as an African and spoke the local dialect. The message, as at Medjugorje, spoke of prayer, fasting and penance; and here, too, were warnings of imminent catastrophe. Similar reports have come from Kinelo in Uganda.

In 1985 at Oliveto Citra, a small town south of Naples, the Virgin appeared to twelve boys aged between eleven and twelve. Later she appeared to numerous people, among them two middle-aged fathers of families, a car mechanic, a road construction worker, a housewife, a waitress, a fourteen-year-old schoolgirl and two younger children. The message, the signs, the healings, and the apocalyptic are all as at Medjugorje. History seems to be repeating itself. Even as I write this, there are reports from the Ukraine in the Soviet Union that Our Lady has been seen there. As Professor Franco Ferrarotti has noted, there seems to be "a correlation between such so-called supernatural phenomena and the needs of people at a time of crisis. It's a question of giving meaning to existence, and of psychic compensation for social groups who feel themselves rejected or marginalised by society."

All of which is rather an embarrassment for the modern Church which during the Second Vatican Council (1962–3) tried so hard to drag itself into the twentieth century. The days of Catholic triumphalism ended with the death of Pope Pius XII in 1958; and the more extreme Marian doctrines perished with it. Pope John XXIII applied the brakes. "The Madonna is not pleased," he said sternly, "when she is put above her Son." In the hope of mending its fences with the estranged Christian churches, the Council declared that Mary's significance derived wholly from her Son, and insisted that her role must not "take away or add anything to the dignity and efficacy of Christ, the one Mediator". As Peter Hebblethwaite has recently written, "Mary does not embody the female element in God. She reminds us that it is there."[8]

Many of those outside the Roman Catholic Church who could not accept Mary as Theotokos have found it easier to accept her in the role of first Christian, a role model for the Christian life and spiritual mother of mankind.[9] The stress is on her identification with the human race. As though in reaction to four centuries of deprivation, the last two decades have seen a resurgence of devotion to Mary in the Reformed Churches – just as it has been declining in the Roman Church. There is now a flourishing Ecumenical Society of the Blessed Virgin Mary, born of the question: Can Mary, who for so long has symbolised the division among the churches, become at last in the twentieth century a symbol of reconciliation?

Is there a place for apparitions in all this? Many Catholics answer the question with a resounding "No". Revelation, they say, ended with the death of the last Apostle. They quote St Thomas Aquinas who warned against letting the faith become a laughing-stock. The new rationalism in the Church is suspicious of the supernatural, regards miracle cures as psychosomatic and dismisses visions as hallucinatory. In today's climate, claims René Laurentin, even Lourdes would probably not stand a chance of being accepted.

Even some who admit that apparitions are possible complain that they are unhelpful and tend to make the Church look foolish. Cardinal Jozef Ratzinger of the Congregation for the Doctrine of Faith tries to span the divide between the two factions:

> No apparition is indispensable to faith. Revelation ceased with Jesus Christ. He alone is Revelation. But this does not stop God speaking to our times through simple people and through extraordinary signs which point to the short-comings of our prevailing rationalistic culture.[10]

As Laurentin has pointed out, Medjugorje does not lay claim to being a Mount Sinai, only to being a place of grace.

Unless one categorically denies that apparitions are possible, the claims of Medjugorje must be taken seriously. It is surely not impossible that in our hour of great danger, some messenger of the divine may be trying to get through to warn us. But then one comes up against the sheer insipidity of some of the messages, the unnerving frequency of the apparitions, and the inordinately long time they have continued. Has the vision got stuck in a time warp? Are the messages being correctly interpreted? And what about the secondary phenomena – the woman-shaped clouds, disappearing crosses and dancing suns? However startling they are, the only real response to such oddities is: so what? Where do they lead us, what are they telling us, these

> acoustic ghosts
> that could as well be mineral
> signalling to mineral
> as immortal mind communicating with itself.[11]

As for the healings, it may well be true that they are psychosomatic. But we could also put that in more theological terms and say that the power of love is able to liberate the natural healing process. Medical science is still in its infancy with regard to such things. And why is such stress placed on proving that the visionaries are normal? Is normality a necessary proof? After all, other, greater visionaries, like Teresa of Avila and John of the Cross, have been prey to neuroses and deep psychological problems. "God is not bound by medical evidence and does not bestow His gifts exclusively on healthy souls," commented a Croatian critic.[12]

The same writer, a theologian, has even greater reservations:

> Whoever believes, like Laurentin, that the Madonna has truly appeared to the Medjugorje visionaries – not once or twice but well over a thousand times – needs to note the historical fact that even the noblest Divine initiatives have on occasion ended badly, because they were thwarted by various naïve and fanatical individuals and their deplorable propaganda.

The warning acts as a reminder that visionaries are no more than mediums, and have not always lived up to their visions. Maximin, one of the children at La Salette, for example, led a rootless life and was always in debt; and at Garabandal in Spain (1970s) the main visionary finished by denying that she had seen anything at all.

But how important is any of that? "In the final analysis," writes John Cornwell, "the fundamental question remains: does the experience of any set of visions, prophecies, messages or 'secondary phenomena' exert a clear moral power? Does it lead, or add a special resonance to faith? What are the permanent fruits? Are they better than faith unaided? Are they even good?"[13] The Medjugorje message is that of the Gospel: peace is urgently needed; we must work to bring reconciliation into the world; the ways to do this involve faith, prayer and fasting. But has Medjugorje diluted that powerful message, rendered it bland and insipid, reducing it to a request for frequent Confession, a weekly fast and a daily recitation of the Rosary? Surely that isn't the total conversion of mind and spirit that is called for, that "condition of complete simplicity / costing no less than everything", of which Eliot wrote. Doesn't such a view represent a throw-back to the bad old days when being a Catholic meant practising an inward-looking piety? Have we "had the experience but missed the meaning"?

After all, however edifying the initial behaviour of the villagers of Medjugorje may have been (and still is), in some quarters greed is beginning to raise its ugly head in the village; and the temptations of prosperity will be hard to resist. The unedifying dispute between the Franciscans and the bishop shows no sign of abating; and, although Orthodox and Muslim pilgrims do go to Medjugorje in reasonable numbers, the centuries-old religious divide still separates them. One must not forget that the Madonna on the hillside was weeping.

It has been pointed out by fellow-Catholics that their co-religionists who frequent Lourdes, Fatima and Medjugorje, who join charismatic groups and who say the Rosary regularly are not as a rule among those who join in or even applaud the Church's work for justice and peace in the world. (Obviously there are exceptions.) A September 1987 edition of the American *National Catholic Reporter*, while noting that every month 500 pilgrims have gone from New Orleans to Medjugorje, at an estimated cost of $6.6 million, and have returned claiming that they have discovered an inner peace, comments acidly that peace is still sadly lacking in their home-town. New Orleans, the paper claimed, was "a city in pain", beset by drugs and violence, its housing crumbling and fifty-five per cent of its people living below the poverty line. And in an orgy of executions in the state of Louisiana, eight death-row inmates had been electrocuted in the space of a few months.[14]

It is considerations like these that infuriate forward-looking Catholics (let alone atheists and agnostics) and make them see Medjugorje as an old-fashioned reactionary preserve. Yet, as some cooler heads on both sides of the divide see it, Medjugorje could instead be seen as a unifying link. Mary's message, claimed Richard McSorley, an American Jesuit, writing in the journal of Pax Christi, the international Catholic peace movement:

is a gospel formula for integrating peace-making with faith, conversion, prayer and fasting. All the strength to follow Gandhi's search for truth through non-violent action can and does flow from this foundation. Tax resistance, draft resistance, conscientious objection, opposition to death penalty and abortion, marches, boycotts, strikes and all forms of non-violent resistance should be based on faith, love, conversion and fasting . . . Jesus, Gandhi and Martin Luther King all taught what the Blessed Mother is reported to be teaching daily through the young people in Yugoslavia.

There should be no division between prayer and action, between faith and practice. Medjugorje illustrates what happens when the two come together.[15]

Catholic traditionalists may shudder at that, but Chris Maunder, a radical and anti-clerical research student from Leeds University, would agree. He was agreeably surprised by what he found in Medjugorje:

> Pre-conceived ideas from either left or right tend to get drowned in God's will here. I've found that I've been called to reconsider the more traditional elements, the eucharist, fasting, reconciliation through Confession. At the same time, people on the right may have come here expecting Medjugorje to confirm their ideas about Mary and the dogmatic traditions of the Church, but would find here a renewal that went beyond that. I think this place transcends divisions. It's about peace and reconciliation ... Marian devotion tends to be associated with a backward looking Church. But Marian devotion is about renewal that is for everyone. In Medjugorje, I believe God is speaking above the din of conservatives versus radicals.[16]

It is comforting to think that Medjugorje may represent such a renewal. But then another, more chilling thought intrudes. What if, after all, it should prove to have been a hoax? Everything would then fall to the ground. It is a fear which haunts many who would love to believe. "Medjugorje might be a wonderful gift to us Croatians," says an émigré journalist working in London, "but if it's a lie, I'd rather not be given it."

The odds are probably against such an eventuality. Though the Medjugorje Franciscans have certainly made the most of their opportunities, it is hard to see them, as Bishop Žanić and some of the diocesan clergy do, as scheming villains. Nor is it obvious what a disparate non-group of youngsters would have stood to gain from a situation which exposed them to so much harassment and disruption. They have never once wavered from their story – for the most part maintaining a remarkable consensus about its details – and not all the ingenuity of science has yet sufficed to shake or disprove them. They have remained unruffled by either threats or adulation; and have on occasion spoken with a wisdom, an insight, and even a theological self-assuredness that are quite remarkable. They have been more than a match for the bishop! We cannot but conclude, with Hamlet, "there are more things in heaven and earth ..."

For a layman the crucial question is how to distinguish between a subjective experience which is psychic in origin, and divine revelation. The distinction can only be a fine one, and for a psychologist it may not even be worthwhile to look for it. "I can't see that looking for a supernatural explanation helps," says Dr Jill Robson, a psychologist specialising in apparitions, herself a Catholic. "Why should God not act through the normal workings of human psychology? As regards under-standing how the mind works, we are still at a stage equivalent to pre-Newtonian physics."[17]

I find the argument from psychology persuasive. "The Catholic devotion to the Virgin Mary is a part of the visionaries' unconscious dimension," says Jill Robson:

> They almost certainly were brought up hearing about the Annunciation to Mary; the angel's announcement to Zachary about the birth of John the Baptist; Joseph being warned in a dream not to return to Herod. These things will have been stored in their unconscious. There are some people whose psychological make-up is such that they are more accessible to this kind of experience and the high emotional charge which it carries. They experience altered states of consciousness. For such people, the doors of perception are opened.

Devotion to the Blessed Virgin is real and uncomplicated in the com-munity within which the children were raised. It can sometimes happen that certain people – often children whose mind-set is not fixed and who are not yet a prey to prejudices – can pierce through the barriers separating the outer abstract formulation of a religious belief from its inner core of truth. Such people, says Dr Robson, "have living, personal contact with the great doctrines – on behalf of everyone else. What they perceive may speak to humanity's deepest hopes and fears." Perhaps this is what the theologian, Rowan Williams, meant when he spoke of "experiencing the metaphysics from the inside".[18] Or the mariner in another of R. S. Thomas's poems:

> astronaut
> on impossible journeys
> to the far side of the self,
> I return with messages
> I cannot decipher.[19]

It follows that any "apparition" must speak in the visionaries' own language and in a style compatible with their culture and education. It explains why the Virgin of the visions almost always looks like a statue or a holy picture. "To the visionaries," continues Dr Robson, "the experience will appear entirely non-volitional, something coming from the outside. This is perfectly normal. But in fact they may be contacting very deep levels of their own being. They may be being given a genuine religious insight; and other people recognise this and respond to it."

Jungian psychologists would speak (not altogether differently) of the Collective Unconscious and of the great archetypes which lie buried in the human unconscious, tinged with a suggestion of the numinous and more powerful than the individual consciousness of those who – circumscribed by their own history and circumstances – may be called to project them outwards. The visionary will be convinced that the experience is something that he/she is living; but the truth is the other way round: the archetype is living the visionary.

In the case of Medjugorje, any such archetype must be the Eternal Feminine, always evoked at time of crisis. In its early stages this will be projected as a mother figure, but with greater maturity it becomes what Jung called the *anima*, the source of humanity's deepest insights, the key to its capacity to transcend itself, to its self-knowledge and wholeness. Its arousal can only be good. "On Jung's showing," writes Geoffrey Ashe, "devotion to Mary should activate the archetype and help to unlock the treasury of the psychical depths, with results which no rational or dogmatic system can keep under control."[20]

The greater maturity needed to activate the *anima* might lead an over-rationalistic world to understand at last that the God it rejects has never existed outside its own imagination. God is neither up there, out there, nor down here, but actually *is* the knowledge and the insights that we gain, *is* all the creativity, compassion and generosity of which we are capable. Mary merely points us in the direction of this understanding. The psychological explanation does not imply disbelief, but it seems to make an appeal to the supernatural superfluous. "To explain is not the same as to explain away," says Dr Robson. "It seems to me that God's truth cannot be in conflict with psychological truth. It *is* psychological truth. There is no war between religion and science. Here is God being made manifest through the extraordinary capacity of the human subconscious."

If the doors of perception have in this case been breached for the sake of a world in danger of annihilation, why on earth should it have happened in a backwoods village in Yugoslavia? In one sense, perhaps, it doesn't matter where it has happened, so long as it *has* happened. But Yugoslavia with its "two alphabets, three religions, four languages, five nationalities and six constituent republics" seems almost to epitomise both the world's divisiveness and its craving for peace. The Balkan peoples form an uneasy mix, they are volatile, easily provoked and utterly unpredictable. The area has always been one of the world's powder-kegs, and it cannot be without significance that General Sir John Hackett, in his imaginative scenario for a future Third World War, postulated the war as beginning there.[21] The republic of Bosnia-Hercegovina has an especially explosive ethnic and religious mix, and its villages – such as Medjugorje – have been dealt a more than average share of suffering and guilt. If Medjugorje can find the recipe for a true peace and radiate it outwards, then peace should be possible anywhere on earth. There is a long way still to go, but a start has at least been made.

Yugoslavia is a bridge between East and West, a Communist country which looks out on the West across the Adriatic Sea. Upheld ideologically by the East and economically by the West, it has a foot in both camps and is in thrall to neither. It may be true that the Third World War might start there, but is it also possible that from there might come the impetus to prevent it from starting at all? Ten million people have gone as pilgrims to Yugoslavia, and returned convinced of the paramount urgency of peace. But peace will not happen of itself. What they, and the ten million who follow them, and the ten or twenty or thirty million after that, propose to do about it, may prove to be crucial for us all.

Notes

CHAPTER 1   The First Three Days

(1)   Interview transcript for BBC *Everyman*/Westernhanger film, *The Madonna of Medjugorje*
(2)   *Sunday Times*, 6.10.85

CHAPTER 2   In Your Lifetime, Have You Known Peace?

(1), (2), (3), (14)   Vladko Maček, *In the Struggle for Freedom*, Pennsylvania University Press, 1957
(4), (5), (6), (7), (8), (9), (12), (17)   Stella Alexander, *Church and State in Yugoslavia since 1945*, Cambridge University Press, 1979
(10)   *A Short History of Yugoslavia*, ed. Stephen Clissold, Cambridge University Press, 1966
(11), (13), (15), (16)   Nora Beloff, *Tito's Flawed Legacy, Yugoslavia and the West 1939–1984*, Victor Gollancz, 1985
(18)   Fred Singleton, *A Short History of the Yugoslav Peoples*, Cambridge University Press
(19)   Trevor Beeson, *Discretion and Valour*, Collins/Fount, 1982
(20), (21)   Dusko Doder, *The Yugoslavs*, George Allen & Unwin, 1979

CHAPTER 3   A Diabolical Plot?

(1), (3)   Fra Janko Bubalo, *A Thousand Encounters with the Blessed Virgin Mary in Medjugorje: the seer Vicka speaks of her experiences*, Friends of Medjugorje, Chicago, Illinois, 1987
(2)   in Svetozar Kraljević, *The Apparitions of Our Lady at Medjugorje, 1981–3*, Franciscan Herald Press, Chicago, Illinois
(4)   René Laurentin, Henri Joyeux, *Scientific and Medical Studies on the Apparitions at Medjugorje*, Veritas, 1987

CHAPTER 4   The Hill

(1)   Fra Janko Bubalo, *A Thousand Encounters*, op.cit.
(2)   Gitta Sereny, *Sunday Times*, 6.10.85

The quotations from Fra Jozo Zovko are from interviews recorded with him by Fra Svetozar Kraljević.

CHAPTER 5   Growth of a Legend

(1)   Christopher Cviic, "A Fatima in a Communist Land", *Religion in Communist Lands*, vol. 10, no. 1, Spring 1982
(2)   BBC interviews, September 1987
(3)   22.7.81
(4)   *Sunday Times*, 6.10.85
(5)   Fra Janko Bubalo, *A Thousand Encounters*, op.cit.
(6), (7)   Svetozar Kraljević, *The Apparitions of Our Lady at Medjugorje*, op.cit.

CHAPTER 6   Arrest

(1)   Fra Janko Bubalo, *A Thousand Encounters*, op.cit.
(2)   "Our Lady of Yugoslavia", a three-piece article by Richard West in *Spectator*, 2, 9, 16 June 1984
(3), (4)   BBC interviews, September 1986
(5)   Since the signing of the Protocol with the Vatican in 1966, Catholic priests from Yugoslavia were permitted to do pastoral work in the West. Inevitably this involved contact with nationals who had chosen for political reasons not to return to their homeland.

CHAPTER 7   A Place of Pilgrimage

(1), (2)   Svetozar Kraljević, *The Apparitions of Our Lady at Medjugorje*, op.cit.
(3)   Lucy Rooney, SND and Robert Faricy, SJ, *Mary, Queen of Peace*, Fowler Wright Books

CHAPTER 8   The Children

(1)   Author interview
(2)   In Yugoslavia children start school at the age of six or seven and receive eight years of compulsory primary education. These are followed by an optional four years of technical, medical or grammar schooling.
(3)   Fra Janko Bubalo, *A Thousand Encounters*, op.cit.
(4)   Author interview
(5)   The testimonies of Anka Pehar and Fra Janko Bubalo are taken from Appendix 3 in René Laurentin, *Is the Virgin Mary Appearing at Medjugorje?* Word Among Us Press, Washington, 1984
(6)   *Keston Newsletter 154*, 29.7.82

CHAPTER 9   The Bishop and the Friars

(1), (2)   Dr Fra Andrija Nikić, *Franjevci u Hercegovini u doba fra Matije Divkovića* (1563–1631), Mostar, 1985
(3), (4)   Personal interviews
(5), (6)   Jerko Mihaljević, *Hercegovački Slucaj*, Humac, 1976
(7), (8), (9)   Letter from the Hercegovina Franciscans to the Yugoslav Bishops' Conference in Zagreb, 1981

(10)   Stella Alexander, in *Keston Newsletter 188*, 1.12.83
(11)   *"S'il y avait une erreur, ce fut la mienne"*, letter from Tomislav Vlašić to V. de Bernardi, 23.8.84
(12)   Pavao Žanić, *Posizione attuale* . . . 1984

CHAPTER 10   Apocalypse

(1), (3)   Svetozar Kraljević OFM, *The Apparitions of Our Lady at Medjugorje*, op.cit.
(2), (8)   *Sunday Times*, 6.10.85
(4), (9), (10), (12)   "The Present (Unofficial) Position of the Bishop's Curia of Mostar with Regard to the Events of Medjugorje" (30.10.84), quoted in full (in English) by Michael O'Carroll CSSp in *Medjugorje, Facts, Documents, Theology*, Veritas, 1986
(5)   René Laurentin, *Is the Virgin Mary Appearing at Medjugorje?* op.cit.
(6)   There was also (from June 1983), a third group centred on Ivan and Marija.
(7)   This is the kind of thing the Church has always found deeply embarrassing. Revelations of this sort were reported in the second century, in the apocryphal Proto-Evangelium of James, a rich source of popular beliefs about Mary in the early Church. Later "Lives" of the Virgin were reported by various women visionaries in Europe.
(11)   Fra Janko Bubalo, *A Thousand Encounters*, op.cit.

CHAPTER 11   "Pray to be Healed"

(1)   Carolyn Burch, "Update on events and reactions in Medjugorje", *Religion in Communist Lands*, vol. 12, no. 3, Winter 1984
(2)   Richard West, "Our Lady of Yugoslavia", *Spectator*, 9.6.84
(3)   "What Mr Pentecost thinks about Medjugorje", *New Covenant* (Ann Arbor), October 1984. Quoted by Kevin Devlin in a Radio Free Europe Background Report/72 (Yugoslavia)
(4), (5)   René Laurentin, *Is the Virgin Mary Appearing at Medjugorje?* op.cit.

Chapter 12   When the Wind Blows

(1), (2), (3), (4), (6), (7), (9)   Michael O'Carroll CSSp, *Facts, Documents, Theology*, op.cit.
(2), (9)   Bishop Žanić's *Posizione*, quoted from above
(5)   BBC TV interview with Father Dugandžić, September 1986
(6), (7), (13)   René Laurentin, *Medjugorje à l'Heure de la Désinformation*, OEIL, 1985
(8)   This is the only test known to have been carried out by the bishop's Commission
(10)   Lucy Rooney, *Mary, Queen of Peace*, op.cit.
(11), (12)   Richard West, *Spectator*, op.cit.

Chapter 13 Medical Evaluations

(1), (2) René Laurentin and Henri Joyeux, *Etudes Médicales et Scientifiques sur Medjugorje*, Paris, OEIL, 1985. Translated into English as: *Scientific and Medical Studies on the Apparitions at Medjugorje*, op.cit.

(3), (4), (21) René Laurentin, *Dernières Nouvelles de Medjugorje, Vers la fin des apparitions*, OEIL, October 1985

(5), (6) *Etudes*, as above, Appendix 1

(7), (8), (10), (11), (12), (13), (15), (16) all refer to *Scientific and Medical Studies*, as above. This is essential reading for anybody who wishes a fuller and more detailed account of the medical tests carried out on the visionaries. See also: Luigi Frigerio, Luigi Bianchi and Giacomo Mattalia, *Dossier Scientifico su Medjugorje*, Presentazione di Flaminio Piccoli, 1986; and: René Laurentin, *La Prolongation des Apparitions de Medjugorje*, OEIL, 1986

(9) The wife of Professor Henri Joyeux studied six video-cassettes of fifty apparitions and observed these same synchronisms.

(14), (19), (20), (22) René Laurentin, *La Prolongation des Apparitions*, op.cit.

(17), (18) Gitta Sereny, article in *Sunday Times*, 6.10.85

Chapter 14 A Campaign of Disinformation

(1), (4), (5) René Laurentin, *Medjugorje à l'Heure de la Désinformation*, op.cit., Supplément no. 2

(2) *Sunday Times*, 6.10.85

(3), (7), (8), (9), (10) René Laurentin, *Dernières Nouvelles de Medjugorje*, op.cit.

(6) Kevin Devlin, *The Medjugorje Story*, RAD Background Report/72 (Yugoslavia), 25.7.85; also Michael O'Carroll, "Our Lady of Medjugorje – Hallucination or Apparition?" *Sunday Press* (Dublin), 20.1.85

(11) Lucy Rooney, SND and Robert Faricy, SJ, *Medjugorje Unfolds, Mary Speaks to the World*, Fowler Wright Books, 1985

(12) *La Stampa*, 20.6.85. Quoted by Kevin Devlin (see above)

(13) *Sunday Times*, 6.10.85

(14) *Tablet*, 5.6.85

Chapter 15 Miracles or Illusions?

(1) *Sunday Times*, 6.10.85

(2) Mary Kenny, *Tablet*, 13.7.85

(3) Delia Smith, *Catholic Herald*, 19.10.84 and 26.10.84

(4) *Scientific and Medical Studies*, op.cit.

(5), (7), (8), (9) René Laurentin, *Désinformation*, op.cit.

(6) Pavao Žanić, *Posizione*

(10) BBC interview with Fra Jozo Zovko, September 1986

(11) "Visions of the Virgin", *Newsweek*, 20.7.87

Chapter 16   A Time of Grace

(1), (5)   René Laurentin, *La Prolongation des Apparitions*, op.cit.
(2)   Fra Janko Bubalo, *A Thousand Encounters*, op.cit.
(3)   Mary Kenny, *Tablet*, 3.7.85
(4), (6)   Gitta Sereny in *Sunday Times*, 6.10.85

Chapter 17   Five Years On

(1), (3), (4)   René Laurentin, *La Prolongation des Apparitions*, op.cit.
(2)   *The Medjugorje Messenger*, no. 4, October-December 1986

Chapter 18   An Unhealed Wound

(1)   All quotations in this chapter are taken either from transcripts made for the BBC/Westernhanger film, *Madonna of Medjugorje* (BBC1, Sunday, 8th February 1987) or from transcripts of interviews done by myself.

Chapter 20   The Doors of Perception

(1)   Geoffrey Ashe, *The Virgin*, Paladin Books
(2)   Kenneth Clark, *Civilisation*, BBC/John Murray
(3)   Marina Warner, *Alone of All Her Sex*, Weidenfeld and Nicolson, 1976
(4)   Hilda Graef, *Mary: A History of Doctrine and Devotion*, Sheed and Ward
(5)   Peter Hebblethwaite, "The Pope and Fatima", *New Blackfriars*, October 1982
(6)   *Tablet* 27.9.86
(7)   For a longer account of these extraordinary happenings, described as "one of the most dramatic manifestations of the supernatural in two thousand years", see Francis Johnston, *When Millions Saw Mary*, Augustine Publishing Co., Chulmleigh, Devon, November 1980
(8)   Peter Hebblethwaite, *From Mariology to Liberation Theology*, Walsingham, 28.10.86
(9)   Clifford Longley, "Increasing Devotion to Mary", *The Times*, 27.7.87
(10)   *Rapporto sulla Fede*, ed. Paolini, 1985
(11)   R. S. Thomas, *The Tree*, from *Later Poems 1972–1982*, Papermac
(12)   Josip Curić, article in *Život*, a bi-monthly review published by the Jesuit Philosophical-Theological Institute in Zagreb
(13)   John Cornwell, *Tablet*, 29.8.87
(14)   *National Catholic Reporter*, 25.9.87
(15)   "Prayer and Peace: The Message of Medjugorje", in *Justpeace*, Journal of Pax Christi
(16)   BBC *Everyman* transcript

(17)   Author interview. Dr Robson also allowed me to see two papers written by her: (1) *Towards a Psychology of Visions*; and (2) *A Fresh Look at the Visions of the Mystics*

(18)   Rowan Williams, lecture to Theological Society at Nottingham University

(19)   R. S. Thomas, *The New Mariner*, from *Later Poems 1972–1982*, op.cit.

(20)   Geoffrey Ashe, op.cit.

(21)   General Sir John Hackett: *The Third World War*

Bibliography

1. Medjugorje

Bianchi, Luigi, Frigerio, Luigi and Mattalia, Giacomo
   Dossier Scientifico su Medjugorje (distributed by Agenzia Mescat, Milan
Bubalo, Fra Janko
   A Thousand Encounters with the Blessed Virgin Mary in Medjugorje, Friends of
   Medjugorje, Chicago, 1987. (First published in Croatian, 1985)
Hummer, Franz and Jungwirth, Christian
   Medjugorje, Sveta Vaština, Duvno, 1986
Kraljević, Svetozar, OFM
   The Apparitions of Our Lady at Medjugorje, Franciscan Herald Press, 1984
Laurentin, René
   (with Ljudevit Rupčić), *Is the Virgin Mary Appearing at Medjugorje?* The Word
   Among Us Press, Washington, 1984
   Medjugorje à l'heure de la Désinformation: autopsie des fausses nouvelles, OEIL,
   1985
   Dernières Nouvelles de Medjugorje: Vers la fin des Apparitions, OEIL, 1985
   *La prolongation des apparitions de Medjugorje: délai de miséricorde pour un monde en
   danger?* OEIL, 1986
   (with Prof. Henri Joyeux and his team):
   Etudes Médicales et Scientifiques sur Medjugorje, OEIL, 1985
   (in English) *Scientific and Medical Studies on the Apparitions at Medjugorje*,
   Veritas, 1987
   Medjugorje Récit (et Message des Apparitions), OEIL, 1986
Ljubić, Marijan
   La Vierge Marie Apparaît en Yougoslavie, Editions du Parvis, Hauteville/Suisse,
   1984
McKenna, Briege, OSC (with Henry Libersat)
   Miracles Do Happen, Veritas, 1987
O'Carroll, Michael, CSSp
   Medjugorje: Facts, Documents, Theology, Veritas, 1986
Rooney, Lucy, SND, and Faricy, Robert, SJ
   Mary, Queen of Peace: Is the Mother of God appearing in Medjugorje? Fowler
   Wright, 1984
   Medjugorje Unfolds: Mary Speaks to the World, Fowler Wright/Mercier Press,
   1985
   Medjugorje Journal, McCrimmon, 1987

Vlašić, Tomislav and Barbarić, Slavko
Open your hearts to Mary, Queen of Peace, Milan, 1985
Also
Christopher Cviic, "A Fatima in a Communist Land?" *Religion in Communist Lands*, vol. 10, no. 1, Spring 1982
Report by Carolyn Burch in *RCL*, vol. 12, no. 3, Winter 1984
Gitta Sereny, "A Village Sees The Light", *Sunday Times Magazine*, 6th October 1985

2. Virgin Mary and Apparitions (General)

Ashe, Geoffrey
The Virgin, Paladin Books
Clark, Kenneth
Civilisation (Ch. 7: Grandeur and Obedience), BBC
Graef, Hilda
Mary, A History of Doctrine and Devotion, Sheed and Ward
Graves, Robert
The White Goddess, Faber & Faber, 1948 and 1971
Huxley, Aldous
The Doors of Perception, Chatto & Windus, 1954
Küng, Hans
On Being a Christian, Collins, 1976
Marnham, Patrick
Lourdes, A Modern Pilgrimage, Nationwide Book Service
Paul VI, Pope
Marialis Cultus: (To Honour Mary), CTS, 1974
Ratzinger, Cardinal Joseph
Daughter Zion: Meditations on the Church's Marian belief, Ignatius Press, San Francisco, 1983
Rapporto sulla Fede, ed. Paolini, 1985
Warner, Marina
Alone of All Her Sex, Weidenfeld and Nicolson, 1976
Wilkins, Eithne
The Rose-Garden Game, Gollancz
Also
The Way Supplement: Mary and Ecumenism. Papers of the 1981 International Congress of the Ecumenical Society of the Blessed Virgin Mary. In particular:
Gregorieff, Dmitri: "The Theotokos in the Orthodox Tradition and Russian Thought"
Laurentin, René: "Pluralism about Mary: Biblical and Contemporary"
Ross Mackenzie, John A. (of the First Presbyterian Church, Gainesville, Florida): "Honouring the Virgin Mary"
Cardinal Leon-Josef Suenens; "Mary and the Holy Spirit"

Robson, Jill
"Towards a Psychology of Visions": Paper given to the Catholic Psychology Group at the University of Nottingham, September 1984
"A Fresh Look at the Visions of the Mystics": Paper given to the Second International Imagery Conference, April 1985
"Imaging: A Conceptual Anatomy", doctoral thesis 1983

Franciscans

Huber, Very Rev. Raphael M., OFM
A Documented History of the Franciscan Order 1182–1517, Milwaukee, 1944
Moorman, John
A History of the Franciscan Order: from the origins to 1517, Oxford
Also
Jerko Mihaljević: *Hercegovački slučaj*, Humac, 1976
Letter from Hercegovina Franciscans to Yugoslav Bishops' Conference, June 1981
Dr Fra Andrija Nikić: *Franjevci u Hercegovini u doba fra Matije Divkovića (1563–1631)*, 1985

General (Historical)

Alexander, Stella
Church and State in Yugoslavia since 1945, CUP, 1979
Beeson, Trevor
Discretion And Valour: Religious Conditions in Russia and Eastern Europe, Revised edition, Collins/Fount, 1982
Beloff, Nora
Tito's Flawed Legacy, Yugoslavia and the West 1939–1984, Gollancz, 1985
Clissold, Stephen (ed.)
A Short History of Yugoslavia, CUP, 1966
Doder, Dusko
The Yugoslavs, George Allen & Unwin, 1979
Foot, M. R. D.
Resistance, Paladin/Granada, 1978
Lawrence, Sir John
The Hammer and the Cross, BBC, 1986
Lodge, Olive
Peasant Life in Yugoslavia, London, 1942
Maček, Vladko
In The Struggle For Freedom, Pennsylvania State University Press, 1957
Ristić, Dragiša N.
Yugoslavia's Revolution of 1941, Pennsylvania State University Press, 1966

BIBLIOGRAPHY

Singleton, Fred
  A Short History of the Yugoslav Peoples, CUP
Waugh, Evelyn
  Unconditional Surrender, Penguin Books
  The Diaries, ed. Michael Davie, Penguin Books
West, Rebecca
  Black Lamb, Grey Falcon, Collected Writings, Penguin
Also
  Yugoslavia, Vista Books, 1962

Index

INDEX

INDEX